PHOTOGRAPHY BY **JASON LOWE**

LINDSEY BAREHAM

DINNER
IN A DASH

50 DINNERS FOR 6 IN 60 MINUTES

Editorial Director Jane O'Shea
Art Director Helen Lewis
Editor Laura Herring
Designer Miranda Harvey
Photographer Jason Lowe
Food Stylist Claire Ptak
Production Director Vincent Smith
Production Controller Bridget Fish

First published in 2007 by
Quadrille Publishing Limited
Alhambra House,
27-31 Charing Cross Road,
London WC2H 0LS
www.quadrille.co.uk

Text © 2007 Lindsey Bareham
Photography © 2007 Jason Lowe
Design and layout © 2007 Quadrille Publishing Limited

Reprinted in 2007
10 9 8 7 6 5 4 3 2

Cataloguing in Publication Data: a catalogue record for this book
is available from the British Library.

ISBN 978 184400 456 0

Printed in China

CONTENTS

INTRODUCTION

DINNER IN A DASH is a cookery book for people who love to eat well and entertain their friends but who don't always have the time to spend hours shopping, chopping and cooking. It is for people who don't want to confine socializing to the weekend, when cooking and eating can be leisurely and experimental, but who want to entertain spontaneously.

What's special about these menus is that the ingredients are listed as you might make your own shopping list, grouping all the fruit and vegetables together, the groceries, the fish and meat, the creamy stuff and the booze. And, once you get home, the menus are written in a friendly and helpful way, dovetailing the three courses, so you end up with a perfect meal for six within an hour. The instructions are broken down into blocks of 15 minutes, sometimes attending exclusively to one course but, most often, interweaving instructions so that time is used efficiently.

That's not to say that the menus require you to cook like a whirling dervish, far from it, but there are helpful tips for getting ahead with one thing while something else is simmering away in the background. And, for the occasions when you want to mix and match your favourite dishes from the menus, or for when you only want to cook one or two courses, there is an additional section at the back of the book where the menus have been unscrambled into their individual recipes. These are ordered in the more usual way, divided into Soups, Starters, Seafood, Poultry, Meat, Vegetarian, and Hot and Cold Puddings, with their accompanying menu number. All the recipes will serve six people and, although the menus are timed, use the timing as a guideline only, since some people work more quickly than others.

I don't claim a particular style of cooking but I do like to eat interesting, imaginative food that can be prepared easily and it is this that forms the basis of my dinner party menus. You will find 50 stimulating, no-hassle dinners that you and your friends and family can enjoy in a dash.

So, if anyone claims that the dinner party is dead, give them a copy of this book. **DINNER IN A DASH** proves that there is a new kind of dinner party on the circuit, which has nothing to do with starched linen and candelabra. It's quick to shop for, easy to prepare and cook and, in no time at all, you will be serving the kind of food you might expect to eat at a fashionable restaurant but at a fraction of the cost. I hope you enjoy these recipes as much as my friends and I have done and may all your dinner parties be fun.

LINDSEY BAREHAM

THE WELL-DRESSED STORE CUPBOARD

Some ingredients pop up repeatedly throughout the book and I'd like to pass on a few tips and observations about them.

SALT I use ordinary fine salt for cooking unless I specify soft sea salt flakes, such as Maldon, which I use for garnishing and to accompany food. I always use freshly ground black pepper.

OILS I keep several extra-virgin olive oils – from Spain, Italy, Greece and France – plus other fancy oils such as avocado oil, nut oils, Argon oil from Morocco and toasted sesame oil, to give a specific flavour to certain dishes. I also recommend groundnut (peanut), sunflower or sesame oil, all of which are pure and without pronounced flavour, for most other cooking.

VINEGARS Decent red- and white-wine vinegars are vital and so, too, is the best, aged balsamic vinegar you can afford. I particularly like the one made by Belazu, which is syrupy and richly flavoured; ideal for quick dressings with olive oil and a great seasoning for chicken and white fish. It's also useful to add sweet soul to fried onions, garlic, stews and gravies.

HERBS Fresh herbs, particularly basil, flat-leaf parsley, coriander and mint, make food look and taste good. Buy them regularly.

FOR SPICE Tabasco or another chilli sauce is vital for perking up all manner of food and so, too, is Angostura, the rum-based bitters from Trinidad with flavour enhancing powers called umami, which is the so-called fifth taste. Also curry spices, particularly ground cumin. I recommend saffron stamens rather than powder, buying whole nutmeg for grating, vanilla pods (which can be wiped and used again), star anise, cardamom pods and kaffir lime leaves.

FOR STOCKS I often use brown rice miso or Japanese soup sachets instead of stock cubes, particularly for vegetarian soups but otherwise I use chicken stock cubes for everything. I also keep a can or two of consommé/game soup for 'best'.

EXTRAS English mint sauce, tomato ketchup, chilli and tomato relish, soy sauce, Thai fish sauce, smooth Dijon mustard and mayonnaise, black olive paste, Moroccan harissa, quince jelly (membrillo) and runny honey are invaluable store cupboard secrets. Ground almonds are useful for all sorts of thickening jobs but look out, too, for Spanish Marcona almonds and big packets of pine kernels, which will be repeatedly required. And don't forget lemons and limes – their juice and zest is extremely useful, but lay in a plastic bottle of pure lemon and lime juice for emergencies.

Most other ingredients listed in these recipes speak for themselves. A quick word, though, for Eazy onions fried in olive oil, which come in 390g cans. They are the equivalent of about four Spanish onions, chopped and fried until meltingly soft. I buy a few cans whenever I see them. (Phone 01372 375 444 for your nearest stockist.) I am also a big fan of creamed coconut. It comes in a hard block with a long shelf-life. It can be grated directly into food or hacked off the block and dissolved in warm water, milk or stock to make a substitute for coconut milk or coconut cream. It is also very cheap.

USEFUL KIT

KNIVES Good tools make light work and save time. Good, sharp knives are vital. You will need at least one with a small blade and one with a larger blade.

SHARPENERS Most knife-related accidents happen because the knife isn't sharp enough, so buy a knife sharpener, too, and use it little and often – aim to keep your knives so sharp they glide through an onion as though it were butter. The simplest to use replicates a sharpening steel with two crossed steels set on springs. It's small and neat and sits on the work surface and works by sliding the knife through it; mine is made by Chantry but there are other good ones.

UTENSILS At least one potato peeler is essential and a grater (box-style is sturdiest and easiest to use) has many uses, as does a fish slice, palette knife, potato-masher, a couple of plastic spatulas and several wooden spoons. A balloon whisk will save lumpy sauces as well as mixing eggs and other food. You will also need bowls for mixing ingredients, a couple of sieves, a colander, a set of kitchen scales, a measuring jug, a rolling pin and some metal tongs.

PANS Apart from all the usual pots and pans, I find a cast-iron ridged grill-pan with a black matt enamel coating comes in very handy.

EXTRAS Supplies of tinfoil, clingfilm and baking parchment are essential, and you will need wooden and metal kebab sticks for some recipes. I find a hand-held liquidizer/mixer quick and easy to use – and it's also less hassle to wash up – but I would also recommend a Mouli-legumes food-press. This is a sieve-cum-masher, with three different-sized metal discs for puréeing and it makes sublimely smooth mashed potato. A favourite implement for quick, thin slicing of anything from potatoes to cheese is a mandolin. This is a very sharp blade set in a stand – but does require some practise! I would also recommend having at least two chopping boards, either wood or plastic.

THE
MEN

US

SHOPPING LIST

GREEN GROCERIES

2 shallots

6 medium-sized potatoes

750g trimmed green beans

500g podded broad beans

2 medium fennel bulbs

2 large ripe pineapples

3 lemons

1 large garlic clove

GROCERIES

1 tbsp vegetable oil

4 tbsp olive oil

1 tbsp smooth Dijon mustard

2 chicken stock cubes

CREAMY STUFF

50g butter

2 tbsp crème fraîche

FISH

**6 thick fillets undyed
smoked haddock**

BREAD

**Crusty bread and butter,
to serve**

BOOZE

**4 tbsp rum or 1 tbsp
Angostura bitters**

You will also need clingfilm

A friend just back from Sicily inspired this beguiling soup. The pale green and white theme continues with smoked haddock roasted under a cloak of thinly sliced crisp potato. The roasting juices are then stirred with cream and Dijon mustard to make a delicious sauce for the beans. This simple but effective way of preparing pineapple comes from Trinidad; slices of the juicy golden fruit refresh the palate whilst delivering a sneaky alcoholic boost.

0-15 MINUTES: Boil the kettle. Heat the oven to 230°C/450°F/gas mark 8. For **SICILIAN FENNEL AND BROAD BEAN SOUP**, peel and finely chop the shallots and garlic. Soften both in the butter and vegetable oil in a spacious, heavy-bottomed pan over a medium heat. Halve, core and chop the fennel and stir into the shallots and garlic. Add ½ tsp salt, stir again, cover and leave to cook for 5 minutes. Peel, chop and rinse 1 potato. Dissolve the stock cubes in 1.5 litres boiling water.

15-30 MINUTES: Add the chopped potato and stock to the fennel. Bring to the boil, reduce the heat slightly, partially cover the pan and boil for 5 minutes. Add the broad beans. Increase the heat and return to the boil. Boil for 5 minutes. Add 1 tbsp lemon juice then liquidize in batches, pressing the soup through a sieve into a clean pan. Taste and adjust the seasoning with salt and lemon juice. Remove from the heat.

30-45 MINUTES: For the **CARIBBEAN PINEAPPLE**, trim the pineapples and cut into quarters lengthways. Slice off the skin. Slice thinly lengthways and pile onto a platter, collecting any juices to add, too. Sprinkle with the rum, moving the slices to ensure everything is touched by the alcohol. Cover with clingfilm. Chill until required.

45-60 MINUTES: For the **ROAST SMOKED HADDOCK WITH A POTATO CRUST**, smear a heavy-duty baking tray with 1 tbsp olive oil. Place the haddock fillets, skin-side down, about 5cm apart, on the tray. Slice the unpeeled potatoes as thinly as if making crisps – a mandolin is ideal for this. Rinse the slices, shake dry and pile over the fish to entirely cover in a smooth layer. Season with salt and pepper and dribble with the rest of the oil. Boil the kettle. Cook the fish in the oven for 35 minutes – checking after 20 minutes – until most of the potatoes are crusty and all are cooked through. Mix the Dijon and crème fraîche in a warmed serving bowl.

TO SERVE: Reheat the soup and serve very hot with crusty bread and butter. Ten minutes before the fish is ready, boil the beans for 2 minutes in a large amount of salted, boiling water. Drain but retain 1 tbsp of the water to stir into the Dijon mixture together with any juices from the fish. Fold in the beans. Using a fish slice, lift a portion of fish and potato onto 6 warmed plates. Add a lemon wedge and serve the beans separately. Serve the pineapple straight from the fridge.

CARPACCIO OF TUNA WITH THAI AVOCADO SALAD
THYME SPRING CHICKEN
STEM GINGER FOOL

SHOPPING LIST

GREEN GROCERIES

200g trimmed fine beans

400g asparagus spears

3 small ripe, but firm, avocados

10cm cucumber

3 lemons

2 limes

2 garlic cloves

50g bunch flat-leaf parsley

25g bunch coriander

Large bunch of thyme

GROCERIES

3 tbsp olive oil

½ tbsp toasted sesame oil

2 tbsp Thai fish sauce (nam pla)

1 tbsp sweet chilli dipping-sauce preferably Blue Dragon

350g jar stem ginger in sugar syrup

300g jar lemon curd

CREAMY STUFF

175g butter

500g strained Greek yoghurt, preferably Total

FISH AND MEAT

2 x 200g tuna steaks

6 poussins/spring chickens

Carpaccio, in this context, means thin slices of raw tuna. Here, it is served with a contrasting crisp and creamy cucumber and avocado salad, and dressed in a sweet chilli vinaigrette. The meal gathers momentum with roasted spatchcocked spring chicken slathered with garlicky butter and underpinned by delicate greens, and concludes with an intriguingly delicious store cupboard fool.

0-15 MINUTES: Turn the oven to 230°C/450°F/gas mark 8. To begin **THYME SPRING CHICKEN**, snip out and discard the poussins' spines. Open up the birds and flatten slightly with the heel of your hand. Smear generously with the olive oil and season both sides with salt and pepper. Lay the birds over the thyme on roasting trays. Roast for 30-40 minutes.

15-30 MINUTES: Start the **CARPACCIO OF TUNA WITH THAI AVOCADO SALAD** by putting the tuna in the freezer for 15 minutes to firm up and make slicing easier. Peel and finely chop the garlic. Sprinkle with ¼ tsp salt and crush to make a juicy paste. Dice 150g butter. Cream the butter with a squeeze of lemon juice and the garlic paste. Chop the parsley leaves and stir into the butter. Form the butter mixture into a small log, cover with clingfilm and pop into the freezer. Next make the salad. Squeeze the juice of 1 lime into a bowl. Add the sesame oil, fish sauce and sweet chilli dipping-sauce. Mix together.

30-45 MINUTES: Finely slice the tuna, cutting across the grain (as if slicing smoked salmon) and arrange in a single layer on 6 plates. Peel and split the cucumber lengthways. Use a teaspoon to remove the seeds and thinly slice into half moons. Run a knife round the avocados, twist apart and remove the stone and skin. Slice across the avocados and season with the juice of 1 lime. Mix the avocado with the cucumber and pile next to the tuna. Prettily dribble over the dressing. Chill until required.

45-60 MINUTES: Check the poussins and remove from the oven when they are ready. Keep them warm until required. To make **STEM GINGER FOOL**, dice the ginger into a bowl. Add the yoghurt, 4 tbsp of the ginger syrup and the lemon curd. Mix together then transfer to pretty glasses. Add a splash of the remaining syrup. Chill until required. Boil the kettle. Remove the garlic butter from the freezer.

TO SERVE: Garnish the carpaccio with a shower of freshly chopped coriander. Snap off the woody ends of the asparagus and cook the beans and asparagus tips separately in plenty of boiling salted water for 2 minutes. Drain and toss together with 25g butter. Arrange the asparagus and beans in the middle of 6 warmed dinner plates and drape a poussin over the top. Make a couple of slashes in the birds and insert a thick slice of garlic butter. Serve with lemon wedges. Remove the desserts from the fridge 10 minutes before serving.

03

COCKLES WITH TOMATO AND LINGUINE
MISO COD WITH MANGETOUT
FROZEN BERRIES WITH WHITE HOT CHOCOLATE

SHOPPING LIST

GREEN GROCERIES
1 medium onion

400g mangetout or sugar snap peas

4 medium vine tomatoes or
300g cherry tomatoes

2 large garlic cloves

1 red Bird Eye chilli

20g bunch flat-leaf parsley

GROCERIES
2 tbsp olive oil

90g Japanese miso soup paste
sachet, preferably Yutaka

200g jar cooked and pickled
cockles (drained weight 100g)

400g linguine

750g frozen summer fruits

400g organic white chocolate,
preferably Green & Black's

CREAMY STUFF
50g butter

4 tbsp grated Parmesan

400g double cream

FISH
6 fillets cod, haddock or whiting

BOOZE
Glass of white wine, approx. 150ml

You will also need tinfoil

Cooked and pickled cockles in a jar are perfect for this cheat's version of *spaghetti alla vongole*, enlivened with fresh tomatoes, a hint of chilli, linguine, your best olive oil and a shower of chopped parsley. The main course is suitably light and interesting. It uses a clever trick of seasoning grilled white fish with miso, and is served, restaurant-style, over a pile of glistening mangetout. The finale is a stunning idea copied from the fashionable Ivy restaurant, of pouring a hot caramel sauce over frozen summer fruits – an 'ooh ah' dessert if ever there was one.

0-15 MINUTES: Begin with **COCKLES WITH TOMATO AND LINGUINE**. Tip the cockles into a sieve and rinse thoroughly under cold water. Shake dry. Peel, halve and finely chop the onion and garlic. Split the chilli lengthways, scrape away the seeds, slice into batons and then into tiny scraps. Melt 25g butter with 1 tbsp olive oil in a small, heavy-based pan and stir in the onion, garlic and chilli. Cook gently, stirring occasionally for 10–12 minutes until the onion is soft but uncoloured. Meanwhile prepare **MISO COD WITH MANGETOUT**. Line a grill-pan with tinfoil and lightly smear with olive oil. Place the fish fillets onto the foil and spread each one with the miso soup paste, making an even but not overly thick covering. Carefully dust the paste with Parmesan to cover entirely.

15-30 MINUTES: Stir the drained cockles into the onions, add the white wine and bring to the boil. Reduce the heat immediately and cook at a steady simmer for 8-10 minutes until the liquid has reduced by half. Turn off the heat and leave until required. Finely chop the flat-leaf parsley leaves. Rinse the mangetout or sugar snap peas. Boil the kettle. If using vine tomatoes, place them in a bowl and cover with boiling water. Count to 20, then drain, splash with cold water and remove core and skin. Quarter the tomatoes lengthways, scrape away the seeds, slice each piece into 4 strips and then dice. If using cherry tomatoes, cut into quarters and then halve the quarters.

30-45 MINUTES: Prepare the **FROZEN BERRIES WITH WHITE HOT CHOCOLATE** by breaking the chocolate into small pieces and placing in a double boiler or in a metal bowl placed over a pan of simmering water; do not let the water touch the bowl. Add the cream and stir occasionally over the next 5-10 minutes until the chocolate has melted and the sauce is smooth and very hot.

45-60 MINUTES: Cook the linguine in plenty of boiling salted water for 6 minutes or until *al dente*. Drain and return to the pan with 25g butter. Quickly reheat the cockles and stir them into the linguine.

TO SERVE: Stir the tomatoes and parsley into the pasta. Transfer to a warmed serving bowl. To finish the main course, turn the grill very high and cook the fish for 4–8 minutes, depending on the thickness of the fillets, until just cooked through with a crusty topping. Meanwhile, boil the mangetout in plenty of salted water. Drain, arrange in the middle of 6 warmed plates and drape the fish over the top. About 5 minutes before serving the pudding remove the fruit from the freezer and spread out on 6 plates or 2 platters for sharing. Reheat the sauce until very hot, transfer to a jug and pour lavishly over the semi-frozen fruit in front of your guests.

04 PISSALADIERE WITH ROCKET
LAMB KEBABS, SKORDALIA AND PICKLES
AFFOGATO

SHOPPING LIST

GREEN GROCERIES

600g baking potatoes

800g small boiled beetroot (without vinegar)

6 plum tomatoes

1 large cucumber

150g wild rocket

3 lemons

1 lime

5 large garlic cloves, preferably new-season

A few sprigs of rosemary

A small bunch of dill

GROCERIES

300ml olive oil, plus 8 tbsp

Bottles of extra-virgin olive oil and wine vinegar (for the table)

2 tbsp aged balsamic vinegar

2 tbsp white-wine vinegar

3 tbsp red-wine vinegar

2 x 50g anchovy fillets in olive oil

75g pitted black olives

3 tbsp tomato purée

400g can Eazy fried onions

350g puff pastry

Flour for dusting

1 tsp caster sugar

Espresso coffee

CREAMY STUFF

500g good quality vanilla ice cream

MEAT

800g lamb neck fillet

BREAD

120g day-old white bread without crusts

BOOZE

100ml Amaretto

You will also need 2 big sheets of tinfoil and 12 metal kebab sticks

Pissaladière is a gorgeous gooey onion and anchovy tart from Nice where it's sold in slabs and eaten as a snack. This quick version uses canned fried onions, saving about 40 minutes cooking time! It looks pretty with its lattice of anchovy and makes a lovely starter with a simple rocket salad. Lamb is always good with garlic and potatoes and here the two combine in a classic Greek sauce. This innocent looking purée is offset by crisp pickled cucumber, slippery roast tomatoes and silky baby beetroot. Pudding is a small but addictive combination of vanilla ice cream with a shot of Amaretto and hot espresso coffee.

0-15 MINUTES: Heat the oven to 200°C/400°F/gas mark 6. Get started with **LAMB KEBABS, SKORDALIA AND PICKLES**, by halving the tomatoes lengthways. Arrange cut-side up on a baking tin and smear with 1 tbsp olive oil. Roast for 15 minutes until soft and juicy. Set aside until required. For **PISSALADIERE WITH ROCKET**, smear a 24 x 34cm baking tin with 1 tbsp olive oil. Dust a work surface with flour and roll the pastry to fit the baking tin. Pierce the pastry with a fork to stop it rising. Smear with tomato purée then onion, going right up to the edges. Split the anchovies lengthways. Make a wide lattice with the anchovies over the onions. Place an olive in each lattice. Dribble the tart with oil from the anchovies and cook in the oven for about 20 minutes until the pastry is golden. If it billows, pierce it with a knife to deflate. Remove from the oven and leave until required.

15-30 MINUTES: For the skordalia, peel the potatoes and boil until tender. Drain. Meanwhile, for the kebabs, peel and chop 2 garlic cloves. Sprinkle with ¼ tsp salt and crush to a paste. Place in a dish that can accommodate the lamb and whisk in the juice of the lime, 4 tbsp olive oil and the rosemary. Cut the lamb into kebab-sized chunks and stir into the marinade. Cover and chill until required (at least 30 minutes). Place the beetroot on one large sheet of foil, drizzle with 2 tbsp each balsamic vinegar and olive oil. Season with salt and pepper. Place a second sheet of foil on top and seal the edges securely, but not too tightly.

30-45 MINUTES: Tear the bread into pieces and blitz with the remaining 3 peeled garlic cloves in a food processor. Pass the potatoes through a vegetable press (Mouli-Legumes) or mash until smooth. Stir the garlicky crumbs into the potato. Gradually beat in 300ml olive oil. Finish by beating in the red-wine vinegar. Cover with clingfilm until required. Peel the cucumber and slice wafer-thin using a mandolin or the side of a cheese-grater. Dredge with 1 tbsp salt. Leave for 10 minutes. Check the pissaladière is ready and set aside. Chop the dill leaves.

45-60 MINUTES: Thread the kebabs onto the skewers and arrange on a baking tin. Place at the top of the oven and the foil parcel of beetroot at the bottom. Cook both for 15 minutes, turning the kebabs halfway through so they end up crusty. Turn off the oven, open the door and leave both until required. Squeeze as much water as possible out of the cucumber, then wrap in a tea-towel and squeeze again. Dissolve 1 tsp sugar in the white-wine vinegar. Stir the cucumber and dill into the vinegar. Transfer to a serving bowl. Cover and chill until required.

TO SERVE: Serve slabs of warm pissaladière half-covered with rocket, asking guests to garnish with extra-virgin olive oil and vinegar. Serve the kebabs on warmed plates with a dollop of skordalia and a lemon wedge. Offer the pickles and roasted vegetables separately. For the **AFFOGATO** make a pot of strong espresso coffee. At the table, place a scoop of ice cream in 6 espresso cups, or similar. Add a splash of Amaretto and follow with the hot coffee.

SHOPPING LIST

GREEN GROCERIES

1 onion

1kg organic new potatoes, preferably Nicola

1 trimmed leek, approx. 150g

200g extra-fine beans

200g podded broad beans

2 courgettes, approx. 200g

350g young leaf spinach

1 celery heart

150g fresh or frozen raspberries

3 ripe peaches or nectarines

2 lemons

1 garlic clove

2 tbsp chopped flat-leaf parsley

GROCERIES

3 tbsp vegetable oil

2 tbsp olive oil

2 tbsp extra-virgin olive oil

1 vegetable or chicken stock cube

130g carton basil pesto

Tabasco

350g Neopolitan-style tomato sauce

25g flour

1 tbsp runny honey

4 tbsp caster sugar

200g frozen petits pois

CREAMY STUFF

25g butter

250ml milk

6 tbsp freshly grated Parmesan

500g vanilla ice cream

FISH

200g cooked, peeled prawns, preferably North Atlantic

6 salmon tail fillets

BOOZE

250ml white wine

A lovely spring menu that celebrates new-season vegetables. It kicks off with a chunky green vegetable soup enlivened with a garlicky basil pesto and shower of grated Parmesan. The main course is almost fish pie, but cooked as individual portions, served with a generous parsley garnish and a swirl of your best olive oil. No-one can resist Peach Melba; a perfect confection of raspberries, peach and ice cream.

0-15 MINUTES: Heat the oven to 200°C/400°F/gas mark 6. Boil the kettle. For **GREEN MINESTRONE WITH PESTO**, peel and finely chop the onion. Heat 2 tbsp vegetable oil in a spacious pan that can accommodate the finished soup. Stir in the onion and cook gently for 10 minutes. Half fill a medium pan with boiling water, add 1 tsp salt and the broad beans. Boil for 1 minute. Drain, refill the pan with cold water and return the beans to cool and arrest cooking. Trim and finely chop the celery. Slice the leek into thin rounds. Boil the kettle for a second time.

15-30 MINUTES: Begin **ALMOST SALMON PIE WITH LEMON CRUSHED POTATOES** by boiling all but 2 potatoes (approx. 150g) in salted water for 10–15 minutes until tender. Now back to the soup. Stir the celery and leeks into the onions. Add 1 tsp salt, stir again, reduce the heat, cover and cook for 5 minutes. Chop the fine beans into 5cm-lengths. Dice the courgettes. Dissolve the stock cube in 1 litre boiling water. Peel, dice and rinse the reserved potatoes, then stir into the onions. Add the stock and bring the soup to the boil. Reduce the heat and simmer for 15 minutes. Drain the broad beans and, in between other jobs, remove their rubbery skin by nicking the edge with your nail, then squeezing out the bean.

30-45 MINUTES: Heat 1 tbsp vegetable oil in a wok. Add the spinach and stir-fry for a couple of minutes until it has wilted. Tip into a colander, squeeze with the back of a spoon to remove any excess liquid and then divide into 6 salmon-sized mounds close together in a small baking tin. Place the salmon on a plate, smear with olive oil and squeeze the juice of 1 lemon over the top. Arrange the salmon over the spinach. Tip the tomato sauce into a bowl. Stir in the honey and prawns and spoon over the fish. Drain the potatoes. Melt the butter in a pan. Stir in the flour until smooth, then gradually add the milk, whisking as it comes to the boil. Season with salt and pepper and simmer gently for 5 minutes. Leave to cool for 5 minutes then spoon the thick sauce over the fish.

45-60 MINUTES: Skin the potatoes and return them to the pan. Add the juice of 1 lemon and crush lightly with a potato-masher or fork. Pile the potatoes over the fish and dribble with olive oil. Cook in the oven for 25–35 minutes until the potatoes are crusty and the salmon is cooked. Boil the kettle again. Return the soup to the boil. Add the fine beans, courgettes and petits pois. Boil for 5 minutes. Taste and adjust the seasoning with salt, pepper and Tabasco. Peel and chop the garlic and liquidize it with the pesto. Tip into a serving bowl. For **PEACH MELBA** plunge the peaches in boiling water for 30 seconds. Peel off the skin and halve them round their middles. Dissolve the sugar in the wine over a medium heat and cook the peaches in it, covered, for 5 minutes. Place the raspberries in a sieve over a bowl, spoon 4 tbsp of the sugary wine over the top and press through with the back of a spoon.

TO SERVE: Stir the broad beans into the minestrone and serve with the pesto and Parmesan. Use a fish slice to plate the salmon and serve with a scattering of parsley and a splash of extra-virgin olive oil. Place an upturned peach over a mound of ice cream and cover with raspberry sauce.

THAI-STYLE SWEETCORN CHOWDER
THYME-ROAST QUAIL WITH ROSTI
LEMON POSSET WITH RASPBERRIES

SHOPPING LIST

GREEN GROCERIES

1 onion

700g baking potatoes

4 large corn-on-the-cob

1 red pepper

3 little gem lettuce hearts

300g raspberries

150g white seedless grapes, approx. 30 grapes

2 large lemons, plus 1 small lemon

5 garlic cloves

2 red Bird Eye chillies

1 tbsp finely snipped chives

25g bunch thyme

25g bunch coriander

GROCERIES

2 tbsp vegetable oil

2 tbsp olive oil

1 dsp wine vinegar

3½ chicken stock cubes

75g caster sugar

CREAMY STUFF

50g butter

300g double cream, plus 6 tbsp

1 tbsp mayonnaise

MEAT

6 quail

18 rashers pancetta or 12 rashers thin-cut smoked streaky bacon

BOOZE

½ glass white wine, approx. 75ml

There is a surprisingly large amount of meat on little quails but I am never sure whether to serve one or two quail per person. In this menu, one bird is enough as the chowder is quite satisfying and the quail sits on a potato rösti, with salad to follow. The meal finishes with a small but very rich and creamy dessert, topped with a mound of raspberries. I wouldn't say this is a girly menu, but if you are feeding strapping great men, it is probably wise to cook a few extra birds.

0-15 MINUTES: Boil the kettle. Heat the oven to 200°C/400°F/gas mark 6. For **LEMON POSSET WITH RASPBERRIES**, pour 300g double cream into a small pan. Add the sugar and bring slowly to a boil, stirring as it melts. Boil gently for 3 minutes, stirring. Remove from the heat. Stir the juice of a large lemon into the cream. Leave for 5 minutes before dividing between 6 glasses or ramekins, leaving enough space for the raspberries. Chill. For **THYME-ROAST QUAIL WITH ROSTI**, peel then halve 3 garlic cloves. Halve the other large lemon and cut each half into 3 pieces. Rinse out the cavity of the birds, shake dry and season with salt and pepper.

15-30 MINUTES: Pop the halved garlic cloves, sprigs of thyme and pieces of lemon into the quail cavity. Wrap in 3 rashers of pancetta, making sure that the breast is thoroughly covered. Arrange on a baking tray, breast up and with the bacon joins underneath. Dot with butter. For the rösti, smear a heavy baking tray with the vegetable oil. Coarsely grate the potatoes. Squeeze in a cloth to remove as much liquid as possible and place in a mixing bowl. Season with salt and pepper and stir in 6 tbsp of cream. Spoon 6 mounds onto the tray and flatten them out to make ½ cm-thick patties. Place on the top shelf of the oven with the quail below. Cook for 15 minutes. Flip the rösti and cook for 15 more minutes until very crisp. Roast the quail for 25–30 minutes until the pancetta is crisp and shrunken, the breast feels springy when pressed and the legs feel loose. Remove from the oven and keep warm. Turn off the oven but leave in the rösti.

30-45 MINUTES: For **THAI-STYLE SWEETCORN CHOWDER**, peel, halve and finely chop the onion. Cook, stirring occasionally, in a large pan in 2 tbsp olive oil for 5 minutes. Remove the zest from the small lemon in paper-thin scraps. Trim and finely chop the chillies. Chop the garlic. Quarter the pepper, discard the stalk, seeds etc. and cut into small chunks. Stir everything into the onion. Slice down the cobs to remove the kernels. Using water from the kettle, dissolve 3 stock cubes in 1½ litres boiling water. Add the stock and kernels to the pan, return to the boil, reduce the heat, partially cover and cook for 15 minutes until everything is tender. Boil the kettle. Chop the coriander.

45-60 MINUTES: Dissolve ½ a stock cube in 300ml boiling water. Drain most of the fat from the quail pan, leaving about 1 tbsp. Add the wine and simmer briskly for 2 minutes. Add the stock. Simmer for 5 minutes. Halve the grapes lengthways. Add to the pan and cook for 2 minutes. For the salad, place the mayonnaise in a bowl and stir in the vinegar and 2 tbsp olive oil. Separate the lettuce, rinse, shake dry and arrange on a platter.

TO SERVE: Reheat the soup and adjust the seasoning with salt and lemon juice. Stir in the coriander just before serving. Place a rösti in the centre of 6 warmed plates, top with a quail and spoon over the gravy, settling the grapes around the edge. Spoon the vinaigrette over the salad, garnish with chives and serve after the quail. Top the possets with the raspberries and finish with a scoop of cream.

ROAST TOMATO SOUP WITH SAFFRON AND HONEY
PAN-FRIED SALMON TABBOULEH
RASPBERRY AND ROSE-SCENTED SYLLABUB

SHOPPING LIST

GREEN GROCERIES

250g fine beans

2kg medium-sized tomatoes

4 firm medium-sized vine tomatoes, approx. 500g

2 red peppers

125g bunch of spring onions

400g very ripe raspberries

Juice of 1 lemon

80g bunch flat-leaf parsley

25g bunch coriander

GROCERIES

125ml olive oil, plus 4 tbsp

2 tbsp extra-virgin olive oil

6 drips Tabasco

1 tbsp rose water or lemon juice

1 chicken stock cube

Generous pinch saffron stamens

225g bulgar cracked wheat

2 tsp runny honey

3 tbsp caster sugar

175g packet sponge fingers

CREAMY STUFF

300g double cream or whipping cream

FISH

6 salmon fillets

BOOZE

2 large glasses sweet white wine, approx. 300ml

You will also need tinfoil and clingfilm

There is a whiff of the kasbar about this menu. Roast tomatoes are puréed with honey and the saffron and herb-laced bulgar (cracked wheat) is served with crusty, but moist, salmon. The meal concludes with a heady raspberry syllabub scented with rose petals.

0-15 MINUTES: Boil the kettle. Heat the oven to 180°C/350°F/gas mark 4. Begin with **PAN-FRIED SALMON TABBOULEH**. Measure 400ml boiling water into a bowl and stir in the bulgar wheat. Cover and leave until required. Put 6 sundae glasses in the freezer for **RASPBERRY AND ROSE-SCENTED SYLLABUB**. Dissolve 2 tbsp caster sugar in the wine in a small saucepan. Cook gently until reduced by approximately one-third. Leave to cool. For **ROAST TOMATO SOUP WITH SAFFRON AND HONEY**, halve the 2kg tomatoes and lay, cut-side up, on a foil-lined baking sheet. Smear with olive oil. Halve the peppers lengthways and discard the stalk, core and seeds. Arrange, skin-side up, next to the tomatoes. Roast for 45 minutes. Soften the saffron in 2 tbsp boiling water. Dissolve the stock cube in 800ml boiling water.

15-30 MINUTES: Return to the tabbouleh. Place a sieve over a bowl. Quarter the vine tomatoes lengthways and scrape the seeds and juices into the sieve. Press the debris through the sieve, using the back of a spoon to extract maximum juice. Whisk the juice of 1 lemon and 125ml olive oil into the tomato juice. Chop the tomatoes. Finely chop the spring onions. Chop the coriander and parsley leaves. Back to the syllabub, place half the raspberries in a bowl and lightly bruise with the back of a spoon. Sprinkle with 1 tbsp sugar and the rose water or lemon juice. Leave until the sugar has dissolved. Beat the cream until floppy then gradually incorporate the cooled wine, beating gently until all the wine is absorbed to end up with soft peaks. Do not over-beat. Stir 2 large spoonfuls of whipped cream into the bruised raspberries and their juices, mixing thoroughly. Lightly fold the mixture into the cream until streaked with colour then gently fold in the whole raspberries. Spoon the syllabub into the chilled glasses. Chill in the fridge.

30-45 MINUTES: Going back to the soup, lift the burnished skin off the peppers then tip the tomatoes and peppers into the bowl of a food processor. Blitz to make a thick, smooth purée. Pass through a sieve into a suitable pan, pressing and scraping so nothing is wasted – don't forget under the sieve. Add the honey, Tabasco saffron and stock. Reheat and adjust the seasoning with salt, pepper and lemon juice. Boil the kettle.

45-60 MINUTES: Cut the beans in half. Using water from the kettle, boil in salted water for 2 minutes. Drain and set aside. Heat 2 tbsp olive oil in a frying pan over a medium-high heat and fry 3 salmon fillets for 2 minutes each side, pressing down to encourage crusty edges, until just-cooked but still moist. Lift onto a plate and cover with clingfilm. Repeat with the remaining fillets.

TO SERVE: Serve the soup very hot. Give the tomato dressing a final whisk and stir into the bulgar wheat. Add the chopped tomatoes, spring onions, beans and herbs. Stir thoroughly. Serve a pile of the bulgar in the middle of 6 plates and drape a salmon fillet over the top. Decorate with a swirl of extra-virgin olive oil. Serve the syllabubs with sponge fingers.

PORTABELLO BRUSCHETTA
JAPANESE PORK FILLET WITH MISO RICE
MARSALA GRAPES WITH MUSCOVADO YOGHURT

SHOPPING LIST

GREEN GROCERIES
2 medium onions

250g large, flat mushrooms, preferably portabello

500g seedless red grapes

350g seedless white grapes

3 unwaxed lemons

3 large garlic cloves

25g bunch flat-leaf parsley

GROCERIES
6 tbsp olive oil

3 tbsp extra-virgin olive oil

75ml soy sauce, preferably Kikkoman

3 sachets Japanese miso soup paste, preferably Yutaka

100g natural fried breadcrumbs, preferably Goldenfry

400g basmati rice

2 tbsp dark brown muscovado sugar

Flour for dusting

CREAMY STUFF
25g butter

500g Greek yoghurt

4 large eggs

MEAT
2 pork fillets, approx. 500g each

BREAD
6 thick slices sourdough

BOOZE
100ml Chinese cooking wine, preferably Wing Yip

2 tbsp Marsala

A shower of finely chopped garlic with parsley and lemon zest is a delicious complement to any mushrooms but goes particularly well with big, flat portabello mushrooms on garlicky toast. Miso is a useful secret weapon in the kitchen. Here, it combines with other Japanese seasonings to provide a delicious broth thickened with egg. It is spooned over boiled basmati rice and topped with thick slices of crusty pork fillet. The meal ends with a mellow boozy grape salad served with yoghurt stirred with dark, toffee-flavoured muscovado sugar.

0-15 MINUTES: Boil the kettle. To begin **JAPANESE PORK FILLET WITH MISO RICE**, peel, halve and finely slice the onions. Place in a medium-sized pan with the miso soup paste, soy sauce, cooking wine and 400ml boiling water. Simmer for 40–50 minutes until the onions are soft and the liquid has reduced by half. Meanwhile, cut the fillets in half across the middle. Trim any fat or membrane. Sift about 4 tbsp flour into a shallow bowl, put the breadcrumbs in another and crack two eggs into a third bowl. Whisk the eggs lightly until smooth. Roll each piece of fillet first through the flour, shaking away any excess, then the egg and, finally, press into the breadcrumbs.

15-30 MINUTES: Heat the oven to 200°C/400°F/gas mark 6. Heat 4 tbsp olive oil in a frying pan over a medium heat and brown two pieces of fillet at a time, cooking each side for 3 minutes, until crusty and golden. Transfer to a roasting tin. Begin **PORTABELLO BRUSCHETTA** by wiping the mushrooms clean, then slice thickly.

30-45 MINUTES: Wipe out the frying pan, add the butter and remaining olive oil. Place the sliced mushrooms in the pan – you may need to do this in two batches – and cook for a few minutes before turning. Cook for 10–15 minutes until shrunken, juicy and just cooked through. Meanwhile, peel and finely chop 2 garlic cloves. Remove the zest from half a lemon in wafer-thin sheets. Finely chop. Chop the parsley leaves. Make a pile of garlic, lemon zest and parsley, and chop everything together. If necessary, return the first batch of mushrooms to the pan. Add half the parsley mixture. Toss together and turn off the heat.

45-60 MINUTES: Wash the rice. Place in a pan with 600ml cold water. Bring to the boil and immediately turn the heat very low. Cover and cook for 10 minutes. Remove from the heat and leave covered for 10 minutes. For **MARSALA GRAPES WITH MUSCOVADO YOGHURT**, slice the grapes in half lengthways. Place in a pretty bowl and stir in the Marsala. Spoon the yoghurt over the grapes and scatter the sugar over the top. Chill until required. Roast the pork for 15 minutes. Rest for at least 10 minutes before slicing. Crack the remaining eggs into the egg bowl and whisk with any leftover egg.

TO SERVE: Toast the bread. Rub one side with the remaining peeled garlic. Place on plates and dribble with extra-virgin olive oil. Add the remaining parsley to the mushrooms, squeeze over the juice from half a lemon and cook briskly to reheat and absorb the juices. Pile onto the toast and serve with a lemon wedge. Add the beaten egg to the reduced onion gravy and leave to set, then stir once; it will be streaky. Thickly slice the pork. Spoon the rice in the middle of 6 warmed plates or bowls, cover with the dark, eggy gravy and arrange slices of pork on top. Loosely mix the streaked yoghurt into the grapes just before serving.

ASPARAGUS, BROAD BEAN AND PRAWN SALAD
SALMON WITH TOMATO AND CORIANDER VINAIGRETTE
STRAWBERRY VACHERINS WITH BALSAMICO

SHOPPING LIST

GREEN GROCERIES

**500g stringless runner
beans, traditionally sliced
(long, thin and on the diagonal)**

200g podded broad beans

150g sugar snap peas

150g asparagus tips

400g cherry tomatoes

400g strawberries

1 unwaxed lemon

1 large garlic clove

25g bunch mint

50g bunch coriander

GROCERIES

9 tbsp olive oil

1 tbsp red-wine vinegar

½ tbsp aged balsamic vinegar

1 tsp runny honey

1 tbsp sugar

6 meringue nests

CREAMY STUFF

150ml double cream

200g feta cheese

FISH

6 salmon tails

**200g cooked, peeled prawns,
preferably North Atlantic**

You will also need tinfoil

This menu celebrates the arrival of spring. The meal begins with a medley of green spring vegetables tossed with little pink prawns. Continuing with the healthy theme, roast salmon tails are piled over green beans and dressed with a coriander and cherry tomato vinaigrette. The meal goes off the rails at the end with a deliciously unhealthy mound of strawberries, cream and meringue.

0-15 MINUTES: Boil the kettle. To begin **ASPARAGUS, BROAD BEAN AND PRAWN SALAD**, remove the zest from half the lemon and chop finely. Measure 2 tbsp lemon juice into a wide-based serving bowl. Stir in the honey. Add 3 tbsp olive oil and whisk to amalgamate. Stir in the lemon zest. Add the prawns. Pour 5cm-depth of boiling water into a sauté pan or similarly wide-based pan. Add 1 tsp salt and return to the boil. Add the broad beans and boil for 2 minutes. Have ready a bowl of cold water. Scoop the beans out of the pan into the cold water. Add the asparagus tips to the boiling water and boil for 2 minutes. Drain the broad beans. Nick the edge of each bean with your thumb and squeeze the bright green beans into the salad, continuing as you cook the asparagus and then the sugar snap peas, separately for 2 minutes each. Lift the asparagus carefully out of the boiling water and rest on kitchen paper to drain. Add the drained sugar snap peas and asparagus to the salad.

15-30 MINUTES: Boil the kettle. Begin the **STRAWBERRY VACHERINS WITH BALSAMICO**. Hull the strawberries and quarter lengthways. Place in a bowl. Sprinkle over the sugar, tossing to dissolve then add the balsamic vinegar. Toss again and leave until required. Beat the cream until holding soft peaks, taking care not to overdo it. Heat the oven to 200°C/400°F/gas mark 6. Start **SALMON WITH TOMATO AND CORIANDER VINAIGRETTE**. Smear the fish on both sides with olive oil and place on an oven tray. Squeeze over any remaining lemon juice.

30-45 MINUTES: Peel and chop the garlic. Sprinkle with a generous pinch of salt and crush into a paste. Add to a bowl that can accommodate the tomatoes. Stir in the vinegar. Add 4 tbsp olive oil and whisk to amalgamate. Quarter the tomatoes and stir into the dressing. Scoop half the strawberries into a sieve to drain. Tip into a bowl. Into another bowl pass the rest of the fruit and the juices through the sieve, scraping underneath so nothing is wasted, stirring to make a sauce. Transfer to a jug.

45-60 MINUTES: Roast the fish for 15 minutes until just cooked through. Remove from the oven and cover with foil to keep warm. Finely chop the coriander. Stir the coriander into the tomatoes. Boil the runner beans in a large pan of salted water for 2 minutes. Drain and keep warm.

TO SERVE: To finish the salad, set aside 6 of the smallest mint sprigs and finely chop the rest of the leaves. Add the chopped leaves to the salad and carefully toss all the ingredients together. Crumble the feta over the top. Loosely toss before serving. Make a pile of runner beans in the middle of 6 warmed dinner plates. Lay a piece of salmon over the top and spoon the dressing over the fish. Quickly assemble the vacherins by filling the meringue nests with whipped cream. Pile with chopped strawberries, add a little of the sauce and garnish with a sprig of mint. Serve the remaining sauce separately.

SHOPPING LIST

GREEN GROCERIES

2 shallots

400g small boiled beetroot

6 medium-sized tomatoes

200g cherry tomatoes

3 large lemons

4 garlic cloves

50g bunch flat-leaf parsley

80g bunch coriander

GROCERIES

9 tbsp olive oil

3 generous pinches saffron stamens

2 tsp ground coriander

2 tsp ground cumin

175g couscous

70g pitted black olives

150g pot organic hummus

200g ready-made falafel

400g can Eazy fried onions

4 tbsp roasted Marcona almonds

250g packet thin ginger biscuits

1 tsp sugar

CREAMY STUFF

25g butter

200g natural yoghurt

6 eggs

500g tub coffee ice cream

MEAT

12 skinned, boned
chicken thighs

BREAD

2 Greek sesame seed
loaves (daktyla)

This meal begins with a platter of delicious dips and appetisers for people to pile onto their plate and eat with crusty sesame-seed Greek bread. The tagine is served in the traditional Moroccan-style without an accompaniment, but do leave any leftovers from the mezze on the table, because all this food is complementary. The wow-factor pudding is a guaranteed hit with the males round the table.

0-15 MINUTES: Begin **GINGER AND COFFEE ICE CREAM SANDWICHES** by taking the ice cream out of the freezer to soften slightly. Boil the kettle. Heat the oven to 200°C/400°F/gas mark 6. Preheat the grill. For **MIDDLE EASTERN MEZZE,** halve the medium-sized tomatoes, season with salt, pepper, sugar and a splash of olive oil. Grill for 10 minutes, adjusting the heat so they cook evenly, until soft and weeping. Leave to cool. Boil the eggs for 10 minutes for **MOROCCAN CHICKEN, EGG AND ALMOND TAGINE**. Leave in cold water to cool. Now make 12 sandwiches with the ginger biscuits and a generous scoop of ice cream. Pile onto a plate and return to the freezer.

15-30 MINUTES: Continuing with the mezze, peel, chop and crush the garlic with a little salt to make a juicy paste. Place ½ tsp of the paste in a bowl, add the yoghurt and stir in 1 tbsp olive oil and a squeeze of lemon. Halve the beetroot and place on one end of a platter. Season with salt and a squeeze of lemon. Spoon over the yoghurt. Chop 20g coriander and sprinkle on top. Arrange the grilled tomatoes next to the beetroot. Spoon the hummus next to the tomatoes and season both with cumin. Scatter with olives and splash the tomatoes with olive oil. Place the couscous in a bowl, add 250ml boiling water, a pinch of saffron, 1 tbsp lemon juice and 1 tbsp olive oil. Stir, cover and leave for 5 minutes to hydrate. Quarter the cherry tomatoes. Peel and finely chop the shallots. Finely chop the flat-leaf parsley leaves. Mix everything into the couscous. Pile onto one end of a second platter. Cook the falafel in the oven for 10 minutes. Turn off the oven but put the loaves in to get crusty. Place the falafel next to the couscous with 1 lemon, cut into wedges.

30-45 MINUTES: Return to the tagine. Heat 2 tbsp olive oil and the butter in a spacious heavy-bottomed pan over a high heat. Add the onions and stir-fry for 5 minutes. Soften the remaining saffron in a little boiling water. Add the cumin, ground coriander and saffron to the onions. Reduce the heat, cover and leave to cook for about 10 minutes. Meanwhile, cut each chicken thigh into 4 or 5 strips. Stir 3 tbsp olive oil into the remaining garlic paste and smear it all over the chicken. Heat 1 tbsp olive oil in a frying pan and quickly stir-fry the almonds until golden. Drain on kitchen paper.

45-60 MINUTES: Stir the chicken into the onions, increase the heat and stir until all the pieces have turned white. Add just enough water to cover. Bring to the boil, reduce the heat, cover and cook for 15 minutes. Adjust the seasoning with salt, pepper and lemon juice. Chop the remaining coriander.

TO SERVE: Break up the bread to serve with the starter and main course. To finish the tagine, stir in the almonds and chopped coriander, and garnish with halved boiled eggs. Serve the ice cream sandwiches from the freezer.

INSTANT BORSCHT
PORK WITH CRISPY SAGE AND APPLE MASH
APRICOTS WITH VANILLA, ORANGE AND HONEY

SHOPPING LIST

GREEN GROCERIES

8 medium-sized potatoes, approx. 1kg

4 uncooked beetroot, approx. 750g

4 large eating apples

4 large oranges

3 lemons

3 large garlic cloves

50g bunch flat-leaf parsley

18 large sage leaves

GROCERIES

3 tbsp olive oil

2 chicken stock cubes

1½ tsp paprika

1 vanilla pod

2 tbsp honey

500g large, soft, ready-to-eat dried apricots

CREAMY STUFF

50g butter

150ml milk

500g natural yoghurt

150g crème fraîche or soured cream, to serve

MEAT

6 pork chops

A wonderfully comforting menu that begins with an unbelievably quick and easy version of borscht. Pork chops follow, with a luscious frill of crisp fat running round the meat, which cry out for mashed potato. The addition of apple to the mash complements the pork and results in a light, elegant mash that is guaranteed to become a favourite. Soft apricots cooked with vanilla, fresh orange juice and honey, with a dollop of thick, natural yoghurt to help them along, is the perfect conclusion to the meal.

0-15 MINUTES: Begin **PORK WITH CRISPY SAGE AND APPLE MASH**. Peel and finely chop 2 garlic cloves. Chop the flat-leaf parsley leaves. Set aside 2 tbsp parsley to garnish. Cut through the rind of the chops at 2cm intervals towards the meat, to avoid buckling as they cook. Season both sides with salt and paprika. Place in a shallow dish and squeeze 2 lemons over the chops. Scatter chopped garlic and parsley on both sides. Leave to marinate. Peel the potatoes, cut into even-sized chunks and place in a pan with 1 tsp of salt and plenty of water. Bring to the boil while you quarter, peel and core the apples. Cut into chunks and add to the potatoes. Boil for about 15 minutes until tender.

15-30 MINUTES: Meanwhile, get **APRICOTS WITH VANILLA, ORANGE AND HONEY** under way. Place the apricots in a pan. Split the vanilla pod and add to the pan with the honey. Squeeze over the oranges. Cover and simmer gently for 20 minutes, until the apricots are swollen and soft. Tip into a bowl and leave to cool. Drain the potatoes and apples. Heat the butter and milk together. When the butter has melted remove from the heat. Add the potatoes and apples and mash together until smooth. Keep warm. Heat the oven to 200°C/400°F/gas mark 6.

30-40 MINUTES: Boil the kettle. To make **INSTANT BORSCHT**, trim, peel and grate the beetroot using a food processor or the large hole of a cheese-grater. Dissolve the stock cube in 1.2 litres boiling water in a medium-sized saucepan. Stir the beetroot into the boiling stock, return to the boil and boil for 7 minutes. Meanwhile, peel and chop the remaining garlic clove. Sprinkle with ½ tsp salt and crush to make a paste. Squeeze the remaining lemon into a cup. When the 7 minutes is up, stir the garlic and half the lemon juice into the soup. Taste and adjust the seasoning with more lemon juice and salt.

45-60 MINUTES: Heat the olive oil in a frying pan and quickly fry the sage leaves on both sides. Remove and place on some kitchen paper to drain and crisp. Lift the chops out of their marinade and brown them 2 at a time for 2 minutes each side. Transfer to a heavy-duty roasting tray and allow plenty of space between the chops.

TO SERVE: When you serve the soup – with a dollop of crème fraîche and parsley garnish – pop the chops into the oven for 10 minutes, until the fat is crusty and golden. Keep warm until you are ready to serve. Tip the marinade juices into the frying pan, sizzle up and dribble over the chops. Lay 3 sage leaves on each chop. Serve the apricots and their honeyed juices over the yoghurt.

PEAR, SPINACH, GORGONZOLA AND WALNUT SALAD
TURKEY TOM YAM
CHOCOLATE TART WITH CREME FRAICHE

SHOPPING LIST

GREEN GROCERIES

400g extra-fine beans

250g button mushrooms

350g young leaf spinach

5 ripe pears

3 tbsp lemon juice

5 limes

4 red Bird Eye chillies

3 green Bird Eye chillies

2 large garlic cloves

2 lemongrass stalks

25g fresh ginger

80g bunch coriander

GROCERIES

4 tbsp olive oil

7 tbsp Thai fish sauce (nam pla)

1 chicken stock cube

20cm pre-cooked shortcrust pastry case

50g caster sugar

2 tsp white sugar

50g walnut pieces

1 tbsp runny honey

100g dark chocolate (minimum 70% cocoa solids)

Icing sugar, to dust

CREAMY STUFF

75g butter

170g creamy gorgonzola

250g crème fraîche

1 whole egg

2 egg yolks

MEAT

8 turkey steaks

The combination of fresh young spinach leaves, juicy but slightly grainy pear, chunks of creamy gorgonzola cheese and walnut kernels, dressed in lemon juice and olive oil, tastes as interesting as it looks. The main course is really a big soup; one of those highly seasoned Thai soups, a citrus, chilli-flecked broth, with green beans and chunks of turkey breast. It is further enlivened with an oriental pesto made with coriander. The finale is another change of mood: a slice of divinely wobbly dark chocolate tart, the richness counterbalanced by crème fraîche.

0-15 MINUTES: Boil the kettle. Heat the oven to 190°C/375°F/gas mark 5. Begin with **CHOCOLATE TART WITH CREME FRAICHE**. Put the egg yolks, whole egg and caster sugar in the bowl of an electric mixer and beat vigorously until thick and fluffy. Half fill a pan with boiling water and place a metal bowl over the top. Break up the chocolate, cut the butter into pieces and melt together in the bowl, stirring occasionally until smooth. Remove the bowl and leave the chocolate to cool for 10 minutes.

15-30 MINUTES: Begin **TURKEY TOM YAM**. Slice the unpeeled ginger, smash the lemongrass with something heavy and place both in a pan with the red chillies. Dissolve the stock cube in 750ml boiling water and add that, too. Bring to the boil, reduce the heat, cover the pan and simmer for 15 minutes. To finish the chocolate tart, pour the chocolate onto the egg mixture, beating the two together, then pour into the pastry case, right up to the lip. Bake for 10 minutes then leave to cool.

30-45 MINUTES: Wipe the mushrooms. Stir the juice from 2 limes and 2 tbsp Thai fish sauce into the stock then add the mushrooms. Simmer for 5 minutes. Add the turkey. Simmer very gently for 10 minutes then turn off the heat. Cover the pan and leave for 10 minutes. Meanwhile, make the relish for the main course. Remove the coriander stalks. Peel and chop the garlic. Deseed and coarsely chop the green chillies. Place the coriander leaves, garlic, chopped green chilli, sugar, 5 tbsp Thai fish sauce and the juice of 3 limes in a food processor. Blitz until amalgamated. Pour into a serving bowl. Refill the kettle and boil again.

45-60 MINUTES: For the **PEAR, SPINACH, GORGONZOLA AND WALNUT SALAD**, arrange a bed of spinach leaves on 6 starter plates. Peel, core and quarter the pears lengthways. Thickly slice lengthways into a bowl. Toss with 1 tbsp lemon juice to avoid discolouration. Arrange the slices over the spinach. Add slices of cheese and scatter with walnut pieces. Rest the turkey fillets on a chopping board for 5 minutes then slice on the diagonal into 3 or 4 thick pieces. Return to the pan and cover. Cook the beans in boiling water for 2 minutes. Drain then stir into the tom yam. Cover the pan to keep hot.

TO SERVE: Make the dressing by whisking together 2 tbsp lemon juice, the honey and olive oil. Spoon over the salad just before serving. Quickly reheat the tom yam, if necessary, and transfer to a warmed serving bowl. Spoon into wide soup bowls with a scoop of coriander relish. Carefully lift the tart out of the tin onto a plate, dust with icing sugar and serve with crème fraîche.

13

ROASTED PEPPERS WITH FETA AND BLACK OLIVES
HADDOCK WITH A CHIVE AND MUSTARD SAUCE
PASSION FRUIT SYLLABUB

SHOPPING LIST

GREEN GROCERIES
1 kg baking potatoes, preferably King Edward

6 red peppers, preferably pointed variety

7 passion fruit

1 lemon

20g chives

GROCERIES
4 tbsp extra-virgin olive oil

2 tbsp aged balsamic vinegar, preferably Belazu

12 pitted black olives

1 tbsp smooth Dijon mustard

25g flour

2 tbsp caster sugar

CREAMY STUFF
75g butter

600ml milk

200g Greek feta cheese, preferably Pittas

300g double cream

FISH
6 fillets of haddock, cod or smoked haddock

BREAD
Crusty bread and butter, to serve

BOOZE
300ml white wine

You will also need clingfilm

Peppers roasting in the oven is one of the most mouth-watering cooking smells I know and red peppers look particularly attractive on a platter with a crumble of feta cheese and black olives. A simple olive oil and balsamic vinegar dressing makes this a stunning starter. Some ingredients are made for each other and roast haddock with mashed potato and a creamy chive and mustard sauce is a good example. This food is both comforting and elegant and so, too, is this syllabub with sweet but sharp passion fruit.

0-15 MINUTES: Heat the oven to 200°C/400°F/gas mark 6. Boil the kettle. For **PASSION FRUIT SYLLABUB**, put 6 glass bowls or large wine glasses in the freezer to chill. Place the wine and 2 tbsp sugar in a small saucepan and simmer, swirling the pan as the sugar dissolves, until reduced by approximately one-third. Leave to cool. Whisk the double cream in a bowl until fairly stiff. For the **ROASTED PEPPERS WITH FETA AND BLACK OLIVES**, arrange the peppers on a roasting tin and roast for 30 minutes, turning halfway through. Transfer to a plate, cover with clingfilm and leave for 5 minutes.

15-30 MINUTES: For **HADDOCK WITH A CHIVE AND MUSTARD SAUCE**, melt 25g butter in a medium-sized pan and stir in the flour, stirring until smooth. Now stir in the mustard. Remove from the heat and add 500ml milk, return to the heat and stir constantly as the sauce comes to the boil. Any lumps can be quickly dispersed by beating the sauce with a globe whisk. Reduce the heat and simmer for 5 minutes. Taste and adjust the seasoning with salt and plenty of pepper. Remove the skin, stalk and seeds from the peppers and arrange, shiny-side uppermost, on a platter. Zig-zag with balsamic vinegar and extra-virgin olive oil.

30-45 MINUTES: Gradually add the cooled wine to the whipped cream, beating gently until all the wine is absorbed to end up with soft, floppy peaks. Do not over-beat. Scrape the pulp from 4 passion fruit into the cream, folding it in lightly so the cream is irregularly streaked with colour. Spoon the syllabub into the chilled bowls or glasses. Chill in the fridge until required. Arrange the fish on an oiled baking tray. Season with salt, a squeeze of lemon and splash of olive oil. Roast for 15 minutes. Keep warm.

45-60 MINUTES: Peel the potatoes, cut into even-sized chunks and rinse. Boil in plenty of salted water for about 15 minutes until tender. Drain and set aside. Add 50g butter and 100ml milk to the potato pan. Heat the milk and when the butter has melted, remove from the heat. Return the potatoes to the pan and mash. Beat with a wooden spoon to make a fluffy mash, adding a little extra milk or butter as you think fit. Keep warm.

TO SERVE: Crumble the feta over the peppers and scatter with torn black olives. Serve with crusty bread and butter. Spoon the potato into the middle of 6 warmed plates. Top with a piece of fish. Quickly reheat the sauce and spoon over the top. Garnish generously with snipped chives. Halve the remaining passion fruit and scrape half over the top of each syllabub.

STARTER P116 **MAIN** P122 **PUDDING** P139

SHOPPING LIST

GREEN GROCERIES

1 medium red onion

750g new potatoes

400g podded broad beans

9 medium-size ripe vine tomatoes

3 large, firm but ripe avocados

Juice of 1 lemon

1 large garlic clove

25g bunch mint

About 20 basil leaves

GROCERIES

3 tbsp olive oil

6 tbsp extra-virgin olive oil

1 tsp aged balsamic vinegar

½ tsp chilli flakes

400g can chopped tomatoes

150g pudding rice

250g Agen ready-to-eat pitted prunes

1 regular tea bag

1 vanilla pod

1 tsp runny honey

75g caster sugar

CREAMY STUFF

25g butter

900ml milk

4 buffalo mozzarella

150g clotted or double cream

MEAT

75g pancetta or smoked streaky bacon

6 loin pork chops

BREAD

Crusty bread and butter, to serve

BOOZE

½ glass white wine, approx. 75ml

3 tbsp Armagnac, brandy, whisky or rum

Tomatoes, avocado and mozzarella make a classy salad that can look endlessly different. It is vital that the ingredients are perfectly ripe and dressed simply with olive oil and lemon juice – although a smidgen of balsamic vinegar gives the flavours an extra dimension. The main course comes from Mallorca where broad beans are often teamed with bacon and ham, not to mention tomatoes and mint. Prunes plumped up with black tea and Armagnac go wonderfully well with this extremely creamy rice pudding.

0-15 MINUTES: Boil the kettle. Keeping separate piles, peel, halve and finely chop the onion and garlic for **PORK CHOPS WITH MALLORQUIN BROAD BEANS**. Heat the olive oil in a frying pan and gently soften the onion, adding the garlic after 10 minutes. Slice across the pancetta to make skinny strips and stir into the onion. Cook briskly, stirring often, for 5 minutes. Meanwhile, with water from the kettle, boil the broad beans for 1 minute, then drain. Refill the pan with cold water and return the beans.

15-30 MINUTES: Add the wine to the onions and let it bubble away. Stir in the chilli flakes and then the tomatoes. Season with salt and pepper and cook for 10 minutes. Drain the broad beans. In between other jobs, remove their rubbery skin by nicking the edge with your nail, then squeezing out the bean into a bowl. At 2cm-intervals cut into the fat running round the chops towards the meat, to prevent them from buckling during cooking. Now start **ARMAGNAC PRUNES WITH VANILLA RICE PUDDING**. Place the vanilla pod in a pan with the milk and bring to boiling point. Reduce the heat and simmer gently for 5 minutes. Give the vanilla pod a good bash with a wooden spoon to release the seeds. Add the rice to the milk. Simmer very gently, stirring occasionally, for about 20 minutes or until the rice is tender and most of the liquid absorbed.

30-45 MINUTES: Pour 150ml boiling water onto the tea bag. Squish once and remove the bag. Simmer the prunes in the black tea with 25g sugar and the Armagnac for 15 minutes. Tip into a serving bowl and leave to cool. Now make the **INSALATA TRICOLORE WITH BALSAMICO**. Making separate piles, core and thickly slice the tomatoes. Thickly slice the mozzarella. Halve the avocados, twist apart, remove the stone and peel. Slice across the halves thickly. Make individual salads by alternating the slices of tomato, mozzarella and avocado or present on a large platter for sharing. Whisk together the juice of 1 lemon, the honey, a generous seasoning of black pepper, the extra-virgin olive oil and balsamic vinegar and spoon over the salad. Tear the basil leaves over the top.

45-60 MINUTES: Boil the potatoes in salted water until tender. Drain, toss with the butter and keep warm. Stir the remaining 50g sugar into the rice pudding. Add half the cream and cook for a couple of minutes until thick but sloppy. Leave to cool a little (and thicken) in the pan. Stir the podded broad beans into the tomato sauce. Shred the mint leaves. Grill the chops for 8 minutes each side until the fat border is splayed and golden. Season both sides with salt and pepper. Keep warm until required.

TO SERVE: Serve the salad with crusty bread and butter. Reheat the tomato and bean sauce, stir in the mint and spoon it over the chops. Serve the potatoes separately. Remove the vanilla pod from the rice pudding and stir in the rest of the cream before transferring to a serving bowl. Serve the warm rice topped with a scoop of prunes.

STARTER P116 **MAIN** P132 **PUDDING** P135

15 ASPARAGUS RISOTTO WITH PARMESAN
BABY SQUID WITH GARLIC AND LEMON
FRUIT PLATTER WITH VANILLA CREAM

SHOPPING LIST

GREEN GROCERIES

1 shallot or small onion

750g fine green beans

750g asparagus

1 yellow melon

1 large ripe pineapple

500g strawberries

500g cherries

4 large lemons

6 large garlic cloves, preferably new-season

80g bunch flat-leaf parsley

A few sprigs of mint

GROCERIES

2 tbsp olive oil

½ chicken stock cube

250g arborio rice

1 tsp vanilla essence

Icing sugar for dusting

CREAMY STUFF

125g butter, plus extra knob

4 heaped tbsp freshly grated Parmesan, plus extra for serving

350g crème fraîche

FISH

1 kg baby squid, cleaned, tentacles tucked inside the sac

BREAD

Crusty bread and butter, to serve

BOOZE

Glass Noilly Prat vermouth or white wine, approx. 150ml

What nicer way to start a summery menu than with an elegant risotto? The light main course of baby squid cooked in garlicky butter is finished with lemon juice and masses of chopped flat-leaf parsley. I love this combination of textures and flavours, accompanied by a mound of green beans and some good crusty bread and butter to mop up the juices. It's good, sometimes, to serve fresh fruit as a sharing platter. And here, it's a do-it-yourself fruit salad, with individual bowls of vanilla dipping cream.

0-15 MINUTES: Boil the kettle. Begin with **ASPARAGUS RISOTTO WITH PARMESAN**. Trim the asparagus, discarding the woody ends. Snap off the tips. Cut the stalks into 5cm-lengths. Boil the tips in 1.2 litres boiling water for 2 minutes. Scoop the tips out of the water and set aside. Boil the stalks for 4–6 minutes until tender, then put into the bowl of a food processor with a cupful of cooking water and a generous knob of butter. Blitz into a smooth purée. Pass the purée through a sieve into a small pan, scraping underneath so nothing is wasted. Season with salt, pepper and lemon juice. Dissolve the stock cube in the asparagus water and leave on a low heat.

15-30 MINUTES: Peel and finely chop the shallot. Melt 25g butter in a heavy-based, wide saucepan and gently cook the shallot for 3 minutes until soft but uncoloured. Add the rice and cook, stirring constantly, for a couple of minutes until glistening and semi-translucent. Add the vermouth, stirring as it seethes and bubbles into the rice. Add a ladleful of the hot stock. Stir as it sizzles until the rice has absorbed most of the liquid. Add a second ladleful of stock and continue to stir until all the liquid has been absorbed, adjusting the heat to maintain a gentle simmer. Continue in this way until the rice is almost tender but firm to the bite; 17–20 minutes in total.

30-45 MINUTES: Meanwhile, start **FRUIT PLATTER WITH VANILLA CREAM**. Rinse the strawberries. Trim the pineapple, quarter lengthways and remove the skin and woody core. Slice across the pieces into large bite-sized chunks. Quarter the melon, scrape out the seeds and cut off the skin. Use a melon-baller or cut into bite-sized pieces. Arrange the strawberries, cherries, pineapple and melon on a serving dish. Decorate with the mint. Beat the vanilla essence into the crème fraîche. Decant into 6 ramekins. Chill until required. Boil the kettle.

45-60 MINUTES: Prepare **BABY SQUID WITH GARLIC AND LEMON**. Pick the leaves off the parsley and chop finely. Chop the garlic, sprinkle with ½ tsp salt and crush to a paste. Trim the green beans. Remove the tentacles from inside the squid sacs. Split the tentacles and slice the sac into 1cm-wide rings. Quickly reheat the asparagus purée and stir it into the risotto. Cook for a few more minutes until the risotto is creamy and porridge-like. Stir in the asparagus tips, 50g butter and the cheese. Cover and leave for 5–10 minutes to settle. Using the kettle water, boil the beans with 1 tsp salt for 2 minutes. Drain and keep warm.

TO SERVE: Give the risotto a final stir and serve on warmed plates with a dusting of the extra Parmesan. Melt the remaining 50g butter with the olive oil in a large frying pan. Stir in the garlic paste. Let it sizzle briefly before stirring in the squid. Stir-fry over a high heat for about 5 minutes until just cooked and very tender. Toss with half the parsley. Serve immediately, sprinkled with the rest of the parsley, giving each person half a lemon to squeeze over the top, and the beans in a separate bowl. Serve with crusty bread and butter. Serve the fruit platter with a dusting of icing sugar and individual bowls of the vanilla dipping cream.

STARTER P116 **MAIN** P123 **PUDDING** P139

SPINACH SOUP WITH CORIANDER DUMPLINGS
CHEAT'S CHICKEN CONFIT WITH RED ONION MARMALADE
CARAMELIZED PEAR COMPOTE

SHOPPING LIST

GREEN GROCERIES

6 medium red onions

1.5kg floury potatoes,
plus 2 medium potatoes

500g young leaf spinach

6 ripe but firm pears,
preferably Conference

1 lemon

25g bunch coriander

GROCERIES

7 tbsp olive oil

1 tbsp aged balsamic vinegar

2 chicken stock cubes

¼ tsp freshly grated nutmeg,
plus extra to season

3 heaped tbsp seedless raisins
or sultanas

200g caster sugar

½ tbsp dark brown muscovado
sugar

Sea salt flakes, preferably Maldon

CREAMY STUFF

100g butter

125ml milk

75g mascarpone

75g soft goats' cheese

150ml double cream

250g rich pouring cream,
preferably Channel Islands

MEAT

18 chicken drumsticks or
12 large thighs

Creamy dumplings flecked with coriander bob about in a pool of dark green, combining into a sublime mix of flavours. The main course of very crisp, roast-chicken drumsticks with a sweet and mellow onion marmalade and exceptionally buttery mashed potatoes is one of my favourite combinations. The meal concludes with diced pear, lightly cooked in caramel, with lashings of cream. So quick, so easy and so inexpensive – a classic example of what this book is all about.

0-15 MINUTES: Trim, quarter and peel the onions for **CHEAT'S CHICKEN CONFIT WITH RED ONION MARMALADE**. Slice them very thinly. Heat the oven to 230°C/450°F/gas mark 8. Heat 3 tbsp oil in a wok over a high flame, add the onions and toss constantly for 5 minutes, stir-frying until they wilt and glisten. Add ½ tsp salt, stir-fry for a further 5 minutes then tip into a 2-litre capacity heavy-bottomed pan. Add sufficient water to just cover. Bring to the boil, reduce the heat, cover and simmer for 10 minutes.

15-30 MINUTES: Add the raisins. Boil, uncovered, for 10 minutes until most of the water has evaporated. Stir in ½ tbsp muscovado sugar. When melted add the balsamic vinegar. Boil for 5 minutes until thick. Leave to cool. Meanwhile, make **SPINACH SOUP WITH CORIANDER DUMPLINGS**. Peel, halve and thinly slice the 2 extra potatoes, rinse and drain. Melt 25g butter with 2 tbsp olive oil in a spacious pan. Add the potatoes to the buttery oil and cook for about 5 minutes until tender, stirring to avoid sticking. Fold in the spinach until it has wilted. Add 1.2 litres cold water and crumble the stock cubes over the top, together with ½ tsp salt and ¼ tsp nutmeg. Bring to the boil and simmer for 5 minutes.

30-45 MINUTES: Liquidize the soup and return to a clean pan. Stir in the double cream, reheat and adjust the seasoning. Returning to the main course, smear the drumsticks with olive oil and sprinkle generously with sea salt. Roast on a cake rack placed over an oven tray for 30 minutes until the skin is crisp and golden. Meanwhile, peel the 1.5 kg potatoes and cut into even-sized chunks. Rinse, then boil for 15 minutes in salted water until tender. Drain. Heat the milk with 75g butter. Remove from the heat then mash the potatoes into the pan to a fluffy, creamy consistency. Season with nutmeg and keep warm.

45-60 MINUTES: Squeeze the lemon into a mixing bowl to start **CARAMELIZED PEAR COMPOTE**. Quarter the pears lengthways. Core, peel and then chop them into 1cm-cubes, adding them to the bowl as you go. Cook the caster sugar in a dry, wide-based, heavy-bottomed pan over medium heat. Swirl the pan occasionally until the sugar melts and turns a deep golden colour. Remove from the heat and carefully add the pears and lemon juice, stirring with a wooden spoon. Return to the heat and cook, stirring constantly, for a couple of minutes, so the pears colour but retain their bite. Tip into a serving bowl and leave to cool.

TO SERVE: While the soup reheats, chop the coriander leaves and mix with the mascarpone and goats' cheese. Pour the soup into 6 bowls and drop 2–3 spoonfuls of the coriander mixture into each bowl. To serve the main course, make a mound of mashed potatoes in the centre of 6 warmed plates, spoon over a dollop of onion marmalade and top with 3 drumsticks. Serve the compote with the pouring cream in a jug.

AVOCADO WITH TOMATO MAYONNAISE
CHILEAN STEAK WITH PIMIENTO
CRUSHED RASPBERRY PAVLOVA

SHOPPING LIST

GREEN GROCERIES

1 red onion

1 shallot or small red onion

2 medium vine tomatoes

500g plum tomatoes

2 red sweet pointed peppers

6 firm but ripe small avocados

3 passion fruit

200g raspberries

1 lemon

3 garlic cloves

2 red chillies

50g bunch flat-leaf parsley
or coriander

15g chives

GROCERIES

3 tbsp olive oil

7 tbsp groundnut oil

2 tbsp red-wine vinegar

1 tbsp mayonnaise, preferably
Hellmann's

1 bay leaf

½ chicken stock cube

100g pimiento-stuffed green
olives

400g basmati rice

75g raisins

½ tbsp caster sugar

6 meringue nests

CREAMY STUFF

150g double cream

BREAD

Thinly sliced brown bread and
butter, to serve

MEAT

1 kg rump steak

BOOZE

1 glass white wine, approx. 150ml

This menu is a treat for the eye as well as the taste buds. The avocado salad is a new twist on an old favourite while the main course is a colourful vegetable-heavy stew with intriguing flavours. The meal ends with meringues piled high with crushed raspberry cream finished with a tumble of passion fruit.

0-15 MINUTES: Begin with **CHILEAN STEAK WITH PIMIENTO**. Boil the kettle. Peel and chop the onion. Heat 4 tbsp groundnut oil in a spacious heavy-based pan and cook the onion with the bay leaf for 5-6 minutes. Meanwhile, peel and thinly slice the garlic. Trim, deseed and chop the chillies. Dice the peppers, discarding the seeds and stalk.

15-30 MINUTES: Stir the garlic, chilli and peppers into the onion. Cook, stirring occasionally for 10 minutes while you trim the steak and slice into 3cm-long strips, approx. 1½cm wide. Heat 3 tbsp groundnut oil in a wok and quickly stir-fry the beef, in uncrowded batches, until browned all over, transferring to a plate as you go.

30-45 MINUTES: Dissolve the stock cube in 300ml boiling water. Add the olives and raisins to the onions together with the meat, wine and the stock. Season with salt and pepper. Stir well, bring to the boil then establish a gentle but steady simmer. Partially cover the pan and cook for 20 minutes. Place the plum tomatoes in a bowl and cover with boiling water. Count to 30, drain and remove core and skin. Chop the tomatoes and transfer to a bowl. Chop the flat-leaf parsley and add to the tomatoes. Wash the rice and place in a lidded pan with 600ml cold water. Bring to the boil, reduce the heat immediately to very low, cover and cook for 10 minutes (set the timer). Remove from the heat but leave covered for 10 minutes.

45-60 MINUTES: Begin **CRUSHED RASPBERRY PAVLOVA** by whisking the cream until it forms soft peaks. Dust the raspberries with the caster sugar. For **AVOCADO WITH TOMATO MAYONNAISE** peel, halve and finely chop the shallot. Place in a bowl and just cover with the vinegar. Pour boiling water over the vine tomatoes. Count to 30, drain, halve, remove the skin and scrape away the seeds. Dice finely. Run a sharp knife round the avocados. Twist apart, remove the stone and peel, then slice across the halves to make 1cm-wide half-moons. Pile the avocado onto 6 plates and season with lemon juice to avoid discolouration. Place the mayonnaise in a bowl. Drain the shallots, reserving ½ tbsp of the vinegar. Add the drained shallot and the reserved vinegar to the mayonnaise then beat in the olive oil to make a thick and creamy dressing. Scatter the diced vine tomatoes liberally over the avocado and spoon over the dressing. Finely slice the chives and scatter over the top. Give the beef a stir and then simmer uncovered for 10–15 minutes.

TO SERVE: Serve the avocado and tomato mayonnaise with slices of brown bread and butter. Stir the plum tomatoes and chopped parsley into the beef, quickly reheat, check the seasoning and serve from the dish. Fork up the rice and transfer to a serving dish to serve with the beef. Lightly crush the raspberries and stir into the cream. Pile into the meringue cases. Halve the passion fruit and scrape over the top.

STARTER P116 **MAIN** P132 **PUDDING** P139

18 ROAST AUBERGINE WITH ASIAN DRESSING
CARAMELIZED RED ONION TARTS
GOLDEN FRUIT SALAD WITH LEMONGRASS SYRUP

SHOPPING LIST

GREEN GROCERIES

6 medium-large red onions

4 aubergines, long rather than fat

200g organic wild rocket

1 large ripe pineapple

3 navel oranges

1 red grapefruit

1 large lemon, plus 2 tbsp lemon juice

2 large garlic cloves

4 red Bird Eye chillies

4 kaffir lime leaves (fresh or Bart's Spices)

2 lemongrass stalks

4 tbsp chopped coriander

About 20 small mint leaves

GROCERIES

4 tbsp olive oil

3 tbsp peanut oil

1 tbsp aged balsamic vinegar

1 tbsp Thai fish sauce (nam pla)

75g white sugar

2 tsp caster sugar

½ tbsp dark brown muscovado sugar

Flour for dusting

500g ready-made puff pastry

CREAMY STUFF

200g Dolcelatte

44

This is a fabulous menu for entertaining vegetarian friends or for those occasions when you don't want to serve meat or fish. Each course is light and elegant, although the cheese makes the tart surprisingly satisfying. The fruit salad zings the taste buds back into action so be sure to serve a well-balanced dessert wine to stand up to the tropical flavours.

0-15 MINUTES: Heat the oven to 200°C/400°F/gas mark 6. Begin with **CARAMELIZED RED ONION TARTS**. Trim, quarter and peel the onions. Slice them thinly. Heat 3 tbsp oil in a wok over a high flame, add the onions and toss constantly for 5 minutes, stir-frying until they begin to wilt and glisten.

15-30 MINUTES: Add ½ tsp salt, stir-fry for a further 5 minutes then tip into a 2-litre heavy-bottomed pan and add sufficient water to just cover. Bring to the boil, reduce the heat, cover and simmer for 10 minutes. Boil, uncovered, for 10 minutes until most of the water has disappeared. Stir in the muscovado sugar and, when melted, add the balsamic vinegar. Boil for 5 minutes until thick and luscious. Leave to cool until required. Meanwhile, begin **ROAST AUBERGINE WITH ASIAN DRESSING** by quartering the aubergines lengthways. Arrange the aubergine pieces, cut-side up, on a roasting tin and roast for 20 minutes until the flesh is tender and scorched. Leave to cool. Turn up the oven to 220°C/425°F/gas mark 7.

30-45 MINUTES: Whisk together the lemon juice and peanut oil. Finely chop two chillies discarding the seeds. Peel and finely chop the garlic and crush to a paste with a little salt. Add the chopped chillies, garlic, caster sugar and half the Thai fish sauce. Stir thoroughly. Taste and add the remaining fish sauce if you think the dressing isn't sufficiently salty. Stir in the chopped coriander. Bruise the lemongrass for the **GOLDEN FRUIT SALAD WITH LEMONGRASS SYRUP** and place in a pan with the 2 remaining chillies, lime leaves, sugar and 400ml cold water. Swirl the pan to melt the sugar as it comes to the boil, reduce the heat and simmer for 15 minutes. Leave to cool. Meanwhile, trim and quarter the pineapple lengthways and cut out the core. Peel and slice thinly across each section (a mandolin is perfect for this). Slice the skin off the citrus fruit and cut into thin, bite-sized slices. Transfer to a serving bowl with all the juices.

45-60 MINUTES: Strip the skins off the aubergine and cut into 2cm cubes. Pile onto a platter and spoon over the dressing. Cut the pastry into 6 equal pieces. Dust a work-surface with flour and roll the pieces to approximately 16cm x 12cm. Etch a 2cm-border then prick the pastry inside the border with a fork. Oil two baking sheets and lay out the pastry oblongs with space between them. Spread with the onion. Divide the cheese into 6, cut each piece into 4 or 5 chunks and put on top of the onions.

TO SERVE: Finish the aubergine salad with a scattering of mint leaves. Bake the tarts for 15 minutes, or until the pastry border is puffed and golden. Serve with a handful of rocket. Strain the cooled syrup over the fruit salad. Finely chop one chilli and stir thoroughly through the salad. (Leftover syrup makes a great vodka cocktail.)

STARTER P117 **MAIN** P134 **PUDDING** P139

SHOPPING LIST

GREEN GROCERIES

750g small new potatoes

18 young carrots

400g fine green beans, trimmed

400g podded broad beans

18 bulbous spring onions

225g seedless white grapes

800g small strawberries, preferably English

5 lemons

6 large garlic cloves, preferably new-season

20g curly parsley

A few sprigs of mint, to serve

GROCERIES

350ml olive oil

8–10 tbsp extra-virgin olive oil

3 tbsp white-wine vinegar or sherry

100g blanched almonds

Bowl of caster sugar, to serve

Bowl of sea salt flakes, to serve

CREAMY STUFF

500g whipping cream

6 large eggs

2 large egg yolks at room temperature

FISH

6 cod fillets, 175–200g each

BREAD

225g day-old white bread without crusts

You will also need clingfilm

I love playing around with colour themes in my menus and this one is almost completely white. White gazpacho is also known as garlic soup and grape soup because it contains both but is made like its more familiar red relative (see page 64) with stale bread, vinegar, olive oil and water. It is always served chilled. The main course is a treat for all the senses and makes a great sharing dish of poached fish with hard-boiled eggs and seasonal vegetables, all eaten with garlicky aïoli. This pretty summer menu is a garlic fest, ending with a palate cleansing bowl of strawberries and another of whipped cream.

0-15 MINUTES: Begin with the **WHITE GAZPACHO**. Peel 4 garlic cloves. Place them in the bowl of a food processor with the almonds, vinegar, 6 tbsp extra-virgin olive oil and 1 tsp salt. Blitz furiously. Have ready 900ml cold water. Tear the bread into pieces. Add some bread, then some water to the food processor, and continue in this way until the bread and water is used up and you have created a thick, white purée. Taste and adjust the seasoning with more vinegar, salt and olive oil. Pour into a bowl. Peel then halve the grapes lengthways, if time permits. Stir them into the soup, cover with clingfilm and chill.

15-30 MINUTES: To make **LE GRAND AIOLI**, peel 2 garlic cloves. Finely chop, sprinkle with ¼ tsp salt and work into a paste. Place in a bowl with the 2 egg yolks. Beat together with a wooden spoon until thick and creamy. Add the 350ml olive oil gradually, alternating with the juice of 1 lemon, until thick and wobbly. Cover and keep at room temperature. Boil the kettle. Heat the oven to 200°C/400°F/gas mark 6.

30-45 MINUTES: Rinse and hull the strawberries for **STRAWBERRIES AND CREAM**. Pile them into a bowl. Pour the cream into another bowl and whip lightly until it forms soft peaks. Cover and chill.

45-60 MINUTES: Continuing with le grand aïoli, boil the potatoes and eggs until the potatoes are tender. Drain. Using water from the kettle, separately boil the carrots, beans, broad beans and onions for 2 minutes. Keeping them apart, drain and keep warm. Arrange the fish on a baking tray, squeeze over the juice of 1 lemon and splash with a little olive oil. Season with salt and pepper. Roast for 15 minutes. Turn off the oven and leave the door open. In between other jobs, remove the rubbery skin covering the broad beans by nicking the edge with your nail, then squeezing out the bean into a bowl.

TO SERVE: Give the soup a final stir and splash with a little extra-virgin olive oil. Peel and halve the eggs. Halve the lemons. Arrange the fish on a platter and intersperse with piles of all the vegetables, eggs, lemon wedges and parsley. Splash the vegetables with extra-virgin olive oil. Serve the aïoli and a bowl of sea salt separately. Decorate the strawberries with a few sprigs of mint and serve with the cream and a bowl of caster sugar.

STARTER P113 **MAIN** P123 **PUDDING** P139

SHOPPING LIST

GREEN GROCERIES

500g Chantenay or regular carrots

5 red grapefruit

1 navel orange

2 pomegranates

4 limes

4 large garlic cloves

3 green chillies

100g fresh ginger

80g bunch coriander, stalks trimmed

25g bunch mint

GROCERIES

5–6 tbsp vegetable oil

1 tbsp mustard seeds

½ tsp cayenne pepper

2 tsp ground cumin

400g basmati rice

198g block creamed coconut

4 tbsp caster sugar

CREAMY STUFF

500g natural yoghurt

FISH

6 whiting, plaice or sole fillets

BREAD

4 garlic and coriander mini naan breads

You will also need tinfoil

Chantenay carrots are small, squat and very sweet. They look charming, but any carrot is fine for this Asian-inspired way of cooking them. The little carrots are delicious scooped up with crusty garlic naan bread and creamy yoghurt. Ideally the fish parcel would be made with banana leaves, but tin foil does the job just as efficiently – if not as prettily. It is quite a surprise to open the packet and discover fillets of fish covered in an aromatic green sauce to spill over some simply boiled basmati rice. The meal concludes with a pretty palate cleanser: segments of red grapefruit dressed with orange juice and tossed with pomegranate and mint.

0-15 MINUTES: Begin with **ASIAN CHANTENAY CARROTS**. Rinse the carrots. If using regular carrots scrape and cut into 6cm-long, chunky pieces. Boil in salted water for 5 minutes until *al dente*. Drain. Meanwhile, peel the ginger. Set aside half and slice the rest into thin pieces no larger than a shirt button. Coarsely chop and set aside 2 tbsp coriander. Now start on **FISH IN A PACKET WITH GOAN GREEN SAUCE**. Crumble or grate the creamed coconut into a bowl. Moisten with 100–150ml hot water, stirring to make a thick cream. Peel the garlic and coarsely chop the reserved ginger. Set aside a few small mint leaves. Trim and split the chillies, and scrape away the seeds. Place the rest of the coriander, mint leaves, garlic, ginger, chilli, cumin and coconut cream in the bowl of a food processor. Blitz for several minutes to make a stiff green paste. Squeeze the juice of 1 lime into a cup.

15-30 MINUTES: Cut 12 pieces of tinfoil approx. 24cm-square. Lightly oil the centre of 6 pieces of foil. Generously pile the green paste onto the fish then fold the ends together, pressing to make a sandwich. Divide between the oiled sheets of foil. Cover with a second sheet, folding the sides to make a secure but not overly tight parcel. Place on a baking sheet. Heat the oven to 200°C/400°F/gas mark 6.

30-45 MINUTES: Wash the rice and place in a lidded pan with 600ml cold water. Bring to the boil then turn the heat very low. Cover and cook for 10 minutes. Turn off the heat and, without removing the lid, leave for 10 minutes. Heat 3 tbsp oil in a wok or large frying pan. Add the mustard seeds and ginger and stir-fry for 60 seconds before adding the carrots, cayenne and the lime juice. Stir-fry for 2 minutes.

45-60 MINUTES: For **RED GRAPEFRUIT AND POMEGRANATE SALAD**, squeeze the orange juice into a bowl. Stir in the sugar to dissolve. Slice the ends off the grapefruit, then the remaining skin in a few downward sweeps. Slice the fruit off the 'core' in 3 or 4 large pieces. Cut across each piece into 2 or 3 chunky slices. Pile into a serving bowl as you go. Squeeze the juice from skin, core etc. over the top. Halve the pomegranates, discard the pith and scrape out the seeds. Scatter the seeds over the grapefruit. Add the orange juice and garnish with the reserved mint leaves. Chill until required. Cook the fish in the oven for 15 minutes.

TO SERVE: Sprinkle the naan with water and grill for 1 minute each side. Cut into quarters. Give the carrots a final stir-fry to ensure that they are piping hot. Pile onto a serving dish and scatter with the chopped coriander. Serve the carrots with the naan and yoghurt. Fork up the rice and divide between 6 plates. Serve the parcels individually, with a wedge of lime, for guests to open themselves. Serve the fruit salad chilled from the fridge.

CORN ON THE COB WITH CHILLI AND LEMON BUTTER
CHICKEN KEBABS WITH GREEK POTATO SALAD
PEACH FIZZ

SHOPPING LIST

GREEN GROCERIES

1 medium red onion

1 kg small new potatoes

6 corn-on-the-cob

6 ripe tomatoes

2 red peppers

6 perfect peaches, preferably white

2 lemons

3 limes

4 garlic cloves, preferably new-season

2 red Bird Eye chillies

80g bunch coriander

4 sprigs thyme

GROCERIES

3 tbsp olive oil

3 tbsp extra-virgin olive oil

4 tbsp Greek or other fruity olive oil

2 tbsp wine vinegar

1 tbsp aged balsamic vinegar

3 tbsp caster sugar

CREAMY STUFF

150g butter

MEAT

1 kg skinless chicken fillet

150g sliced chorizo

BOOZE

1 bottle of chilled fizzy white wine

You will also need 12 metal kebab sticks and clingfilm

Hot sweetcorn slathered with butter is a favourite summer treat. Here it is given a grown-up twist with flecks of chilli and lemon juice in the butter. This lovely menu continues with chicken kebabs with slices of chorizo and chunks of red pepper. Kebabs love salads, and I've chosen a simple but stunning tomato salad and a punchy potato salad, with red onion, garlic and masses of chopped coriander. The meal concludes with a perfect white peach in a glass of fizzy white wine.

0-15 MINUTES: Begin with the **CHICKEN KEBABS WITH GREEK POTATO SALAD**. Slice the chicken into kebab-sized pieces. Peel and chop 3 garlic cloves. Dust with ½ tsp salt and use the flat of a knife to work to a juicy paste. Transfer the garlic paste to a suitable container that can hold the chicken. Add the thyme. Stir in 1 tbsp lemon juice and the olive oil. Mix the chicken into the marinade, stirring to coat all the pieces thoroughly. Cover and chill until required. For the **CORN ON THE COB WITH CHILLI AND LEMON BUTTER**, trim and finely chop the chillies. Dice the butter and cream together with a squeeze of lemon and the chopped chilli. Form into a log, cover with clingfilm and pop into the freezer. Halve the sweetcorn.

15-30 MINUTES: To make the Greek potato salad, scrub the potatoes, rinse and boil in salted water until tender. Drain. Meanwhile, peel, halve and finely slice the onion and the remaining garlic. Pour the wine vinegar into a salad bowl and add a generous pinch of salt and several grinds of pepper. Swirl the vinegar around the bowl until the salt dissolves. Whisk in the Greek olive oil to make a thick and luscious dressing. Stir in the garlic and onion. Trim the coarse stalk from the coriander and, keeping the bunch shape, finely chop the stalks. Let the chopping get progressively coarser as you work up the bunch into the leaves. Stir the hot potatoes into the dressing.

30-45 MINUTES: Heat the oven to 200°C/400°F/gas mark 6. Quarter the peppers, discarding the stalk, seeds and white membrane. Chunk. Thread the chicken onto skewers, interspersing with a folded slice of chorizo and piece of pepper, shaking off any excess marinade. Arrange the skewers on a cake-rack, resting on a baking tray. Core and thickly slice the tomatoes. Arrange on a platter. Season with salt and pepper then zig-zag with balsamic vinegar and extra-virgin olive oil. Halve the limes. Boil the kettle.

45-60 MINUTES: Place the lime halves next to the kebabs and cook in the oven for about 15 minutes, turning the kebabs halfway through, until crusty; take care not to overcook. Use water from the kettle to boil the sweetcorn for 5–8 minutes until tender. Boil the kettle again. Drain the sweetcorn. Remove the butter log from the freezer. For **PEACH FIZZ**, place the peaches in a bowl and cover with boiling water. Count to 20. Drain, splash with cold water and remove the skin. Place the peaches in 6 wine glasses. Chill until required.

TO SERVE: Serve the sweetcorn with pats of chilli butter. Add the chopped coriander to the potato salad and give it a final stir just before serving with the tomato salad, kebabs and lime wedges. Advise guests to sprinkle their peach with a little sugar then cover (carefully!) with fizzy wine. Look at it, drink it, and eat the peach.

SHOPPING LIST

GREEN GROCERIES

1 shallot

6 sprays of cherry tomatoes on the vine

750g ripe, flawless cherries with stalks

½ lemon

1 large garlic clove

1 tsp finely chopped thyme leaves, plus a few sprigs

2 tbsp coarsely chopped oregano or marjoram

GROCERIES

3 tbsp olive oil

2 tbsp aged balsamic vinegar

3 x 400g cans of borlotti beans

1 bay leaf

½ chicken stock cube

4 sweet-sour pickled cucumbers

18 silverskin pickled onions

200g dark chocolate (70% cocoa solids)

75g dark brown sugar

CREAMY STUFF

75g butter

150g double cream

FISH AND MEAT

6 haddock fillets, approx. 200g each

400–500g chicken livers

BREAD

6 slices sourdough or crusty bread for toast

BOOZE

2 tbsp brandy, whisky, sherry, port or white wine

You will also need tinfoil

Nobody bothers to make chicken liver pâté these days. But why not? It's desperately simple and such a treat. I love it with a thin butter crust, and serve it, Sixties-style, with Melba toast. This is easily made by lightly toasting crustless bread, halving it horizontally and grilling the untoasted side until it curls. The main course is a chuck-it-all-in-one-pan-and-wait-for-the-compliments-style dish. Dipping cherries – or strawberries – into chocolate sauce is a fun conclusion to the meal.

0-15 MINUTES: Begin with **CHICKEN LIVER PATE WITH PICKLES**. Peel and chop the shallot very, very finely. Peel and chop the garlic. Sprinkle with a little salt and use the flat of a knife to work into a paste. Gently soften the shallot in 25g butter in a frying pan. Meanwhile, sort through the livers, discarding any sinew and fatty bits. Coarsely chop the livers and season with salt, pepper and chopped thyme. Tip into the pan with the shallot, increase the heat and quickly brown all over. Add the garlic. Toss again and then add the booze. Cook for a few more minutes, stirring and tossing, as the juices turn syrupy. Tip into a food processor and add 100g cream. Blitz briefly until smooth. Pour into a 600ml/1pt-capacity gratin dish and smooth the top. Decorate with the bay leaf and thyme. Melt 50g butter and pour over the top to cover thinly. Pop in the freezer for 20 minutes (set the timer!) so the butter sets. Chill in the fridge until required. Boil the kettle.

15-30 MINUTES: Preheat the oven to 220°C/425°F/gas mark 7. Now begin **ROAST HADDOCK WITH BORLOTTI BEANS**. Tip the beans into a sieve or colander, rinse with cold water and shake dry. Place the drained beans in a medium-sized saucepan. Dissolve the stock cube in 300ml boiling water. Add the stock, half the oregano and 1 tbsp olive oil to the pan. Season lightly with salt and generously with pepper. Stir well and leave to simmer gently. Meanwhile, smear the base of a large oven tray with olive oil and lay out the fish fillets. Arrange the sprays of tomatoes around them and splash everything with the remaining olive oil. Sprinkle the fish with the balsamic vinegar and squeeze the lemon half over the top. Season with salt and pepper.

30-45 MINUTES: Remember to move the pâté to the fridge. For the **CHOCOLATE-CHERRY FONDUE**, half fill a pan with boiling water and place over a high heat. Break the chocolate into small pieces into a metal bowl that fits over the pan. Add the brown sugar and 50g cream. Beat with a wooden spoon as the chocolate melts, ensuring everything is thoroughly mixed and melted. Remove from the heat. Remove the beans from the heat and cover.

45-60 MINUTES: Roast the fish for 10-15 minutes, depending on the thickness of the fillets, until they are just cooked through and the tomatoes are beginning to split and weep. Carefully drain all the juices into the beans and stir well. Cover loosely with foil, and keep warm in the bottom of the oven (turned off, with the door open). Drain the silverskins into a bowl. Slice 4 pickled cucumbers on the slant and mix them in with the silverskins.

TO SERVE: Serve the pâté with hot toast and pickles. Quickly reheat the beans. Divide between 6 large, shallow bowls. Arrange a piece of fish on top and decorate with a spray of tomatoes. If necessary, reheat the chocolate sauce and pour into 2 bowls. Serve the cherries on a platter for people to dip and eat.

STARTER P117 **MAIN** P123 **PUDDING** P139

ORANGE AND AVOCADO SALAD
PINK PASTA WITH LEMON-GRILLED FETA
PEACH AND RASPBERRY CRUMBLE WITH CLOTTED CREAM

SHOPPING LIST

GREEN GROCERIES

125g bunch salad/spring onions

6 little gem lettuce hearts

350g boiled beetroot
(without vinegar)

4 firm but ripe large avocados

5 medium-large oranges,
preferably navel

5 ripe peaches or
nectarines

400g raspberries

125g redcurrants

3 large lemons

25g bunch chives

GROCERIES

12 tbsp olive oil

8 tbsp extra-virgin
olive oil

4 tbsp smooth
Dijon mustard

400g quick-cook
spaghetti

2 tsp runny honey

2 tbsp caster sugar

100g amaretti macaroons
(about 10)

CREAMY STUFF

25g butter

2 x 250g Greek feta, preferably Pittas

300g clotted or double cream

1 large egg yolk or 1 tbsp
mayonnaise, preferably Hellmann's

BREAD

Crusty bread and butter, to serve

You will also need tinfoil and clingfilm

Orange, pink, peach: a veritable artist's palette of a menu. The orange and avocado combination is a Spanish idea but this surprising way of dyeing pasta with beetroot is more elusive. The result is a stunning pink spaghetti salad that goes deliciously well with lemony grilled feta. The heat softens the feta whilst burnishing the edges. Amaretti biscuits are the crumble for this lovely summer dessert, eaten warm with a greedy dollop of thick cream and a pretty raspberry sauce.

0-15 MINUTES: Begin with **PEACH AND RASPBERRY CRUMBLE WITH CLOTTED CREAM.** Heat the oven to 200°C/400°F/gas mark 6. Cut the peaches into small chunks. Rinse the raspberries and redcurrants. Strip the redcurrants from the stalks directly into a suitable gratin-style china dish. Add half the raspberries and the peaches. Mix together, sprinkle with 1 tbsp sugar and mix again. Tip the macaroons into a dish and use the end of a rolling pin to crush into coarse lumps. Melt the butter in a frying pan and stir in the macaroons so that they are coated with butter.

15-30 MINUTES: Spoon the macaroon crumbs over the fruit. Cook in the oven for 15 minutes. Turn off the oven and leave the crumble until required. Meanwhile, place the remaining raspberries in a bowl and sprinkle with 1 tbsp sugar. Stir, then leave for a few minutes until the sugar has dissolved. Tip into a sieve placed over a bowl and use the back of a spoon to force the raspberries through the sieve. Stir, scraping under the sieve so that nothing is wasted, to make a thick coulis. Boil the kettle. For **PINK PASTA AND LEMON-GRILLED FETA**, slice each block of feta lengthways into 4 slabs. Cover the grill-rack with foil and lay out the 8 slabs. Season with a squeeze of lemon and splash of olive oil.

30-45 MINUTES: Place 2 tbsp Dijon mustard in a mixing bowl. Mix with the runny honey, the juice of 2 lemons, a generous pinch of salt and several grinds of black pepper. Gradually beat in 10 tbsp olive oil until thick and creamy. Trim and finely slice the spring onions and stir into the dressing. Finely dice the beetroot and add that, too. Using water from the kettle, boil the spaghetti according to packet instructions – 5-10 minutes. Drain. Return to the pan with 2 tbsp olive oil. Toss thoroughly. Tip the spaghetti into the beetroot. Use tongs to turn and mix until the pasta is evenly pink. Cover with clingfilm. Finely chop the chives.

45-60 MINUTES: For the **ORANGE AND AVOCADO SALAD**, squeeze the juice from 1 orange into a mixing bowl. Beat in the egg yolk and 2 tbsp mustard, then add 8 tbsp extra-virgin olive oil, beating until thick and glossy. Trim, separate, rinse and shake dry the lettuce hearts. Arrange the best leaves into a 'nest' on 6 plates. Peel and cut segments from the oranges (leaving segment skin behind). Peel the avocados and cut into big chunks. Arrange the orange and avocado in and around the lettuce. Spoon over the dressing. Season with freshly ground black pepper.

TO SERVE: Serve the starter with bread and butter. Just before serving, grill the feta for 2–3 minutes under a fierce heat until it softens and burnishes. Toss the pasta. Serve 6 portions of pasta on warmed plates, ensuring an even share of beetroot. Tip the rest onto a platter. Shower everything with chives. Arrange a slab of hot, molten feta over each portion of pasta and lay the remaining slices on the excess – for second helpings! Serve the crumble with a dollop of cream, topped with the coulis.

LIME-PICKLED PRAWNS WITH FENNEL
COD WITH PUY LENTILS AND SALSA VERDE
GREEN FRUIT SALAD SURPRISE

SHOPPING LIST

GREEN GROCERIES

1 small onion

2 medium-sized red onions

2 firm but ripe avocados

150g seedless green grapes

2 ripe pears

3 passion fruit

3 lemons

5 tbsp lime juice

2 large garlic cloves

80g bunch flat-leaf parsley

60g bunch coriander

GROCERIES

150ml olive oil, plus 3 tbsp

Extra-virgin olive oil, to serve

1 tbsp red-wine vinegar

1 chicken stock cube

1 tsp fennel seeds

1 tsp dried chilli flakes

1 clove

1 bay leaf

350g Puy lentils

1 tbsp smooth Dijon mustard

1 tbsp capers in vinegar

6 anchovy fillets

1 tbsp caster sugar

CREAMY STUFF

2 tbsp crème fraîche or
Greek yoghurt

FISH

6 cod fillets

400g cooked, frozen extra-large
shelled prawns, preferably North
Atlantic

BREAD

Crusty bread and butter, to serve

You will also need clingfilm

The taste buds are in for a treat with this deliciously herby meal. Fennel adds aniseed-y intensity to this pretty prawn salad and masses of flat-leaf parsley and coriander unite with olive oil and a few choice seasonings to make a rich, luscious sauce for poached cod and lentils. The surprise under the green fruit salad is a question to ask your guests.

0-15 MINUTES: Begin with **LIME-PICKLED PRAWNS WITH FENNEL**. Cover the prawns with warm water for a few minutes to defrost. Drain, sprinkle with ¼ tsp salt and leave. Measure 3 tbsp lime juice into a mixing bowl. Add the vinegar, fennel seeds, chilli, ½ tsp salt and several grinds of pepper. Whisk in 3 tbsp olive oil. Peel, halve and slice the red onions wafer-thin. Stir the onions into the dressing and leave until required. Stir occasionally; you want them limp, soft and pale. Boil the kettle.

15-30 MINUTES: Next start **COD WITH PUY LENTILS AND SALSA VERDE**. Rinse and drain the lentils. Place in a pan with 700ml boiling water. Crumble the stock cube over the top. Peel the small onion, use the clove to spear the bay leaf into the onion then bury it in the lentils. Bring to the boil, reduce the heat, partially cover the pan and simmer for 30 minutes. Leave covered until required. Peel the garlic, coarsely chop and dust with a generous pinch of salt. Use the flat of a knife to work into a paste. Transfer to the bowl of a food processor together with the mustard, anchovies, squeezed capers and flat-leaf parsley leaves. Blitz briefly, scraping down the inside of the bowl then, with the motor running, add the olive oil in a thin stream to make a thick, rustic sauce. Season with salt and pepper. Transfer to a serving bowl. Remember to give the onions a quick stir. Boil the kettle.

30-45 MINUTES: For **GREEN FRUIT SALAD SURPRISE**, run a knife round the avocados, twist apart, discard the stone, and scrape the flesh into the washed bowl of the food processor. Add 1 tbsp lime juice, the sugar and crème fraîche and blitz briefly until smooth. Transfer to a bowl and cover with sagging clingfilm to avoid discolouration. Peel, core and slice the pears into bite-size pieces. Toss in 1 tbsp lime juice. Halve the grapes lengthways. Pile both into a bowl, cover and chill until required.

45-60 MINUTES: Pour a depth of 7.5cm boiling water into a large frying pan and return to the boil. Add 1 tsp salt and the juice of ½ lemon. Immerse the fish in the simmering water, bring back to the boil and switch off. Leave for 5 minutes then lift the fish onto a warmed plate. Cover with clingfilm to keep warm until required. Discard the onion from the lentils and quickly reheat. Finely chop the coriander leaves. Give the prawns a quick squeeze to remove excess water. Stir the prawns and coriander into the onions and transfer to a serving dish or platter.

TO SERVE: Serve the prawns with crusty bread and butter. Spoon the lentils into the middle of 6 warmed dinner plates and cover with a fillet of cod. Top with a scoop of salsa verde and decorate with a swirl of extra-virgin olive oil and a lemon wedge. Divide the avocado cream between 6 pretty glass dishes. Top with a share of pear and grapes. Halve the passion fruit and scrape the juices over the top. Serve immediately.

STARTER P117 **MAIN** P124 **PUDDING** P139

VIETNAMESE DUCK SALAD
CRAB AND PRAWN JAMBALAYA
PINEAPPLE CARPACCIO WITH MINT

SHOPPING LIST

GREEN GROCERIES

3 red onions

400g fine green beans

2 medium carrots

500g ripe tomatoes

2 red peppers

½ cucumber

2 little gem lettuce hearts

2 very ripe pineapples

1 lemon

3 tbsp lime juice

2 garlic cloves

25g mint leaves

A few sprigs of coriander

25g bunch flat-leaf parsley

GROCERIES

2 tbsp vegetable oil

2 tbsp rice-wine vinegar

2 tbsp Thai fish sauce (nam pla)

1 chicken stock cube

Tabasco

1 bay leaf

1 tsp chilli flakes

300g basmati rice

1 tbsp sugar

FISH AND MEAT

3 dressed crabs, producing about 250g brown crabmeat and 200g white crabmeat

200g cooked extra-large prawns, preferably North Atlantic

2 duck breasts

You will also need clingfilm

Vietnamese salads are vibrant, fresh affairs, always made with mint and a good contrast of crunchy ingredients. The clean flavours of this salad pave the way for a luscious, spicy jambalaya, a signature dish of Louisiana. I like it served risotto-style with green beans on the side. I've come across this elegant way of serving pineapple in Italy and Spain and the smell of fresh mint with sweet aromatic pineapple is extremely seductive. It is a winning combination after any rich meal.

0-15 MINUTES: Heat the oven to 200°C/400°F/gas mark 6. Boil the kettle. Begin with **VIETNAMESE DUCK SALAD**. Place the duck breasts skin-side down in an oven-proof pan over a high heat and cook for 2–3 minutes until the skin is crisp. Turn to seal the other side, cooking for 1–2 minutes. Transfer to the oven and cook for 10–15 minutes (for pink meat) until they feel springy when pressed. Remove the breasts to a plate. Cover with clingfilm and leave until required. Meanwhile, prepare **PINEAPPLE CARPACCIO WITH MINT**. Trim and quarter the pineapples lengthways. Remove the skin and woody core. Use a mandoline to slice wafer-thin. Pile into a serving bowl, catching any juices. Tear about 20 mint leaves over the top, toss, cover with clingfilm and chill.

15-30 MINUTES: For **CRAB AND PRAWN JAMBALAYA**, peel and finely chop 2 onions and all the garlic. Heat the oil in a large frying pan or similarly wide-based pan and stir in the onions and garlic. Cook gently for about 5 minutes while you chop the peppers, discarding the stalk, seeds and white membrane. Stir the pepper into the onions, together with the bay leaf and chilli flakes, cooking for about 15 minutes until the onion is soft and slippery and the pepper partially softened. Meanwhile, place the tomatoes in a bowl and cover with boiling water. Count to 20, drain, peel and chop. Rinse the rice in several changes of water. Dissolve the stock cube in 600ml boiling water from the kettle.

30-45 MINUTES: Stir the rice into the vegetables then add the brown crabmeat. Cook for a couple of minutes then add the tomatoes, ½ tsp salt and plenty of pepper. Now add the stock. Bring the liquid to the boil, stir, reduce the heat, cover the pan and cook for 15 minutes. Turn off the heat and leave the pan without removing the lid for 10 minutes – the rice will finish cooking in the steam that is generated. In a salad bowl, mix together the lime juice, fish sauce, rice-wine vinegar and sugar. Peel, halve and finely slice the remaining onion. Stir into the dressing. Peel the cucumber, split lengthways, scrape out the seeds and slice finely. Scrape the carrots and slice finely on the diagonal. Stir both into the dressing. Separate the lettuce leaves.

45-60 MINUTES: Boil the kettle again. Stir the white crabmeat and prawns into the rice. Heat through, taste the juices and adjust the seasoning with salt and lemon juice, adding a shake or two of Tabasco if it isn't hot enough. Using water from the kettle, boil the beans for 2 minutes. Drain. Chop the parsley.

TO SERVE: Slice the duck thickly on the diagonal. Make a nest with the lettuce in the middle of 6 plates. Spoon the dressed salad into the nest, top with a few mint leaves and the duck. Garnish with coriander and any remaining dressing. Stir the parsley into the jambalaya before serving risotto-style with the beans served separately. Remove the (now juicy) chilled pineapple from the fridge.

SMOKED SALMON AND FENNEL SALAD
PORCINI AND PORK STROGANOFF
RHUBARB AND PASSION FRUIT COMPOTE

SHOPPING LIST

GREEN GROCERIES
3 medium onions

2 plump fennel bulbs

½ cucumber

500g fresh or frozen rhubarb

2 oranges

4 passion fruit

Juice of 1 lemon, plus 2 tbsp

1 tbsp finely snipped chives

1 tbsp finely chopped dill

GROCERIES
100ml vegetable oil, plus 1 tbsp

2 tsp smooth Dijon mustard

½ chicken stock cube

2 heaped tsp paprika

500g dried tagliatelle

100g dried porcini (funghi porcini secchi)

3 tbsp runny honey

CREAMY STUFF
75g butter

400ml soured cream

FISH AND MEAT
6 slices smoked salmon or trout

1 kg pork fillet/tenderloin

BREAD
Crusty bread, to serve

A pretty, no-cook starter means there is plenty of time to concentrate on getting the main course right. The important point about this inexpensive take on a luscious Sixties favourite, is to cook the onions until they are meltingly soft. Dried porcini give the creamy juices a powerful mushroom flavour, which is perfectly counterbalanced by the fresh zing of dill fronds and slippery *al dente* tagliatelle. Rhubarb stewed with orange and honey, finished with a cascade of passion fruit, is the perfect conclusion to this rich and satisfying meal.

0-15 MINUTES: Put the kettle on. Tip the rhubarb onto a plate to defrost for **RHUBARB AND PASSION FRUIT COMPOTE**. For **PORCINI AND PORK STROGANOFF** peel, halve and finely slice the onions. Melt 50g butter with 1 tbsp vegetable oil in a spacious, wide-based, heavy-bottomed pan and stir in the onions. Cook, stirring occasionally, for about 15 minutes until limp and soft. Meanwhile, tip the porcini into a bowl and just cover with boiling water. Cover with a plate and leave until required.

15-30 MINUTES: Trim the pork and cut into ribbons, approx. 5cm x 1cm x ½cm thick. Season well with salt and pepper. Increase the heat under the onions and stir in the pork, stirring until all the pieces are white. Drain the porcini (keep the liquid) and add to the pot together with the paprika. Stir thoroughly to cook the paprika. Add 200ml of the porcini water plus 200ml boiling water and the crumbled stock cube. Bring to the boil, reduce the heat and simmer gently for 10 minutes.

30-45 MINUTES: Place the rhubarb in a pan. Squeeze the juice from the oranges over the top and add the honey. Cover and simmer gently for a few minutes until just tender. Tip into a serving bowl and leave to cool. For **SMOKED SALMON AND FENNEL SALAD**, split the cucumber lengthways and use a teaspoon to scrape out the seeds. Slice into 5cm-batons. Trim and halve the fennel, cut out the core and slice thinly across the middle. Chop any fronds. Make a dressing with 2 tbsp lemon juice, salt, pepper, mustard and 100ml vegetable oil. Place a slice of salmon in the middle of 6 plates. In separate bowls toss the fennel and cucumber in the dressing. Pile fennel followed by cucumber onto the salmon. Garnish with chopped fennel fronds and chives.

45-60 MINUTES: Stir the soured cream into the pork and reheat. Add the juice of 1 lemon, taste and adjust the seasoning with salt and pepper. Have ready a large pan of boiling, salted water for the pasta.

TO SERVE: When you serve the starter, with crusty bread, add the pasta to the boiling water and cook according to packet instructions – probably around 10 minutes. Drain, return to the pan and toss with 25g butter. Stir the dill into the stroganoff just before serving. To finish the dessert, halve the passion fruit and scrape the seeds and juice over the rhubarb.

GREEK SALAD WITH LIME HALLOUMI
HARISSA CHICKEN WITH GREEN COUSCOUS
STRAWBERRY TART WITH RASPBERRY RIPPLE

SHOPPING LIST

GREEN GROCERIES

1 medium red onion

200g mangetout

6 ripe tomatoes

150g wild rocket

1 small cucumber

750g small ripe strawberries

200g raspberries

5 tbsp lemon juice

4 limes

2 red Bird Eye chillies

80g bunch coriander

GROCERIES

4 tbsp olive oil

10 tbsp extra-virgin olive oil

1 chicken stock cube

3 tbsp harissa

2 generous pinches saffron stamens

20 pitted black olives

350g couscous

250g puff pastry

300g frozen petits pois

Flour for dusting

1 tsp caster sugar

Icing sugar, for dusting

CREAMY STUFF

Knob of butter

250g halloumi cheese, preferably Pittas

500g Greek strained yoghurt

300g double cream

MEAT

6 organic chicken legs, jointed and skinned

BREAD

Crusty bread, to serve

You will also need clingfilm

The curious rubbery texture of halloumi cheese melts slightly when it's fried and develops delicious crusty edges. With a little chilli and a squeeze of lime it is perfect mezze food, and an interesting change from feta with Greek salad. The main course is equally colourful, with Moroccan harissa asserting its spicy flavour on to roast chicken. It goes very well with couscous laced with peas, mangetout and masses of coriander. A dollop of Greek yoghurt and a juicy roast lime to squeeze on top completes the dish. The meal ends with an easy, but extremely special, strawberry tart.

0-15 MINUTES: Heat the oven to 200°C/400°F/gas mark 6. For **STRAWBERRY TART WITH RASPBERRY RIPPLE**, dust a work surface with flour and roll out the pastry to fit a liberally buttered baking sheet approximately 25 x 30cm. Prick the pastry all over with a fork. Bake for 15 minutes until the surface is brown and semi-risen. Use an egg slice to flip the pastry over. Press down to flatten and then return to the oven for a further 5 minutes, until flaky and golden. Slip onto a cake-rack and leave to cool. Warm the raspberries in the oven for a couple of minutes then press through a sieve with a generous squeeze of lime juice and the caster sugar. Scrape underneath so nothing is wasted. In between jobs, rinse and hull the strawberries.

15-30 MINUTES: For **HARISSA CHICKEN WITH GREEN COUSCOUS**, line a roasting tray with foil. Mix the harissa with 1 tbsp Greek yoghurt and smear over the chicken. Arrange on the roasting tray. Next start on **GREEK SALAD WITH LIME HALLOUMI**. Rinse the rocket and shake dry. Peel then split the cucumber lengthways, scrape out the seeds with a teaspoon, and slice into chunky half-moons. Peel and halve the onion and slice wafer-thin. Quarter the tomatoes. Chop 1 tbsp coriander. Place everything in a salad bowl with the olives. Cover with clingfilm and chill. Trim and finely chop the chillies. Place in an egg cup and cover with 2 tbsp olive oil. For the lime halloumi, cut the halloumi into 18 chunky slices, approximately 1cm thick. When the pastry is done remove from the oven and roast the chicken for 15 minutes. Halve 3 limes and add to the tray. Return to the oven for a further 15 minutes. Remove the chicken and limes from the oven and keep warm. Boil the kettle.

30-45 MINUTES: For the couscous, dissolve the stock cube and saffron in 550ml water from the kettle in a spacious serving bowl. Stir in the couscous with 2 tbsp each of olive oil and lemon juice. Cover. Halve the mangetout on the diagonal, lengthways. Use the remaining kettle water to boil the peas and mangetout for a couple of minutes until tender. Drain. Set aside a few sprigs of coriander and chop the rest.

45-60 MINUTES: Heat a non-stick frying pan over a high heat and brown the halloumi in two batches, cooking for about 30 seconds on each side, until crusty and golden. Slip onto a platter and glaze with the chilli and its oil, a generous squeeze of lime and a splash of extra-virgin olive oil.

TO SERVE: Whisk 3 tbsp lemon juice with 7 tbsp extra-virgin olive oil. Pour over the salad and toss at the table. Serve with the halloumi and crusty bread. Fork up the couscous and stir in the peas, mangetout and coriander. Transfer to a platter. Zig-zag with 2 tbsp extra-virgin olive oil. Arrange the chicken and lime wedges around the couscous. Decorate with sprigs of coriander. Dribble with any juices. Serve with the yoghurt. Lightly whisk the cream and spread thickly over the pastry. Cover with strawberries, dribble with raspberry purée and dust with icing sugar.

28
GAZPACHO
CUMIN MACKEREL WITH GOOSEBERRY COUSCOUS
SUMMER BERRY TART

SHOPPING LIST

GREEN GROCERIES

1 red onion

1kg very ripe tomatoes,
plus 3 vine or plum tomatoes

2 red peppers

1 cucumber

400g strawberries

200g raspberries

250g blueberries

3 lemons

3 large garlic cloves

1 red chilli

50g bunch of coriander

20 mint leaves, plus a few sprigs

GROCERIES

3 tbsp olive oil

100ml extra-virgin olive oil,
plus 2 tbsp

2 tbsp sherry or wine vinegar

1 chicken stock cube

2 tbsp ground cumin

Generous pinch of saffron
stamens

2 tbsp blanched almonds

350g couscous

2 x 200g cans gooseberries,
drained

250g puff pastry

Icing sugar, for dusting

CREAMY STUFF

25g butter

250g mascarpone

FISH

12 small fresh mackerel fillets

BREAD

150g white bread, without crusts

You will also need 300ml iced
water and tinfoil

This is a sharing menu; first the soup is served from a tureen with a series of do-it-yourself garnishes, then the main course arrives on a platter decorated with lemon wedges and sprigs of coriander, and the last course is a generously piled summer berry fruit tart.

0-15 MINUTES: Heat the oven to 200°C/400°F/gas mark 6. Begin with **GAZPACHO**. Peel the garlic. Tear the bread into pieces. Place both in the bowl of a food processor and blitz to make fine breadcrumbs. Meanwhile, peel the cucumber. Halve it horizontally and use a teaspoon to scrape out the seeds. Chop half of it roughly. Trim and split the chilli and remove the seeds. Set aside half of one red pepper and chop the rest, discarding the seeds and white filament. Peel and halve the onion. Coarsely chop one half and add to the breadcrumbs, together with the chopped cucumber, chilli and chopped red pepper.

15-30 MINUTES: Remove the cores from the 1kg tomatoes and roughly chop. Add to the food processor bowl, together with the vinegar, iced water, most of the mint, 100ml olive oil, ½ tsp salt and a generous seasoning of black pepper. Blitz for several minutes until liquidized. Keeping separate piles, finely dice the remaining cucumber and red pepper and finely chop the remaining red onion. Quarter the vine tomatoes, discard the seeds and finely chop the flesh. Taste the gazpacho and adjust the seasoning with salt, pepper and lemon juice. Whisk in the 2 tbsp extra-virgin olive oil. Transfer to a serving bowl and chill until required. Boil the kettle.

30-45 MINUTES: For **SUMMER BERRY TART**, dust a work surface with icing sugar. Roll the pastry thinly to fit a liberally buttered baking sheet approximately 25 x 30cm. Prick the pastry all over with a fork and bake for 15 minutes until the surface is brown and semi-risen. Use an egg slice to flip the pastry over. Press down to flatten and return to the oven for a further 5 minutes until flaky and golden. Slip onto a cake-rack to cool.

45-60 MINUTES: For **CUMIN MACKEREL WITH GOOSEBERY COUSCOUS** dissolve the stock cube in 550ml boiling water in a mixing bowl. Stir in the saffron, 2 tbsp each of olive oil and lemon juice and the couscous. Cover the bowl and leave to hydrate. Quickly stir-fry the almonds in the remaining 1 tbsp olive oil until golden. Tip onto a fold of kitchen paper to drain. Cover the grill-pan with foil and smear with the butter. Lay the fish, skin-side down, and dust liberally with cumin.

TO SERVE: Serve the gazpacho with the garnishes in small bowls, adding the mint to the chopped tomato. Preheat the grill and cook the mackerel for 2–4 minutes – depending on the thickness of the fillets – until just cooked through. Fork up the couscous, stir in the almonds and loosely fold in the drained gooseberries. Pile into the middle of a warmed platter and arrange the fish around the couscous. Decorate with a few sprigs of coriander and lemon wedges. Finish the tart by beating the mascarpone and spread it thickly over the cold, crisp pastry, right up to the edges. Arrange the fruit over the top, dust with icing sugar and garnish with the sprigs of mint.

MINTED PEA AND LEMON SOUP
ROAST SALMON WITH PESTO POTATOES
PEARS POACHED IN WHITE WINE, HONEY AND LAVENDER

SHOPPING LIST

GREEN GROCERIES

1 kg scrubbed small salad potatoes

350g trimmed extra-fine green beans

6 sprays cherry tomatoes on the vine

125g spring/salad onions

6 even-sized, firm but ripe pears

4 lemons

**6 lavender flower heads or
2 sprigs of thyme**

GROCERIES

2–3 tbsp olive oil

2 chicken stock cubes

**1 tbsp concentrated English
mint sauce**

130g basil pesto

Tabasco (optional)

1 kg frozen petits pois

3 tbsp runny honey

CREAMY STUFF

50g butter

**250g rich pouring cream,
preferably Channel Island**

FISH

6 salmon tail fillets

BREAD

**Crusty bread and butter,
to serve**

BOOZE

600ml white wine

Frozen peas make surprisingly delicious, quick and easy soups ready within 20 minutes of the kettle boiling. The main course is one of those clever, restaurant-style, quick-assembly dishes, organised in advance and put on to cook as you begin the meal. Poaching pears in white wine turns them prettily translucent and adding honey and lavender, or some fresh thyme, imbues the golden juices with a delicate flavour and heady scent. The pears are best eaten lukewarm or cold, with or without cream.

0-15 MINUTES: Put the kettle on for **MINTED PEA AND LEMON SOUP**. Trim, peel and finely slice the onions. Pare fine strips of zest from half a lemon. Melt the butter in a medium-sized pan and stir in the onion and lemon zest. Season with salt and pepper. Cover and cook over a medium-low heat for about 5 minutes, until soft. Measure 2 litres boiling water into a jug. Add the stock cubes, stirring to dissolve. Add the stock then peas to the pan, increase the heat and boil for 5 minutes, until the peas are tender. Add the mint sauce. Liquidize in batches and pour into a clean pan. Reheat and adjust the seasoning with salt, lemon juice and just a smidgen of Tabasco.

15-30 MINUTES: Next prepare **PEARS POACHED IN WHITE WINE, HONEY AND LAVENDER**. Pour the wine and honey into a lidded pan that can hold the pears in a single layer. Add 2 paper-thin strips of lemon zest and the lavender or thyme. Bring gently to the boil over a medium-low heat, swirling the pan a few times until the honey dissolves. Allow to simmer while you carefully peel the pears, leaving the stalk intact. Cut out the core in a small cone shape and smear the fruit with lemon juice to avoid discolouration. Place the pears in the pan and reduce the heat. Cover and cook until tender – about 20 minutes – turning them halfway through cooking.

30-45 MINUTES: Now get **ROAST SALMON WITH PESTO POTATOES** under way. Boil the potatoes in salted water until tender. Turn off the heat and leave in the hot water. Rinse then halve the beans. Smear the salmon with olive oil and arrange on a heavy-duty baking tray. Arrange the 6 sprays of tomatoes next to the fish. Pierce each tomato to avoid bursting. Heat the oven to 200°C/400°F/gas mark 6.

45-60 MINUTES: Stand the pears in a serving dish. Cook the liquid at a steady simmer until reduced by half and slightly syrupy. Strain it over the pears. Put the pesto into a large bowl. Boil the kettle again.

TO SERVE: Reheat the soup, stirring. Pop the salmon in the oven and set the timer for 15 minutes. Serve the soup with crusty bread and butter. When the starter has been eaten, boil the beans in salted water for 2 minutes. Stir the drained beans and potatoes into the pesto and pile in the middle of 6 warmed dinner plates. Arrange the salmon on top and drape each piece with a tomato spray. Dribble any fish juices over and finish with a swirl of your best olive oil and a lemon wedge. Serve the pears with the cream.

STARTER P113 **MAIN** P124 **PUDDING** P140

ROASTED RED PEPPER SOUP WITH SAFFRON
LAMB WITH SPINACH POLENTA
VANILLA PLUMS IN RED WINE

SHOPPING LIST

GREEN GROCERIES

3 medium-small red onions

6 large plum tomatoes

6 red sweet pointed peppers, preferably Ramiro

500g young leaf spinach

6 dark red plums

2 lemons

1 red Bird Eye chilli

GROCERIES

5 tbsp olive oil

1 chicken stock cube

300g 1-minute polenta, preferably Merchant Gourmet

Generous pinch saffron stamens

1 vanilla pod

2 tbsp sugar

1 tsp runny honey

CREAMY STUFF

75g butter

100g grated Parmesan, plus 2 tbsp

300ml crème fraîche

MEAT

6 lamb chump chops

BREAD

Crusty bread and butter, to serve

BOOZE

2 glasses red wine, approx 300ml

You will also need tinfoil and clingfilm

A whiff of saffron mingles with the gorgeous smell of roasting peppers in this stunning bright orange-red soup. The red theme continues throughout the meal with roast tomatoes providing the perfect juicy sidekick to creamy, Parmesan-rich spinach polenta and pink chump chops. The meal concludes with dark red plums poached in red wine with vanilla, served lukewarm with lemony crème fraîche.

0-15 MINUTES: Heat the oven to 200°C/400°F/gas mark 6. Boil the kettle. For **ROASTED RED PEPPER SOUP WITH SAFFRON**, arrange the peppers on a baking sheet. Halve the onions and position them near the edges. Place the chilli in the middle of the peppers. Dissolve the stock cube in 750ml boiling water. Add the saffron. For **LAMB WITH SPINACH POLENTA** cover a second baking sheet with foil. Halve the tomatoes lengthways, and lay them out, cut-side up on the foil. Smear the cut surfaces with olive oil.

15-30 MINUTES: Put the peppers on the top shelf of the oven and the tomatoes on the bottom shelf and cook for 30 minutes. For **VANILLA PLUMS IN RED WINE**, run a sharp knife round the plums, twist apart and remove the stones – if they are firmly embedded, leave them; they can be removed later. Place the plums in a ceramic gratin dish that can hold them in a single layer. Sprinkle with sugar, pour on the wine and tuck the vanilla pod between the plums. Cover loosely with a double fold of foil. Place the plums next to the tomatoes in the oven and cook for 30 minutes or until very soft but still holding their shape. Remove from the oven but leave covered.

30-45 MINUTES: Pour boiling water into a large pan and return to the boil. Add 1 tsp salt and the spinach. Boil for 1 minute. Drain and leave to cool. Continuing with the soup, lift the peppers onto a plate and cover with clingfilm. Leave for 5 minutes and then peel off the skin. Remove the core and seeds. Scrape the soft onion flesh out of the skin. Place the peppers, onions and what remains of the chilli (discard the stalk and seeds) in the bowl of a food processor. Add the saffron stock and blitz. Pass through a sieve into a suitable pan, scraping underneath so nothing is wasted. Reheat and adjust the seasoning with salt, pepper, lemon juice and honey.

45-60 MINUTES: Trim excess fat from the chops. Smear both sides lavishly with olive oil and set aside. Have ready the grated Parmesan and butter. Refill the kettle and boil. Check the tomatoes: when they are soft and weeping but still holding their shape, remove from the oven and leave to cool. Squeeze the spinach between your hands to remove excess water. Heat the griddle and when very hot cook 2 chops at a time for 2 minutes each side. Transfer to a warmed plate, season with salt and pepper and cover with clingfilm. Check the plums are tender and remove from the oven to cool.

TO SERVE: Reheat the soup and serve with crusty bread and butter. Polenta-cooking must be done at the last minute: measure 1.2 litres boiling water into a spacious pan. Add 1 tsp salt and return to the boil. Add the polenta in a steady stream, reduce the heat immediately and stir for 1 minute as it thickens instantly. Stir in the butter and 100g Parmesan and then stir in the spinach. Divide between 6 warmed dinner plates. Dust with extra grated Parmesan before adding a chop and 2 tomato halves. Swirl with olive oil and add a lemon wedge. Serve the warm plums with crème fraîche.

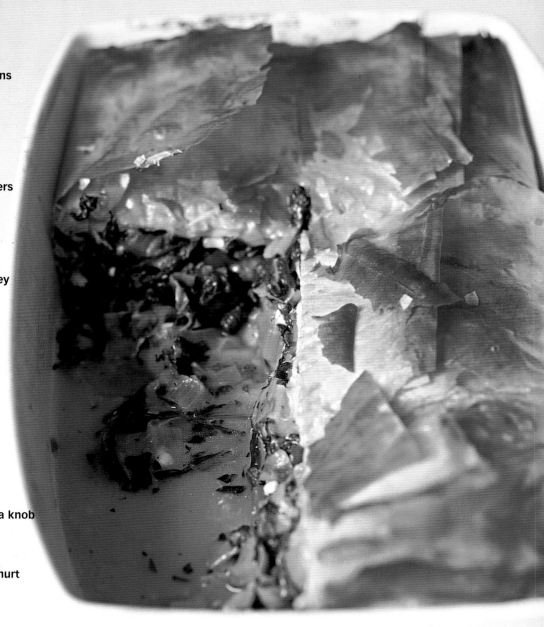

31 PIEDMONTESE PEPPERS
SPANAKOPITTA
HONEY-ROAST FIGS WITH GREEK YOGHURT

SHOPPING LIST

GREEN GROCERIES

200g trimmed green beans

500g trimmed leeks

600g young leaf spinach

6 plum or other firm ripe tomatoes

400g cherry tomatoes

3 decent-sized red peppers

12 ripe figs

1 lemon

3 large garlic cloves, preferably new-season

80g bunch flat-leaf parsley

25g bunch mint

GROCERIES

10 tbsp olive oil

1 tbsp aged balsamic vinegar

½ tsp grated nutmeg

6 anchovy fillets

75g pitted black olives

200g filo pastry

4 tbsp runny honey

CREAMY STUFF

125g butter, plus an extra knob

200g Greek feta cheese

2 tbsp grated Parmesan

500g Greek strained yoghurt

4 large eggs

BREAD

Crusty bread and butter, to serve

Roast peppers stuffed with slivers of garlic and tomatoes, with an anchovy garnish, is one of the simplest and most delicious ways to start a meal. Spanakopitta is a Greek pie made with layers of filo pastry encasing tender spinach leaves and leeks in a feta cheese and herby egg custard. It is perfectly matched with a salad of gently weeping grilled cherry tomatoes with green beans and black olives. The meal concludes with warm figs sweetened with honey and Greek yoghurt.

0-15 MINUTES: Heat the oven to 200°C/400°F/gas mark 6. Begin the **SPANAKOPITTA**. Trim and finely slice the leeks. Agitate in a sink full of cold water and drain. Heat 2 tbsp olive oil and 25g butter in a large, lidded pan over a medium heat. Stir in the leeks and season with ½ tsp salt. Cover and cook, stirring halfway through, for 8 minutes. Stir in the spinach, increase the heat and cook for 2-3 minutes until the spinach wilts. Tip into a colander to drain. Finely chop the flat-leaf parsley and mint leaves. Beat the eggs in a bowl and crumble in the feta. Add the herbs, Parmesan, nutmeg and drained vegetables. Stir well.

15-30 MINUTES: For **PIEDMONTESE PEPPERS**, halve the peppers, slicing evenly through the stalk. Remove any white membrane and seeds. Rinse the peppers and arrange, cut-side uppermost, on a heavy, shallow baking tray. Peel the garlic and slice in super-thin rounds. Lay the slices in the peppers and season with salt and pepper. Put the tomatoes in a bowl, pour boiling water over them, count to 20 and drain. Cut out the cores in a pointed plug shape and peel. Halve the tomatoes lengthways and place 2 pieces, cut-side down, in the peppers, covering the slices of garlic and nudged up closely together. Splash with olive oil. Bake the peppers for 30–40 minutes until tender and charred at the edges. Split the anchovies lengthways. Decorate the peppers with an anchovy cross and leave to cool in the baking tray. Boil the kettle. Melt 100g butter in a small pan.

30-45 MINUTES: Brush an approximately 23 x 30 x 5cm oven dish with olive oil. Use half of the filo pastry to make layers in the dish, spreading each layer with melted butter and leaving an overhang. Keep the rest covered to avoid drying out. Tip the filling into the pastry case and smooth the top. Tuck the overhang in towards the middle and continue making layers of filo as before, finishing with a generous smear of olive oil. Use a sharp knife to cut portion-sized squares or diamonds, going through a couple of layers of filo. Bake in the oven for 30–45 minutes until the pastry is puffed and golden and the filling feels set but still moist and juicy.

45-60 MINUTES: For the salad, trim and halve the beans. Boil for 2 minutes. Drain. Place the cherry tomatoes in a frying pan with 3 tbsp olive oil and the aged balsamic vinegar. Grill for about 5 minutes until the tomatoes soften and the skins begin to split but before they disintegrate. Remove from the heat, tip into a serving bowl and stir in the black olives and beans. To make **HONEY-ROAST FIGS WITH GREEK YOGHURT**, cut a deep cross in the top of the figs and squeeze the sides. Place in an oven dish. Add a knob of butter then spoon over the honey. Squeeze the lemon over the top. Roast for 15 minutes. Keep warm.

TO SERVE: Use a fish slice to scoop the peppers onto a serving platter and spoon over the juices. Serve with crusty bread and butter. Cut the pie into portions and toss the tomato salad before serving. Serve the warm figs with their juices and Greek yoghurt.

STARTER P118 **MAIN** P135 **PUDDING** P136

ASPARAGUS WITH LEMON BUTTER
CRAB LINGUINE WITH WILTED CUCUMBER
STRAWBERRY FOOL WITH BALSAMICO

SHOPPING LIST

GREEN GROCERIES

800g asparagus, preferably British

1 small or ½ large cucumber

800g strawberries, preferably British

3 large lemons

2 red Bird Eye chillies

50g bunch flat-leaf parsley

GROCERIES

8 tbsp extra-virgin olive oil

1 tbsp aged balsamic vinegar

500g linguine

2 tbsp caster sugar

CREAMY STUFF

200g butter

300g whipping cream

FISH

**375–400g dressed crab,
brown and white meat**

Few menus are more perfect for early summer evenings than this one. Asparagus with lemon butter is a marriage made in heaven and so, too, is fresh crab with slivers of cucumber, hints of chilli and masses of flat-leaf parsley stirred into piping hot linguine. The finale is a grown up take on strawberries and cream.

0-15 MINUTES: Begin with **CRAB LINGUINE WITH WILTED CUCUMBER**. Trim and split the chillies and scrape away the seeds. Slice into long, skinny batons and then into tiny scraps. Place in a small bowl and cover with 2 tbsp extra-virgin olive oil. Place the white and brown crabmeat in a mixing bowl. Coarsely chop the flat-leaf parsley leaves. Boil the kettle.

15-30 MINUTES: Prepare the strawberries for **STRAWBERRY FOOL WITH BALSAMICO**. Rinse, shake dry and hull them using a small sharp knife. Quarter the large berries, halve medium ones and leave small fruit whole. Place in a bowl and dust with the sugar. Begin **ASPARAGUS WITH LEMON BUTTER** by snapping the woody ends off the asparagus spears – they will magically snap exactly where tender meets woody. Melt the butter in a small pan and remove from the heat. Give the strawberries a stir to encourage the sugar to melt then stir in the balsamic vinegar.

30-45 MINUTES: Add the chilli and chopped parsley to the crab. Season lightly with salt and generously with freshly ground black pepper. Add the juice from 1½ lemons and mix thoroughly. Slowly stir in 4 tbsp extra-virgin olive oil to make a thick but slack mixture. Use a potato peeler to remove the skin from the cucumber. Split it in half lengthways and use a teaspoon to scrape out the seeds. Slice into thin half-moons. Pour the cream into a pretty glass serving bowl and whip into soft peaks. Set aside a quarter of the strawberries and strain the juices into a jug. Fold the strawberries loosely into the cream and top with the reserved strawberries. Chill until required.

45-60 MINUTES: Boil the kettle. Cook the asparagus in 2 batches in plenty of salted boiling water for 4 minutes until *al dente*. Lift onto kitchen paper to drain.

TO SERVE: Arrange the asparagus on two serving platters. Quickly remelt the butter, whisk in 2 tbsp lemon juice and divide between 2 small jugs. Pour some of the butter over the tips and serve the rest for people to help themselves. Cook the pasta in plenty of salted boiling water until *al dente*. About 2 minutes before the end of cooking add the cucumber. Drain, return to the saucepan and stir in the remaining 2 tbsp extra-virgin olive oil. Add the crab mixture and stir well, adding more lemon juice, oil or black pepper to taste. Remove the fool from the fridge. Dribble each serving with the strawberry juices in the jug.

SHOPPING LIST

GREEN GROCERIES

4 shallots

125g salad/spring onions

4 Little Gem lettuces

½ large or 1 small cucumber

1 unwaxed lemon

2 garlic cloves

25g bunch flat-leaf parsley

15g chives

GROCERIES

300ml vegetable oil

6 tbsp olive oil

2 tbsp red-wine vinegar

1 tbsp smooth Dijon mustard

300g Camargue wild red rice

2 x 400g cans chopped tomatoes

2 x 400g cans lychees in syrup

4 meringue shells or nests

CREAMY STUFF

100g feta cheese

400g fromage frais

MEAT AND FISH

6 free-range chicken legs

**400g cooked, peeled prawns,
preferably North Atlantic**

BOOZE

3 tbsp whisky

You will also need tinfoil

Crumbled feta cheese and flecks of flat-leaf parsley against pink prawns with tomatoes and wild red rice looks very pretty. It is also a delicious complement of flavours. The main course is necessarily light and fresh and an extremely clever way of turning roast chicken portions into a really special treat. Lychee fool – made with fromage frais instead of cream, and canned lychees instead of fresh – is a revelation and certain to become a favourite quick dessert.

0-15 MINUTES: Begin with **LEMON AND TOMATO PRAWNS WITH WILD RED RICE**. Set the timer and boil the rice in plenty of salted water for 40 minutes. Trim and finely slice the spring onions, including the green. Peel and finely chop the garlic. Remove the zest from half the lemon and chop it finely. Finely chop the parsley leaves. Heat the oven to 220°C/425°F/gas mark 7.

15-30 MINUTES: Heat 1 tbsp olive oil in a medium-sized, heavy-bottomed pan and stir in the prawns. Add the whisky and squeeze over the lemon. Bubble up for 30 seconds then tip into a bowl. Warm 3 tbsp olive oil in the pan then add the spring onion and garlic. Cook for 5 minutes, stirring a couple of times. Add 1 tbsp chopped parsley and the lemon zest. Add the tomatoes, stir well and simmer for 10 minutes. Return the prawns and their juices. Cook for 5 minutes. Turn off the heat. Add the remaining parsley and crumble the feta over the top.

30-45 MINUTES: Begin **CHICKEN WITH SHALLOT VINAIGRETTE** by smearing the chicken legs with olive oil and laying them out on a baking tray. Roast for 35 minutes until the skin is golden. Meanwhile, peel, halve and finely chop the shallots. Place in a bowl. Put the mustard, vinegar and a decent seasoning of salt and pepper in a blender. Add 3 tbsp water and blend together. With the motor running, pour in 300ml vegetable oil in a thin stream until thick and homogenized. Transfer to a bowl.

45-60 MINUTES: Drain the rice, return to the pan, cover to keep warm until ready to serve. Separate then rinse and dry the lettuce leaves. Arrange them lengthways on a platter. Peel and thinly slice the cucumber and scatter over the top. Finely snip the chives over the salad. To make **LYCHEE FOOL**, tip the fromage frais into a mixing bowl. Drain the lychees reserving 2 tbsp juice. Beat the reserved juice into the fromage frais then stir in the lychees. Remove the chicken from the oven. Scatter the shallots over the chicken pieces and lavishly cover with some of the vinaigrette. Cover loosely with tinfoil. Leave for 10 minutes before serving.

TO SERVE: Divide the hot rice between 6 warmed plates. Give the prawns a quick blast of heat whilst folding in the parsley and feta then serve over the rice. Spoon the remaining dressing over the salad before serving with the plated chicken and shallot vinaigrette. Finish the dessert by giving the lychees a final stir then spoon into pretty dessert glasses. Crumble the meringues over the top.

TENDERSTEM WITH PARMA HAM
TERIYAKI SALMON WITH SESAME NOODLES
LITTLE CHOCOLATE POTS

SHOPPING LIST

GREEN GROCERIES

600g tenderstem or purple sprouting broccoli

4 x 125g bunches salad/spring onions

GROCERIES

4 tbsp extra-virgin olive oil

1 tbsp toasted sesame oil/ oriental sesame oil

1 tbsp aged balsamic vinegar

200ml teriyaki sauce

2 tbsp soy sauce

½ tsp vanilla extract

2 tbsp sesame seeds

375g medium egg noodles

2 tbsp demerara sugar

175g dark chocolate (70% cocoa solids)

CREAMY STUFF

250g double cream

150g single cream, for pouring

2 egg yolks

MEAT AND FISH

6 salmon fillets

12 slices Parma ham

You will also need tinfoil

Tenderstem can be treated like asparagus and this simple way of dressing it with balsamico and olive oil, with a slice or two of Parma ham, works beautifully for both vegetables. The main course changes mood with a nod towards Japan in one of those moreish noodle salads, here, topped with highly seasoned, grilled salmon and a sesame seed garnish. After two healthy courses, what could provide a better finale than a small, but wickedly rich, chocolate indulgence?

0-15 MINUTES: Begin with **LITTLE CHOCOLATE POTS**. Break the chocolate into a small pan. Add the double cream, demerara sugar and vanilla extract and heat gently, stirring as the chocolate melts, until smooth. Beat the egg yolks until pale and fluffy. Pour the chocolate gradually over the egg yolks whilst beating continually. Pour into 6 small ramekins, glasses or cups. Chill until ready to serve the main course. Put the kettle on to boil.

15-30 MINUTES: Now start **TERIYAKI SALMON WITH SESAME NOODLES**. Trim the spring onions, retaining the pale green and white. Heat a frying pan over a medium heat and stir-fry the sesame seeds for a couple of minutes until pale golden. Tip onto a saucer. Pour the teriyaki sauce into the pan. Add the spring onions and simmer for 3–4 minutes until tender. Scoop the spring onions onto a plate and cover to keep warm.

30-45 MINUTES: For **TENDERSTEM WITH PARMA HAM** half fill a large, wide-based pan with boiling water. Establish a fast boil. Add 1 tsp salt and the tenderstem. Boil for 3-4 minutes until just tender. Drain carefully in a colander. Arrange bundles of tenderstem in the middle of 6 plates. Whisk together the balsamic vinegar and extra-virgin olive oil and spoon most of it over the top.

45-60 MINUTES: Boil the teriyaki sauce for a few minutes until it is thick and has reduced to about one-third. Line the grill-pan with foil and lay out the salmon. Boil the noodles in plenty of salted water for 4 minutes, stirring a couple of times to loosen the noodle coils. Drain and return to the pan with the toasted sesame oil, 2 tbsp soy sauce and half the sesame seeds. Stir and keep warm. Baste the salmon liberally with the reduced teriyaki sauce. Turn the over-head grill to its highest setting.

TO SERVE: Finish the starter by draping a couple of crumpled slices of ham over the tenderstem. Dribble over the remaining dressing. When the starter is finished, place the salmon under the grill. Cook for 2 minutes, baste again and then cook for a further 2–3 minutes until just cooked through. Toss the noodles again and place in the middle of 6 warmed plates or shallow bowls. Top with the warm spring onions and lay a fillet of salmon over the top. Sprinkle the remaining sesame seeds over the salmon. Remove the chocolate pots from the fridge and serve the single cream in a jug to pour over the top.

STARTER P119 **MAIN** P125 **PUDDING** P141

BANG BANG CHICKEN
CHINESE WHITE FISH WITH COCONUT RICE
ORIENTAL FRUIT SALAD

SHOPPING LIST

GREEN GROCERIES

1–2 carrots

200g spring/salad onions

½ cucumber, approx. 300g

1 ripe pineapple

3 ripe mangoes

4 passion fruit

6 limes

2 garlic cloves, preferably new-season

50g fresh ginger

50g bunch coriander

GROCERIES

4 tbsp vegetable oil

4 tbsp toasted sesame oil

5 tbsp soy sauce

150g smooth peanut butter

1 tbsp sweet chilli dipping-sauce preferably Blue Dragon

2 tbsp sesame seeds

400g basmati rice

100g creamed coconut

FISH AND MEAT

6 fillets cod, haddock, whiting or huss

4–6 cooked chicken thighs, approx. 400g

You will also need 12 pieces tinfoil, approx. 24cm-square

All these dishes are favourites from Chinese restaurants and together make an effortlessly stylish dinner party. Bang Bang Chicken was made fashionable by Le Caprice in the Eighties and its combination of cold chicken with raw carrot and cucumber with a sesame-flecked peanut sauce is spot on. There is something magical about opening an aromatic parcel at the table and in this one, white fish is cooked with garlic, ginger and coriander, and served with rice flavoured with coconut. A golden fruit salad is the perfect end to this interesting menu.

0-15 MINUTES: Boil the kettle. Heat the oven to 200°C/400°F/gas mark 6. Begin with **CHINESE WHITE FISH WITH COCONUT RICE**. Lay out 6 sheets of tinfoil. Smear the middle with a little of the vegetable oil. Peel and finely chop the garlic. Sprinkle with ¼ tsp salt and crush to a paste. Place in a bowl, add 1 tbsp vegetable oil, 5 tbsp soy sauce and 1 tbsp sesame oil. Trim and slice 150g spring onions on the slant, including the green. Peel and finely slice the ginger. Arrange the fish over the smear of oil. Scatter with spring onions and ginger and spoon over the dressing. Set aside a few sprigs of coriander and arrange the rest over the top. Place a second sheet of foil on top and fold the edges firmly, but not too tightly, to secure. Place on a baking sheet.

15-30 MINUTES: For **BANG BANG CHICKEN**, begin with the peanut sauce. Place the peanut butter in a metal bowl placed over a small pan half-filled with boiling water. Stir in 1 tbsp sweet chilli dipping-sauce then gradually beat in 3 tbsp toasted sesame oil and 2 tbsp vegetable oil to make a thick pouring sauce. Set aside. Briefly stir-fry the sesame seeds in a frying pan until lightly golden. Discard the chicken skin and shred the flesh into 5cm-lengths.

30-45 MINUTES: Peel and cut the carrots into 5cm-batons. Split the cucumber lengthways and remove the seeds with a teaspoon. Cut into 5cm-batons. Trim and finely slice the remaining spring onions into 5cm lengths. Mix the carrot, cucumber and onion together with the juice of 1 lime. Arrange in the middle of 6 plates. Place the chicken on top. Rinse the rice and place in a pan with 600ml cold water. Crumble the creamed coconut over the top. Bring to the boil, stirring to dissolve the coconut. Reduce the heat to very low and cover the pan. Cook for 10 minutes. Turn off the heat, do not remove the lid and leave for 10 minutes.

45-60 MINUTES: For the **ORIENTAL FRUIT SALAD**, peel the mangoes and slice into a serving dish. Trim, quarter, then peel the pineapple and remove the woody core. Slice thickly and add to the mango. Squeeze the juice of 3 limes over the fruit. Toss well and chill until required. Bake the fish parcels for 15 minutes. Leave, oven off, door open, until required.

TO SERVE Spoon the peanut sauce over the chicken and garnish with sesame seeds. Serve the fish packages for guests to open themselves. Fork up the rice, transfer to a serving platter and decorate with lime wedges and sprigs of coriander. Halve the passion fruit and scrape over the fruit salad.

STARTER P119 **MAIN** P125 **PUDDING** P141

36

POACHED CELERY WITH CAPERS AND ANCHOVY SAUCE
CUMIN-CRUSTED LAMB WITH BROWN RICE PILAFF
GRILLED PINEAPPLE WITH ANGOSTURA

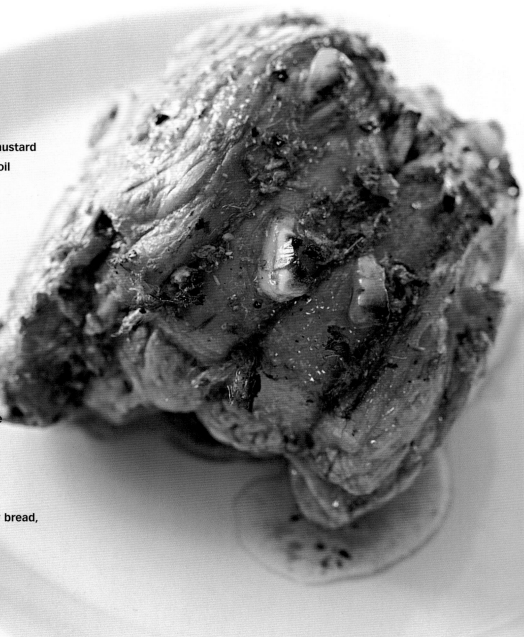

SHOPPING LIST

GREEN GROCERIES

2 onions

4 celery hearts

2 ripe pineapples

12 garlic cloves

About 20 mint leaves

GROCERIES

10 tbsp olive oil

1 scant dsp smooth Dijon mustard

75g anchovy fillets in olive oil

3 tbsp capers in vinegar

1 chicken stock cube

4 tbsp ground cumin

1 tsp ground cinnamon

400g brown rice

3 tbsp flaked almonds

3 tbsp raisins or sultanas

**6 tbsp muscovado or
other dark brown sugar**

CREAMY STUFF

125g butter

500g Greek yoghurt

250g crème fraîche, to serve

MEAT

**2 x ½ legs lamb, fillet end,
800g each**

BREAD

**2 x ciabatta, or other crusty bread,
and butter, to serve**

BOOZE

2 tbsp Angostura bitters

You will also need tinfoil

The subtle flavour of celery is brought to life with this tangy, deeply savoury sauce. It's quick and easy to prepare and is the perfect palate-teaser before cumin-crusted roast lamb. I like to serve it in thick slices so that the flavours and textures combine in every forkful: fragrant, tender lamb, nutty rice pilaff and a dollop of creamy yoghurt laced with fresh mint. This moreish way of cooking pineapples comes from Trinidad, home of Angostura bitters. Prepared in advance it is cooked in a flash at the last moment.

0-15 MINUTES: Heat the oven to 220°C/425°F/gas mark 7. Boil the kettle. For the **CUMIN-CRUSTED LAMB WITH BROWN RICE PILAFF**, peel the garlic and quarter 4 cloves lengthways. Stab each joint in 8 places with a sharp knife, then stuff with the garlic pieces. Crush 4 more garlic cloves and mix with 2 tbsp olive oil. Place the joints in a roasting tin, smear lavishly with the garlicky olive oil then dust liberally with ground cumin. Roast in the oven for 10 minutes.

15-30 MINUTES: Once the lamb is in the oven, start the pilaff. Finely slice the onions and 2 garlic cloves. In a frying pan heat 2 tbsp olive oil and when very hot stir in the sliced onions and garlic. Cook, stirring, for 2 minutes, then turn the heat low. Cook until limp, golden and shrivelled (about 30 minutes). Don't rush this. When the lamb has been cooking for 10 minutes, reduce the heat to 200°C/400°F/gas mark 6. Cook for a further 30 minutes (longer if you don't like your lamb pink), turning halfway through cooking. Wash the rice. Melt 50g butter in a medium-sized, lidded pan. Stir in the almonds and stir-fry until golden. Stir in the washed rice, the raisins and 800ml water. Crumble the stock cube into the pan. Bring to the boil, stir to dissolve the cube then reduce the heat. Cover the pan and simmer gently for about 45 minutes until the rice is tender and the liquid absorbed.

30-45 MINUTES: While the lamb and rice are cooking, prepare **POACHED CELERY WITH CAPERS AND ANCHOVY SAUCE**. Cut the celery into 8cm-lengths and boil in salted water for 10 minutes. Drain and spread on a platter. To make the sauce, melt 75g butter in a small pan, stir in the remaining 2 crushed garlic cloves and cook gently while you chop the anchovy. Add the anchovy and continue stirring for a few minutes until smooth. Add the mustard then beat in the last 6 tbsp olive oil. Remove from the heat.

45-60 MINUTES: Prepare **GRILLED PINEAPPLE WITH ANGOSTURA**. Trim the pineapples and cut into quarters lengthways. Slice off the skin, cut off the woody core and slice each quarter lengthways into 3 chunky pieces. Cover the grill-pan with tinfoil and lay out the pieces. Shred the mint leaves and stir into the yoghurt. When the lamb is done, remove from the oven and rest for 15 minutes while gently reheating the anchovy sauce. Stir the cinnamon into the onions and garlic and cook for a further minute.

TO SERVE: Spoon the anchovy sauce over the celery, scatter capers over the top and serve with crusty bread and butter. After the starter, pile the rice onto a platter and fork in the onions. Carve the lamb thickly, slicing towards the bone so the cumin crust is equally shared. Pour the juices over the lamb and serve with the yoghurt in a separate bowl. About 10 minutes before you are ready for pudding, season the pineapple lavishly with Angostura and then dredge with sugar. Preheat the grill to its highest setting and cook for 7–10 minutes, until the sugar has melted and the pineapple is very juicy. Serve with crème fraîche.

37

HUMMUS WITH DUKKAH AND TOMATO TOAST
MALAYSIAN CHICKEN RENDANG WITH BASMATI
ROAST PEACHES WITH AMARETTI

SHOPPING LIST

GREEN GROCERIES
2 onions

400g fine green beans

6 very ripe tomatoes

6 ripe peaches

1 large lemon

2 limes

1 large garlic clove

8 red Bird Eye chillies

20g fresh ginger

2 lemongrass stalks

50g bunch coriander

GROCERIES
2 tbsp vegetable oil

About 10 tbsp extra-virgin olive oil

35g Egyptian Dukkah, preferably
Seasoned Pioneers

600g organic hummus

1 tsp ground turmeric

1 tsp ground coriander

400g basmati rice

400ml can coconut milk

4 tbsp desiccated coconut

1 vanilla pod

4 amaretti macaroons

CREAMY STUFF
350g crème fraîche

MEAT
1 kg chicken thigh fillets

BREAD
6 slices sourdough or
similarly rustic bread

BOOZE
Approx. 250ml Amaretto

Dukkah is an Egyptian spice mix made with roasted and ground sesame seeds, hazelnuts, coriander and cumin seeds. It's delicious sprinkled lavishly over hummus, hidden under a cloak of chopped coriander, to be scooped onto garlicky, tomato-rubbed toast. Rendang, by contrast, is a chilli-hot, medium-dry curry softened with coconut milk. Its red-flecked, terracotta sauce looks very pretty against green beans and white basmati. Drunken peaches, roasted with vanilla and almond-flavoured Amaretti, are a suitably light and luscious finale.

0-15 MINUTES: For **MALAYSIAN CHICKEN RENDANG WITH BASMATI,** peel and quarter the onions. Peel the ginger. Remove the tough outer layers from the lemongrass and coarsely chop the tender inner stem. Trim and split the chillies. Scrape away the seeds and coarsely chop. Place everything in the bowl of a food processor and add 150ml cold water. Blitz to make a smooth, carrot-coloured purée flecked with red chilli. Add the turmeric, ground coriander and 1 tsp salt and blitz briefly to blend. Heat the vegetable oil in a spacious, wide-based pan over a medium heat and stir in the purée. Cook briskly, stirring occasionally, for 10–15 minutes until the water evaporates, the purée darkens and turns paste-like and all the ingredients cook thoroughly.

15-30 MINUTES: Meanwhile, cut the chicken into chunky, bite-sized strips. Stir the chicken into the paste, cooking until it is sealed. Stir in the coconut milk and bring the sauce to the boil. Adjust the heat so the curry simmers steadily but gently. Cook, stirring often, for about 20 minutes until the chicken is cooked through and the sauce has thickened considerably and darkened in colour. Taste and adjust the seasoning with salt and lime juice. Stir-fry the desiccated coconut in a frying pan, until evenly golden brown. Tip onto a plate to cool and arrest cooking. Heat the oven to 200°C/400°F/gas mark 6.

30-45 MINUTES: For **ROAST PEACHES WITH AMARETTI**, run a sharp knife round the middle of the peaches, twist apart and discard the stones. Split the vanilla pod, scrape out the seeds and stir into the Amaretto. Arrange the peaches, cut-side up, on a small roasting tin. Fill the cavities with some of the Amaretto and roast for about 30 minutes until tender. Transfer to a serving dish. Spoon the rest of the Amaretto and vanilla over the fruit and leave to cool. Boil the kettle. Trim the beans and cut them in half. Wash the rice and place in a pan with 600ml cold water. Bring to the boil, turn down the heat, cover and cook for 10 minutes. Leave, without removing the lid, for 10 minutes.

45-60 MINUTES: Finely chop the coriander. Set aside a few sprigs to garnish the curry. Spoon the hummus into two shallow dishes for **HUMMUS WITH DUKKAH AND TOMATO TOAST**. Douse with extra-virgin olive oil and lemon juice, scatter with the Dukkah and cover with chopped coriander. Toast the bread and cut the tomatoes in half. Rub one side of the toast with garlic and then with cut tomato, rubbing until only the tomato skin remains.

TO SERVE: Season the tomato bread with salt and extra-virgin olive oil and serve with the hummus. Boil the beans for 2 minutes. Drain. Stir the juice of 1 lime into the curry, followed by the desiccated coconut and beans. Taste and adjust the seasoning with more lime juice and salt. Garnish with the reserved coriander. Fork up the rice. Crumble the macaroons into the cavities of the peaches and serve with crème fraîche.

STARTER P119 **MAIN** P129 **PUDDING** P136

BROCCOLI AND LEMON SOUP WITH GARLIC BREAD
COD NICOISE WITH GREEN BEANS
PLUM AND PORT FOOL

SHOPPING LIST

GREEN GROCERIES

1 medium onion

2 red onions

500g fine green beans

2 red peppers

500g red plums

2 lemons

3 large garlic cloves

25g bunch flat-leaf parsley

GROCERIES

1 tsp vegetable oil

4 tbsp olive oil

2 chicken stock cubes

1 scant tsp chilli flakes

2 x 400g cans chopped tomatoes

150g jar pitted black olives in brine,
preferably Cypressa

1 kg frozen broccoli florets

3 tbsp demerera sugar,
or more to taste

3 tbsp toasted flaked almonds

CREAMY STUFF

25g butter

60g grated Parmesan

400g crème fraîche,
plus more to serve

FISH

6 cod fillets

BREAD

3 garlic baguettes

BOOZE

3 tbsp port

Frozen broccoli is perfect for soup and here its cabbagey flavour is lifted with lemon and served with a scoop of crème fraîche and crusty garlic bread. A gorgeous stew of onions, peppers, tomatoes and black olives is delicious with big flakes of lightly cooked cod, offset by crisp green beans. Red plums and port go together sublimely and there is nothing foolish about swirling them into whipped cream with a topping of toasted almonds.

0-15 MINUTES: Begin with **BROCCOLI AND LEMON SOUP WITH GARLIC BREAD**. Boil the kettle. Peel, halve and finely chop the onion and 1 garlic clove. Melt the butter with the vegetable oil in a spacious frying pan. Stir in the onion and garlic. Cook briskly, stirring, for 5 minutes. Meanwhile, use a zester to remove the zest from half a lemon and add to the pan together with 1 tsp salt. Stir, reduce the heat, cover and cook for 10 minutes. Measure 1.3 litres boiling water and dissolve the stock cubes. Boil the kettle again. Begin the **COD NICOISE WITH GREEN BEANS**. Lightly season the fish fillets with salt and set aside.

15-30 MINUTES: Peel, halve and chop the red onions. Peel and thinly slice 2 garlic cloves in rounds. Heat 3 tbsp olive oil in a spacious, heavy bottomed pan and stir in the onion and garlic. Cook briskly, stirring frequently, for 5 minutes. Reduce the heat, add 1 tsp salt, cover and cook for a further 5 minutes. Use a potato peeler to remove the bulk of the skin from the peppers, then discard the stalk, seeds and white filament. Coarsely chop the flesh and add to the pan. Cook, covered, for a further 10 minutes. Add the stock to the onions for the soup, followed by the broccoli. Return to the boil – this will take several minutes – and boil for 5 minutes.

30-45 MINUTES: Liquidize the soup in batches and return to a clean pan. Add the juice from 1 lemon and adjust the seasoning with salt. Heat the oven to 200°C/400°F/gas mark 6. Begin **PLUM AND PORT FOOL**. Cut the flesh off the plum stones in big pieces directly into a pan. Add 100ml water, sugar and the Port. Heat gently until the sugar has dissolved. Increase the heat, cover the pan and boil for 6–8 minutes until very soft. Tip into a sieve over a bowl and cool, reserving the juice. Beat three-quarters of the crème fraîche in a mixing bowl until smooth.

45-60 MINUTES: Stir the chilli flakes into the onions and peppers and then add the chopped tomatoes. Drain the olives and cut in half. Add them to the pan. Cook briskly, stirring occasionally, for 10 minutes. Coarsely chop the parsley. Lay the garlic loaves on an oven tray, prise apart the slices and dredge them generously with grated Parmesan. Bake the garlic bread for 10 minutes. Pat the fish fillets dry with some kitchen paper. Arrange them on an oiled baking sheet and brush first with olive oil and then with a squeeze of lemon. Roast for 15 minutes then keep warm. Stir the parsley into the sauce. Boil the beans in plenty of salted water for 2 minutes.

TO SERVE: Reheat the soup and serve in bowls with a scoop of crème fraîche and the hot garlic bread. Serve the fish topped with the sauce, and the beans separately. Finish the fool by stirring the plums loosely through the crème fraîche then transfer the mixture to pretty glass dishes or glasses. Garnish with the toasted almonds. Pour the cooled juices into a jug and serve separately.

HUMMUS SOUP WITH MINT AND GARLIC
SESAME PORK WITH CHINESE GREENS
TREACLE TART WITH CREME FRAICHE

SHOPPING LIST

GREEN GROCERIES

800g pak choi

4–5 tbsp lemon juice

50g garlic, plus 3 large cloves

50g fresh ginger

25g bunch mint

25g bunch flat-leaf parsley

GROCERIES

9 tbsp olive oil

4 tbsp extra-virgin olive oil

6 tbsp sesame oil

100ml Kikkoman soy sauce

100ml oyster sauce

8 tbsp sesame seeds

3 x 400g cans chickpeas

4–6 tbsp golden syrup

20cm pre-cooked shortcrust pastry case

CREAMY STUFF

250g crème fraîche, to serve

MEAT

12 pork medallions

BREAD

100g white bread, without crusts

Crusty bread, to serve

BOOZE

100ml Chinese cooking wine

You will also need clingfilm

This is one of my favourite autumnal menus, which coincidentally happens to be super-convenient because both the starter and main course use store-cupboard ingredients. The meal begins in Spain, where puréed chickpea soups are popular, moves on to the Orient, and finishes with a cheat's version of British treacle tart made with a ready-made pastry case. The secret of its deliciousness is a hint of lemon in the lightly crusted top and a luscious soft, gooey filling.

0-15 MINUTES: For **HUMMUS SOUP WITH MINT AND GARLIC**, peel and roughly chop the 3 garlic cloves. Drain the liquid from the chickpea cans into a measuring jug and make up the amount to 1.3 litres with water. Heat, then purée in batches in a blender with the chickpeas, chopped garlic, olive oil and 3 tbsp lemon juice. Simmer for 5 minutes. Season to taste with salt, pepper and lemon juice. Finely chop the mint and parsley leaves.

15-30 MINUTES: To prepare **SESAME PORK WITH CHINESE GREENS**, pat the pork medallions dry with kitchen paper. Spread the sesame seeds out on a plate and press the medallions into the seeds to cover entirely. Transfer to a plate, cover with clingfilm and chill until required. Carefully remove the clingfilm from the pastry case for **TREACLE TART WITH CREME FRAICHE.** Tear the bread into pieces and blitz to crumbs in a food processor. Tip the crumbs into the pastry case and smooth the surface. Working from the outside, spoon golden syrup over the crumbs until they are completely covered. Squeeze about 1 tbsp lemon juice over the top. Leave in a warm place for the syrup to soak into the crumbs.

30-45 MINUTES: Separate the pak choi leaves and wash thoroughly in several changes of water. Peel and thinly slice the ginger then cut into matchsticks. Peel and finely chop the 50g garlic. Quickly stir-fry the ginger and garlic in 2 tbsp sesame oil in a wok or frying pan until light golden. Add the oyster sauce, soy sauce and Chinese cooking wine and simmer for a few minutes. Turn off the heat. Heat the oven to 180°C/350°F/gas mark 4. Put the kettle on. Bake the tart for 20 minutes. Turn off the oven, leaving the door open, until the tart is required.

45-60 MINUTES: Heat the remaining sesame oil in a frying pan over a medium heat and cook the seeded pork medallions in batches of 4, allowing a couple of minutes on each side, until golden and just cooked through. Transfer to a plate and cover with a tight stretch of clingfilm to keep them warm. Drop the pak choi into a large pan of boiling water and boil for 30 seconds. Drain carefully and keep warm.

TO SERVE: Reheat the soup and when it is very hot stir in the herbs. Serve with a swirl of your best olive oil and some crusty bread. Reheat the soy sauce, then add the greens and cook for a minute or so, turning them through the sauce. Plate the pork medallions and serve the greens on a warmed platter. Use an egg slice to remove the tart from its foil container and slip onto a plate. Serve with crème fraîche.

STARTER P114 **MAIN** P133 **PUDDING** P136

40 LEEKS VINAIGRETTE WITH EGG AND CHIVES
MOROCCAN SPATCHCOCK WITH TZATZIKI
CARAMELIZED ROAST APPLES

SHOPPING LIST

GREEN GROCERIES

1 kg trimmed long, thin leeks

1 medium-large cucumber

6 small eating apples,
such as Cox's

4 lemons

7 large garlic cloves

25g bunch coriander

1 tbsp snipped chives

GROCERIES

About 10 tbsp olive oil

**150ml peanut oil or other
flavourless oil**

2 tbsp red-wine vinegar

1 chicken stock cube

1½ tbsp smooth Dijon mustard

**4 tbsp ras al hanout (Moroccan
spice mix)**

350g couscous

½ tsp saffron stamens

400g can chickpeas

2 tbsp sultanas

3 tbsp golden syrup

3 tbsp soft brown sugar

CREAMY STUFF

50g butter

500g Greek yoghurt

250g pouring cream, to serve

2 eggs

MEAT

6 poussins/spring chickens

BREAD

Crusty bread, to serve

You will also need tinfoil

Leeks vinaigrette go down well at any time of the year but are the perfect light entrée to this enticingly aromatic autumn menu. Ras al hanout, a Moroccan spice-mix with rose petals, sends wafts of Morocco around the kitchen as the spatchcock poussins cook. It's a hands-on main course, so supply plenty of paper napkins and finger bowls with rose petals or slices of lemon. There should just be room enough afterwards for this elegant take on a favourite old-fashioned British pudding.

0-15 MINUTES: Heat the oven to 220°C/425°F/gas mark 7. Boil the kettle. Fill the sink with water. To start **LEEKS VINAIGRETTE WITH EGG AND CHIVES**, trim and cut the leeks into approximately 10cm-lengths. Agitate in the water. Boil the leeks in salted water for about 6 minutes until tender. Stand in a colander to drain. Boil the eggs for 10 minutes. Crack under running water and peel.

15-30 MINUTES: To begin **MOROCCAN SPATCHCOCK WITH TZATZIKI**, place the sultanas and saffron in a cup and cover with boiling water. Peel and chop the garlic and pound to a paste with ½ tsp salt. Set aside 1 tsp paste in a serving bowl. Mix the remaining garlic with 2 tbsp lemon juice and 6 tbsp olive oil, then stir in the ras al hanout. Use scissors to remove the poussins' spines. Open out the birds and flatten slightly with the heel of your hand. Smear generously with the spice-mix and lay on a couple of heavy-duty roasting trays. Dribble with olive oil. Roast the poussins on the upper shelves, juggling the shelves if necessary for even cooking, for 30-40 minutes.

30-45 MINUTES: Dissolve the stock cube in 550ml boiling water in a serving bowl. Add the sultanas and saffron, the couscous and 2 tbsp each olive oil and lemon juice. Stir thoroughly then cover. Rinse the chickpeas in a colander. Make the tzatziki by stirring 1 tbsp each olive oil and lemon juice into the garlic paste in the serving bowl. Beat in the yoghurt. Peel the cucumber, split lengthways and scrape out the seeds with a teaspoon. Cut into chunky pieces. To make the vinaigrette, briefly blitz the mustard, 3 tbsp warm water and the vinegar in a blender. With the motor running, add the peanut oil in a thin stream until thick and creamy.

45-60 MINUTES: Remove the poussins from the oven. Cover with foil to keep warm. Adjust the oven to 190°C/375°F/gas mark 5. For **CARAMELIZED ROAST APPLES**, core and halve the apples. Lay, cut-side up, on a lightly buttered oven tray. Spoon over the golden syrup and dredge with sugar. Top each apple with a piece of the remaining butter. Bake for 20 minutes until tender.

TO SERVE: Halve the leeks lengthways, discarding the outer layer if it is stiff. Arrange cut-side up on a platter and drizzle with the vinaigrette. Grate the eggs over the top and sprinkle with chives. Serve with crusty bread. For the main course, fork up the couscous and mix in the chickpeas. Chop 1 tbsp coriander. Serve the poussins draped over the couscous with the lemon wedges and the remaining sprigs of coriander. Stir the cucumber and the reserved 1 tbsp chopped coriander into the yoghurt, and serve separately. Serve the apples with the syrup spooned over the top. Serve the cream separately.

CRUDITES WITH BOCCONCINI AND ANCHOVY SAUCE
GREEN SALMON WITH CAULIFLOWER CREAM
CRANACHAN

SHOPPING LIST

GREEN GROCERIES

500g stringless runner beans, sliced long, thin and diagonally

1 very large cauliflower

1 small cucumber

3 little gem lettuce hearts

200g small green tomatoes, preferably Tiger tomatoes

2 large, ripe but firm avocados

400g ripe raspberries

4 lemons

3 large garlic cloves

50g bunch flat-leaf parsley

GROCERIES

6 tbsp olive oil

4 tbsp vegetable oil

1 dsp smooth Dijon mustard

75g anchovy fillets in olive oil

50g jumbo or ordinary porridge oats

4 tbsp flour

2 tbsp runny honey

CREAMY STUFF

75g butter

100g double cream

300g whipping cream

100g grated mature Cheddar

250g bocconcini

2 large eggs

FISH

6 salmon fillets or tails

BREAD

150g white bread, without crusts

BOOZE

3 tbsp whisky

You will also need clingfilm

Crudités are a good idea but they can often end up quite dull. Here the vegetables are a mix of soft and crisp with a few bocconcini to liven matters up. They are served Italian-style, with a hot and creamy anchovy sauce. Salmon covered with a crisp shell of green breadcrumbs looks stunning and the creamy white cauliflower purée on the side will have your guests guessing. Cranachan is an intriguing Scottish way of serving raspberries – the best come from Scotland – with toasted oats, whisky and cream.

0-15 MINUTES: Begin with **CRANACHAN**. Sprinkle the oats over a wide, heavy-based frying pan and place over a moderate heat, shaking occasionally, until toasted and golden. Tip onto a plate to cool. Pour the whipping cream into a mixing bowl and whip with the honey until it begins to form peaks. Fold in the whisky, then half of the raspberries and half of the toasted oats. Divide between 6 glass dishes or transfer to a suitable serving bowl. Chill until required.

15-30 MINUTES: Boil the kettle. For **GREEN SALMON WITH CAULIFLOWER CREAM**, cut the cauliflower into florets. Cook, covered, in boiling salted water for about 5 minutes until soft. Drain, but reserve 2 tbsp of the cooking water. Place the cauliflower, reserved water, the double cream and grated Cheddar into the bowl of a food processor and blitz to make a smooth, thick, creamy white purée. Scrape into a pan. Taste and adjust the seasoning with salt and a squeeze of lemon, adding extra cream if the mixture is too stiff.

30-45 MINUTES: Remove the zest from a lemon. Tear the bread into chunks and place in the food processor together with 25g parsley leaves and the lemon zest. Blitz to make green crumbs. Tip the crumbs into a cereal bowl. Sift the flour into a second bowl and whisk the eggs in a third. Pat the salmon fillets dry, then dip each one first in the flour, shaking off any excess, then in the egg and finally, press into the crumbs. Lay out on a plate as you go. Cover with clingfilm and chill until required. Peel and crush the garlic cloves to a paste. Boil the kettle.

45-60 MINUTES: To make the sauce for **CRUDITES WITH BOCCONCINI AND ANCHOVY SAUCE**, melt the butter in a small pan. Stir in the garlic paste and cook gently while you chop the anchovy fillets. Add the anchovies to the butter and continue stirring for a few minutes until smooth. Stir in the mustard and then beat in the olive oil. Quarter the avocados lengthways, remove the skin and stone and halve each quarter. Trim and quarter the lettuce hearts. Peel the cucumber, halve lengthways, scrape away the seeds and slice thickly on the diagonal. Halve the green tomatoes. Divide the vegetables and bocconcini between 6 plates or arrange on a platter. Season with lemon juice and black pepper. Chop the remaining parsley and scatter over the top.

TO SERVE: Reheat the anchovy sauce and serve it in a separate bowl. Fry the fish in batches in hot oil for a couple of minutes each side until nicely crusty and cooked through. Meanwhile, using water from the kettle, boil the beans for 2 minutes. Drain. Quickly reheat the cauliflower cream and serve alongside the salmon, adding a lemon wedge, with beans served separately. Garnish the cranachan with the remaining raspberries and oats. A wee dram on the side and a dribble of whisky over the top turns it into an extra special finale.

BRUSCHETTA OF RED PEPPER AND GOATS' CHEESE
POACHED CHICKEN WITH CHERRY TOMATO VINAIGRETTE
PISTACHIO CREAMED RICE WITH ORANGE SALAD

SHOPPING LIST

GREEN GROCERIES

2 onions

1 kg scrubbed small salad potatoes

200g trimmed fine beans

2 carrots

250g cherry tomatoes

6 navel oranges

3 large garlic cloves

A few sprigs of thyme or rosemary

Handful of basil, mint, coriander or flat-leaf parsley leaves

GROCERIES

300ml extra-virgin olive oil

½ tbsp red-wine vinegar

4 black peppercorns

1 bay leaf

340g jar roasted red peppers/pimientos in olive oil

Generous pinch ground cinnamon

4 cloves

2 tbsp orange blossom/flower water

2 x 400g cans creamed rice

Handful of shelled pistachio nuts

1 tbsp runny honey

CREAMY STUFF

150g soft fresh goats' cheese

4 tbsp thick cream

MEAT

6 free-range chicken leg portions

BREAD

8 thick slices sourdough bread

BOOZE

2 glasses white wine, approx. 300ml

You will also need clingfilm

Silky glistening sheets of roasted red pepper hide a thick layer of creamy goats' cheese and garlic-rubbed toast, making a light but satisfying start to the meal. The main course is one of my favourite quick suppers and tastes as sublime as it looks – the herby tomato vinaigrette tumbling over plump chicken legs. The meal finishes with a Moroccan-inspired cheat's rice pudding with a pretty and delicately flavoured orange blossom, honey and cinnamon-scented orange salad.

0-15 MINUTES: Begin **POACHED CHICKEN WITH CHERRY TOMATO VINAIGRETTE** by skinning the chicken. Peel, halve and thickly slice the onion and carrot. Place in a large pot with the chicken, thyme, peppercorns, bay leaf, cloves and 2 tsp salt. Add the white wine and sufficient cold water to cover. Put on a high heat and bring to the boil. Skim the surface to remove any grey froth, turn down the heat and leave to simmer gently for 30 minutes. Cover and leave until required. Quarter the tomatoes and place in a medium-sized bowl. Peel the garlic, set aside one clove and slice the other two into wafer-thin rounds. Add the garlic and vinegar to the tomatoes. Season with salt and pepper. Toss together and leave to macerate for 30 minutes.

15-30 MINUTES: Boil the potatoes in plenty of salted water until tender. Cover and leave until required. Stir 200ml extra-virgin olive oil into the tomatoes and tear the basil leaves over the top. If using mint, flat-leaf parsley or coriander, chop the leaves. Begin **PISTACHIO CREAMED RICE WITH ORANGE SALAD**. Place the pistachios in a plastic bag, seal the end and bash with a rolling pin to break into small pieces. Using a sharp knife, slice the ends off the oranges, then remove the remaining skin in 4 or 5 downward sweeps. Slice the fruit off the 'core' in 3 or 4 large pieces. Cut across each piece into 2 or 3 chunky slices. Pile into a serving dish as you go and squeeze the juice from the skin and core over the top. Dribble the honey over the oranges. Boil the kettle.

30-45 MINUTES: Use some of the water to boil the beans for 2 minutes. Drain and keep warm. Begin making **BRUSCHETTA OF RED PEPPER AND GOATS' CHEESE** by toasting the bread. Thoroughly rub one side with the remaining garlic clove and moisten with a splash of olive oil, then spread lavishly with the goats' cheese and cover with slices of pimientos. Cut into big pieces and arrange on a platter.

45-60 MINUTES: Carefully lift the chicken pieces out of the pan and cover them with clingfilm to keep warm. Drain the potatoes and keep warm.

TO SERVE: Serve the platter of bruschetta for people to help themselves. Make piles of beans in the centre of 6 warmed plates. Place a drained chicken leg on the top. Stir the tomato vinaigrette and spoon over the chicken and beans. Serve the potatoes separately. When you are ready for pudding, tip the rice into a pan and warm through. Stir in the orange blossom water and then, loosely, the cream. Pour into a wide serving bowl. Scatter the pistachios over the top and dust with cinnamon. Serve with the orange salad.

43

MELON SALAD WITH LIME, MINT AND PROSCIUTTO
SQUID WITH TOMATOES AND PEAS
PEACH GALETTE WITH ALMONDS AND CLOTTED CREAM

SHOPPING LIST

GREEN GROCERIES

2 medium onions

12 ripe, firm vine tomatoes, approx. 1 kg

1 cantaloupe melon

1 yellow melon

8 ripe peaches or nectarines

Juice from 2 limes

3 lemons

3 large garlic cloves

50g bunch flat-leaf parsley

20 mint leaves

GROCERIES

4 tbsp olive oil

1 tbsp vegetable oil

250g puff pastry

25g whole, peeled almonds

500g frozen petits pois

Icing sugar, for dusting

CREAMY STUFF

Knob of butter

250g clotted cream

FISH AND MEAT

1 kg small squid, cleaned and tentacles inside the sac

12 slices prosciutto crudo

BREAD

Crusty bread and butter, to serve

You will also need greaseproof paper

If there is a melon-baller at the back of your kitchen drawer, this is the time to whip it out. If not, no matter, because chunks of melon taste just as good as balls, particularly when tossed in lime juice with mint and Serrano ham. The main course is one of the finest ways of eating squid and the dish is blessedly simple to prepare. The galette is a smart name for a super-quick faux posh peach and almond tart guaranteed to wow your guests.

0-15 MINUTES: Heat the oven to 200°C/400°F/gas mark 6. Put the kettle on. Finely chop the onions. Heat the olive oil in a spacious, heavy-bottomed pan that can hold all the ingredients for **SQUID WITH TOMATOES AND PEAS**, and stir in the onion. Cook over a medium heat, stirring occasionally, for 10–15 minutes until it begins to soften and turn golden. Meanwhile, peel and finely chop the garlic. Place the tomatoes in a bowl, cover with boiling water, count to 25, drain, peel and cut them in half. Scrape out the seeds and chop the flesh.

15-30 MINUTES: Stir the garlic into the onion, cook for a couple of minutes then add the tomatoes. Cook at a steady simmer for 15 minutes or until the tomatoes begin to thicken with the onions – don't worry if it seems a bit dry. Meanwhile, remove the tentacles from inside the squid sacs. Cut the tentacle clusters in half. Slice the sacs into 1cm-wide rings. Stir both into the sauce. Season with salt and pepper, stir well, cover and cook gently for about 20 minutes or until the squid is tender. Taste and adjust the seasoning. Refill the kettle.

30-45 MINUTES: To make the **PEACH GALETTE WITH ALMONDS AND CLOTTED CREAM**, lightly dust a work surface with icing sugar and roll out the pastry thinly to fit a liberally buttered baking sheet approximately 25 x 30cm. Prick the pastry all over with a fork, dust with icing sugar and cover loosely with a double fold of greaseproof paper. Bake for 10 minutes until the surface is brown and semi-risen. Remove the paper and cook for a further 5 minutes then use an egg slice to flip the pastry over. Press down to flatten and then return to the oven for 5 minutes more until flaky and golden. Flatten the now thoroughly cooked pastry again if necessary and slip onto a cake rack to cool. Meanwhile, place the peaches in a bowl and cover with boiling water. Count to 25, drain and peel. Slice the peaches into thin wedges.

45-60 MINUTES: To make **MELON SALAD WITH LIME, MINT AND PROSCIUTTO**, quarter the melons and scrape away the seeds. Use a melon-baller or cut the melon into small chunks. Place in a bowl and toss with lime juice. Tear the prosciutto into 5cm-strips. Shred 20 mint leaves. Back to the squid, stir the peas into the squid and cook, uncovered, for 5–10 minutes until tender. Coarsely chop the parsley leaves. Drop the almonds into a small pan of boiling water. Boil for 2 minutes. Drain and slice lengthways into 3–4 pieces. Briefly stir-fry the almonds in hot vegetable oil until golden then tip them onto kitchen paper.

TO SERVE: Make piles of melon in the middle of 6 plates. Spoon over the juices and scatter with the mint and fold the prosciutto on the side. Reheat the squid, stir in the parsley and serve in shallow bowls with a lemon wedge and crusty bread and butter. Spread the cream thickly over the cold, crisp pastry, right up to the edges. Arrange the peach slices over the top. Just before serving, sprinkle with the almonds and dust with icing sugar.

AVOCADO SALAD WITH LIME AND HALLOUMI
ROAST COD WITH WATERCRESS MASH
MANGO WITH RASPBERRY SAUCE

SHOPPING LIST

GREEN GROCERIES

1.4 kg floury potatoes

160g watercress

3 ripe ready-to-eat Hass avocados

5 ripe mangoes

350g fresh or frozen raspberries

3 lemons

4 limes

2 large garlic cloves

25g bunch flat-leaf parsley

A few mint leaves

GROCERIES

6 tbsp extra-virgin olive oil

6 tbsp olive oil

3 tbsp capers in vinegar

2 tbsp caster sugar

CREAMY STUFF

250g halloumi cheese,
preferably Pittas

FISH

6 cod fillets

Minimal cooking is required for this pretty menu. I love the symmetry of colour of the first two courses: chalky white halloumi with pale green avocado and inky green capers, followed by glossy white cod with creamy mashed potato flecked with dark green watercress. The finale is a crescendo of colour: silky saffron-coloured mango with a vivid splash of raspberry pink offset by chopped mint.

0-15 MINUTES: Heat the oven to 200°C/400°F/gas mark 6. Peel the potatoes for **ROAST COD WITH WATERCRESS MASH** and cut them into large, even-sized chunks. Boil in plenty of salted water for about 15 minutes until tender. If using frozen raspberries spread them out on a large plate to defrost for **MANGO WITH RASPBERRY SAUCE**. Season the cod with salt. Leave for 10 minutes then pat dry. Use 1 tbsp olive oil to smear a small, heavy-duty roasting tin that can accommodate the fish. Peel the garlic cloves, chop finely, sprinkle with a little salt and use the flat of a knife to work into a paste. Place the fish fillets in the roasting tin and splash with 2 tbsp olive oil. Squeeze over the juice from 1 lemon and season with salt and pepper.

15-30 MINUTES: When the potatoes are ready, drain them in a colander. Put the garlic paste and 3 tbsp olive oil in the potato pan and stir-fry over a medium-low heat for about 30 seconds without letting the garlic brown. Remove from the heat and return the hot potatoes and watercress to the pan. Use a fork to mash, mix and amalgamate; you want the potatoes crushed rather than mashed smooth, and the watercress to wilt in the heat. Cover and keep warm.

30-45 MINUTES: For **AVOCADO SALAD WITH LIME AND HALLOUMI**, run a sharp knife round the avocados. Twist apart, remove the stone and peel. Place on a board, flat-side down and thinly slice along the length of the avocado. Arrange the slices in the middle of 6 plates and squeeze sufficient lime juice over the top to season and prevent them discolouring. Cut the halloumi into 30 wafer-thin slices. Tear the slices in half and strew over the avocado. Squeeze the capers to remove most of the vinegar and scatter over the top. Zig-zag with extra-virgin olive oil. Chop the flat-leaf parsley. Give the salad a final squeeze of lime and scatter with the parsley.

45-60 MINUTES: Push the soft raspberries through a sieve into a serving bowl with the back of a spoon. Stir in the caster sugar and a squeeze of lime. Peel the mangoes and cut big slices off the stone. Slice the flesh, toss with lime juice and pile over the raspberry sauce. Chill until required. Roast the fish in the hot oven for 10–15 minutes, depending on the thickness of the fillets, until just cooked through. Carefully drain the juices from the cooked fish into the potatoes, season with salt and pepper and give a final mash. Keep warm.

TO SERVE: Squeeze any remaining lime juice over the salad just before serving. For the main course, spoon the mash into the middle of 6 warmed plates and lay the fish over the top. Finish the dish with a generous swirl of extra-virgin olive oil over and around the food. Serve with a lemon wedge. Chop the mint leaves and strew over the mango just before serving.

STARTER P120 **MAIN** P126 **PUDDING** P141

MUSHROOMS A LA GRECQUE
LEMON CHICKEN WITH POTATOES AND SPINACH
ROAST PEARS WITH MARSALA AND CINNAMON

SHOPPING LIST

GREEN GROCERIES
2 medium-large onions

8 medium-sized potatoes

500g young leaf spinach

750g small white cap mushrooms

4 vine tomatoes

6 small pears

2 large lemons

1 garlic clove

1 red Bird Eye chilli

3 sprigs of fresh thyme

80g bunch flat-leaf parsley

GROCERIES
10 tbsp olive oil

2 tbsp extra-virgin olive oil

½ chicken stock cube

1 cinnamon stick

2 tsp coriander seeds

3 bay leaves

1 tbsp dried oregano

2 tbsp dark brown sugar

CREAMY STUFF
300g crème fraîche

MEAT
6 free-range chicken legs

BREAD
6 slices sourdough, to serve

BOOZE
2 glasses dry white wine, approx. 300ml

½ glass white wine, approx. 75ml

2 glasses Marsala, approx. 300ml

You will also need tinfoil

Poaching little mushrooms in a highly spiced vinaigrette and then tossing them with diced tomato and chopped flat-leaf parsley sets the scene for this Greek-inspired meal. Chicken and potatoes are roasted with lemon and more parsley for the main course, leaving just enough room to enjoy roast pears flavoured with Marsala and cinnamon.

0-15 MINUTES: Heat the oven to 200°C/400°F/gas mark 6. Begin with **MUSHROOMS A LA GREQUE**. Wipe the mushrooms. Finely chop the chilli. Using a potato peeler remove the zest from 1 lemon in small scraps. Lightly crush the coriander seeds. Add mushrooms, chilli, lemon zest, coriander seeds, 2 bay leaves, thyme, 3 tbsp olive oil and the dry white wine to a suitably sized pan. Bring slowly to the boil – allow at least 10 minutes. Reduce the heat, stir, cover and simmer for 30 minutes. Tip into a wide serving bowl and leave to cool. Meanwhile, prepare **ROAST PEARS WITH MARSALA AND CINNAMON.** Halve the pears through the stalk and lay, cut-side down, in a ceramic dish that can hold them in a single layer. Scatter over the sugar. Add the ½ glass of wine, Marsala and cinnamon stick. Cover loosely with foil.

15-30 MINUTES: Cook the pears in the bottom of the oven for 30 minutes. Chop the flat-leaf parsley and set aside 2 tbsp. For **LEMON CHICKEN WITH POTATOES AND SPINACH**, peel the potatoes, cut into big chunks and boil in salted water for about 10 minutes until tender. Drain. Meanwhile, heat 3 tbsp olive oil in a lidded frying pan and quickly brown the chicken in batches, turning after a couple of minutes. Transfer to a spacious earthenware or ceramic gratin-style dish that can accommodate the chicken in a single layer. Season with salt and pepper. Scatter over the oregano and most of the chopped parsley.

30-45 MINUTES: While the pears are cooking, peel, halve and finely slice the onions. Heat 2 tbsp olive oil in the frying pan and stir in the onions. Cook briskly, stirring constantly, for a couple of minutes, then add 1 bay leaf and 1 tsp salt. Reduce the heat, cover and cook for 10–15 minutes until soft and slippery. Tip the onions over the chicken and squeeze a lemon over the top. Boil the kettle. Heat 2 tbsp olive oil in the frying pan and briefly brown the potatoes on one side, then squeeze over the juice of 1 lemon. Cook for 5 minutes. Tip the potatoes over the chicken, encouraging them down between the legs. Dissolve the stock cube in 300ml boiling water and add to the dish. Cover with foil and cook in the oven for 30 minutes.

45-60 MINUTES: Remove the foil from the pears and cook for a further 15 minutes. Place the tomatoes in a bowl. Cover with boiling water. Leave for 30 seconds. Drain, halve and remove the skin, core and seeds. Finely chop the flesh. Boil the kettle. Remove the foil from the chicken and cook for a further 10 minutes. Cook the spinach in boiling water for 1 minute. Drain in a colander, pressing with the back of a wooden spoon to extract excess water. Transfer to a warmed bowl and splash with 2 tbsp extra-virgin olive oil.

TO SERVE: Toast the sourdough and rub one side with garlic. Stir the chopped tomatoes and 2 tbsp chopped parsley into the mushrooms. Serve in shallow bowls, with spoons and forks, and the toast. Scatter the remaining parsley over the chicken. Serve from the dish with the spinach. Serve the warm pears with crème fraîche.

STARTER P120 **MAIN** P130 **PUDDING** P136

46
CAULIFLOWER AND LEMON SOUP WITH THYME
DIJON HONEY PORK CHOPS WITH SPINACH
AMARETTI-RASPBERRY FLUFF

SHOPPING LIST

GREEN GROCERIES

1 large cauliflower

600g young leaf spinach

150g spring/salad onions

6 plum tomatoes

600g raspberries

2 lemons

1 large garlic clove

1 tsp chopped fresh thyme

GROCERIES

1 tbsp olive oil

5 tbsp extra-virgin olive oil

2 chicken or vegetable
stock cubes

1 tbsp smooth Dijon mustard

½ tbsp runny honey

6 amaretti biscuits

CREAMY STUFF

25g butter

300g double cream

300g whipping cream

MEAT

6 pork chops

You will also need tinfoil

Cauliflower can be paired with some surprising flavours that work particularly well in soups. This thick and fluffy creamy-white soup is flecked with shards of lemon zest that combine with thyme to scent the soup and excite the appetite. Oregano with pork is an unusual idea borrowed from Greece and it is perfectly complemented by silky spinach and juicy roast tomatoes. Almonds, in the form of crunchy amaretti biscuits, ring the changes with raspberries and cream.

0-15 MINUTES: Heat the oven to 170°C/325°F/gas mark 3. Boil the kettle. Begin **DIJON HONEY PORK CHOPS WITH SPINACH** by halving the tomatoes lengthways. Arrange them, cut-side up, on a foil-covered baking sheet. Smear the cut surfaces with olive oil. Cook in the oven until required, but after 50 minutes check that they are soft and weeping but still holding their shape. To make **CAULIFLOWER AND LEMON SOUP WITH THYME**, cut the cauliflower into small florets, each with a bit of stalk. Trim the spring onions and finely chop, including all the tender green. Peel the garlic and chop coarsely. Remove the zest from 1 lemon in wafer-thin scraps.

15-30 MINUTES: Melt the butter in a 2-litre capacity pan. Stir in the onion, garlic, lemon zest and thyme. Add ½ tsp salt and stir thoroughly. Cover and cook gently, stirring occasionally, for 5 minutes, until the onion has begun to soften. In 1.2 litres boiling water dissolve the stock cubes. Add the cauliflower and stock to the pan and bring to the boil. Immediately reduce the heat, partially cover the pan and cook for 10–15 minutes until the cauliflower is tender. Blitz the soup in batches. Add 100g double cream and reheat. Adjust the seasoning with salt, pepper and lemon juice.

30-45 MINUTES: Begin the **AMARETTI-RASPBERRY FLUFF**. Tip the raspberries onto a plate and pop into the oven for a couple of minutes – this will make them extra juicy. Beat the whipping cream into soft peaks. Crumble the amaretti biscuits between your hands and fold into the cream. Fold in the raspberries. Spoon the dessert into pretty glass dishes (or one large dish) and chill until required.

45-60 MINUTES: Preheat the grill to its highest setting. Cut through the fat at the edge of the chops at 2cm-intervals towards the meat to avoid buckling as they cook. Arrange on the grill pan. Season the side about to be cooked lavishly with salt and freshly milled black pepper. Place 5cm from the heat and cook for 5–8 minutes, depending on their thickness, until the fat is crusty and golden. Turn the chops, season the uncooked side and cook as before. Drain 3 tbsp of the cooking juices into a frying pan. When the chops are done remove and keep warm. Stir 4 tbsp double cream, 1 tbsp mustard, 2 tbsp lemon juice, 2 tbsp water and ½ tbsp honey into the pan. Do not finish the sauce yet. Using water from the kettle, boil the spinach, pushing it under the water, for 1–2 minutes until wilted. Drain thoroughly. Return to the pan and stir with 2 tbsp extra-virgin olive oil. Cover to keep warm.

TO SERVE: Reheat the soup and serve with a swirl of cream. For the main course, arrange 6 mounds of spinach on a platter and top with 2 tomato halves each. Add a lavish swirl of extra-virgin olive oil. Heat the sauce, stirring everything together for about 30 seconds to make a rich, caramel-coloured sauce. Taste and add extra cream or lemon juice if necessary. Plate the chops and spoon the sauce over and around.

AVOCADO LAYER CAKE
DUCK WITH QUICK FRENCH PEAS
CHOCOLATE FONDANT PUDDINGS

SHOPPING LIST

GREEN GROCERIES

125g bunch spring/salad onions

2 Little Gem lettuce hearts

3 large ripe avocados

2 limes

2 large garlic cloves

A few sprigs of coriander

20g bunch flat-leaf parsley

GROCERIES

300g jar hot tomato salsa dip, preferably Doritos

2 x 200g bags tortilla chips

750g frozen petits pois

50g plain flour, to dust

100g golden caster sugar

200g dark chocolate (minimum 70% cocoa solids)

CREAMY STUFF

250g butter, plus an extra knob

150g mature Cheddar cheese

300g soured cream

300g crème fraîche

4 large eggs, plus
3 large yolks

MEAT

4 Gressingham duck breasts with skin, approx. 175g each

You will also need clingfilm

This is a menu for any time of year. It begins with an addictively delicious avocado dip scooped up with tortilla chips and loved by everyone who tries it. I usually serve it on a platter for sharing but making it on individual plates gives fairer portion control! The main course is another example of the joys of frozen petits pois. They are cooked French-style with onions and lettuce, creating a lovely base for quickly cooked duck breast, and resulting in one of those clever, last-minute-assembly dishes, which look more complicated than they really are. The pudding is chocolate heaven with a luxurious lava-like centre.

0-15 MINUTES: Heat the oven to 200°C/400°F/gas mark 6. Boil the kettle. For the **CHOCOLATE FONDANT PUDDINGS**, lavishly butter 6 metal 175ml pudding tins and dust with flour, shaking out the excess. Place on a baking sheet and pop in the freezer. Break the chocolate into a metal bowl fitted over a half-filled pan of simmering water. Add 150g butter and stir occasionally as it melts. Meanwhile, place the eggs, yolks and sugar in an electric mixer (or bowl then use an electric whisk) and whisk at high speed for 3–6 minutes until thick, mousse-like and doubled in volume. Gradually fold the chocolate sauce into the mousse until smooth and slackened, then sift the flour over the top and fold through until smooth. Pour it into the prepared tins. Chill until required.

15-30 MINUTES: For **DUCK WITH QUICK FRENCH PEAS**, trim and coarsely chop the spring onions. Melt 75g butter in a wide-bottomed pan and stir in the onions. Cook for a couple of minutes to soften then add 150ml water and the petits pois. Add a scant tsp salt and a generous seasoning of black pepper. Quarter the lettuce hearts lengthways, rinse, shake dry then shred finely across the quarters. Stir the lettuce into the peas. Simmer uncovered for about 10 minutes until the peas and onion are tender and the lettuce has melted.

30-45 MINUTES: For **AVOCADO LAYER CAKE**, run a sharp knife round the avocados, twist apart, remove the stone and scrape the flesh into a bowl. Peel and finely chop the garlic. Dust with ¼ tsp salt and crush into a paste. Mash the garlic paste and the juice of 1 lime into the avocados. Taste and add more lime juice if you think it needs it. Smooth the avocado onto a platter or in the middle of 6 side plates. Spoon the tomato salsa over the top. Stir the soured cream and gently spread it over the salsa. Grate the cheese over the top and decorate with coriander sprigs. Chill until required.

45-60 MINUTES: Place the duck breasts skin-side down in an ovenproof pan over a high heat and cook for 2–3 minutes until the skin is crisp. Turn to seal the other side, cooking for 1–2 minutes. Transfer to the oven and cook for a further 10–15 minutes (for pink meat) until they feel springy when pressed. Remove the breasts to a plate. Cover with clingfilm and leave until required (at least 5 minutes). Chop the parsley leaves.

TO SERVE: Serve the avocado dip with tortilla chips, advising your guests to scoop through the layers. Slice thickly across the duck fillets on the diagonal. Reheat the peas, stir in 25g butter and, when melted, adjust the seasoning. Stir the parsley into the peas and spoon into the middle of 6 warmed dinner plates. Arrange the duck slices over the peas, adding any juices. Bake the puddings for 12 minutes until risen and set. Rest for 2 minutes. Run a knife around the inside of the moulds, turn onto plates and serve with the crème fraîche.

SMOKED MACKEREL PATE WITH BEETROOT RELISH
SQUID, CHORIZO, CHICKPEA AND BEAN STEW
RHUBARB AND ALMOND CRUMBLE

SHOPPING LIST

GREEN GROCERIES

2 medium onions

400g fine green beans

500g cooked baby beetroot

100g cherry tomatoes

500g fresh or frozen rhubarb

1 large orange

2 lemons

4 large garlic cloves

50g bunch coriander

GROCERIES

4 tbsp olive oil

1 tbsp red-wine vinegar

1 tsp aged balsamic vinegar

1 chicken stock cube

3 tbsp capers in vinegar

4 tbsp creamed horseradish

2 x 400g cans organic chickpeas

2 x 400g cans chopped tomatoes

100g plain flour

100g ground almonds

100g caster sugar, plus 1 tbsp

CREAMY STUFF

100g butter

500g crème fraîche

FISH AND MEAT

150g sliced chorizo

1 kg small prepared squid, tentacles inside the sacs

250g–300g smoked mackerel fillets

BREAD

2 ciabatta or other crusty bread

BOOZE

Approx. 150ml red wine

Smoked mackerel is delicious with creamed horseradish and a simple beetroot salad. Here the mackerel is whipped into a fluffy pâté and served with a pretty, perky beetroot relish. The main course is a gorgeous meal-in-a-bowl stew. This one has a Spanish flavour with chorizo firing out its chilli heat, subdued by chickpeas, green beans and creamily tender squid. Pudding is a light and elegant rhubarb crumble made with ground almonds and served at room temperature.

0-15 MINUTES: Begin with **SQUID, CHORIZO, CHICKPEA AND BEAN STEW.** Peel, halve and finely slice the onions. Peel and slice the garlic in wafer-thin rounds. Heat the olive oil in a spacious, heavy-bottomed pan, stir in the onion and garlic and cook, stirring occasionally for 10–15 minutes until soft. Meanwhile, dissolve the stock cube in 600ml boiling water. Tip the chickpeas into a sieve or colander and rinse thoroughly with cold water. Remove the tentacles from the squid sac and cut the sac lengthways into 3 chunky strips.

15-30 MINUTES: Stir the chorizo into the onions, cook for a couple of minutes then add the squid strips and tentacles. Cook gently, stirring continuously for a few minutes, until the squid begins to curl. Add the wine. Increase the heat and allow to boil before adding the chopped tomatoes and stock. Return to the boil, immediately reduce the heat and leave to simmer gently for 30 minutes. Chop the coriander. Heat the oven to 200°C/400°F/gas mark 6.

30-45 MINUTES: Now make **RHUBARB AND ALMOND CRUMBLE**. Trim the rhubarb, cut into 5cm-lengths and pile into a 2-litre capacity gratin-style ceramic dish. Sprinkle with 1 tbsp sugar and squeeze the orange over the top. Mix together the remaining sugar, flour and almonds in a mixing bowl then cut the butter in small pieces over the top. Rub the butter evenly into the mixture. Tip the crumble mixture over the rhubarb, spreading it out evenly. Cook in the oven for 25 minutes until the crumble is pale golden. If you think the crumble is colouring too quickly, cover it loosely with tinfoil. Leave to cool.

45-60 MINUTES: Make the relish for **SMOKED MACKEREL PATE WITH BEETROOT RELISH** by cutting the beetroot and tomatoes into quarters. Transfer to a serving bowl and mix with the drained capers, red-wine vinegar and balsamic vinegar. Season with salt and pepper and toss thoroughly. Peel the mackerel off its skin in chunks directly into a food processor. Add 100g crème fraîche, the juice of 1 lemon, plenty of black pepper and the creamed horseradish. Blitz briefly until smooth and amalgamated. Transfer to a serving bowl and stir in 100g crème fraîche to make a thick, fluffy pâté. Taste and adjust the seasoning with extra lemon juice and black pepper. Top and tail the beans and cut them in half.

TO SERVE: Serve the pâté with a big pile of hot toasted ciabatta, butter, lemon wedges and the beetroot relish. Stir the chickpeas into the stew, reheat and adjust the seasoning with salt and lemon juice. Boil the beans for a couple of minutes then drain and stir into the stew with the chopped coriander. Serve the warm crumble with the remaining crème fraîche.

LENTILS WITH SPINACH AND POACHED EGG
TUNA WITH CHERRY TOMATO GUACAMOLE
CHOCOLATE CREPES WITH RUM BUTTER

SHOPPING LIST

GREEN GROCERIES
1 medium red onion

2 shallots

150g young leaf spinach

5 medium tomatoes

200g cherry tomatoes

4 large firm but ripe avocados

3 limes

1 large garlic clove

2 red Bird Eye chillies

½ tsp chopped thyme

25g bunch coriander

GROCERIES
2 tbsp olive oil

2 tbsp extra-virgin olive oil

Splash of wine vinegar

1 tbsp aged balsamic vinegar

1 chicken stock cube

2 x 400g cans green lentils
in water

150g demerara sugar

6 ready-made pancakes

200g dark chocolate,
(70% cocoa solids)

CREAMY STUFF
150g unsalted butter

250g crème fraîche

6 large fresh organic eggs

FISH
6 thick tuna fillets

BOOZE
8 tbsp rum

You will also need clingfilm

The earthy flavour of lentils is delicious with eggs and here they are soft boiled, so the yolk spills onto the spinach and tomato-laced lentils. The main course is simple but effective; tuna is quickly griddled to achieve those attractive etched 'tram-lines' but the inside remains moist and melting, and a perfect foil to the guacamole. An indulgent chocolate crépe with a rich rum butter sauce rounds off this lovely meal.

0-15 MINUTES: Boil the kettle. Peel, halve and finely slice the red onion for **LENTILS WITH SPINACH AND POACHED EGG**. Heat 2 tbsp olive oil in a medium-sized pan and stir in the onion. Add the thyme and cook gently, stirring occasionally, for about 8 minutes until slippery and soft. Tip the lentils into a sieve, rinse and shake dry. Dissolve the stock cube in 400ml boiling water. Stir the balsamic vinegar into the onion then add the lentils and stock. Simmer uncovered for 10 minutes.

15-30 MINUTES: For **TUNA WITH CHERRY TOMATO GUACAMOLE**, run a sharp knife around the avocados. Twist apart and remove the stone. Dice the avocados in their shells, then use a spoon to scoop the flesh into a bowl. Squeeze over the juice of 1 lime. Quarter the cherry tomatoes then halve the quarters. Peel and finely chop the shallots. Finely dice the chillies. Peel and chop the garlic. Sprinkle with a little salt and crush into a paste. Coarsely chop the coriander. Stir the garlic into the avocado whilst coarsely mashing it; you want lumpy rather than smooth. Mix in the tomatoes, onion, chilli and coriander then taste and adjust the seasoning with salt, pepper and more lime. Cover with clingfilm, letting it sag against the guacamole to avoid discolouration.

30-45 MINUTES: Stir the spinach into the lentils. When wilted, turn off the heat. Cover the medium tomatoes with boiling water, count to 20, drain and splash with cold water. Remove the skin, cut out the core. Dice the flesh. Pour a 10cm-depth of boiling water into a wide saucepan. Add the wine vinegar. One at a time, crack 4 eggs into a teacup and slip them into the simmering water. Have a bowl of cold water at the ready. Cook the eggs for 1½ minutes until the white is set but the yolk is still soft; press one egg gently to test. Use a perforated spoon to transfer the eggs to the bowl of cold water. Cook the remaining 2 eggs and place in the cold water with the others.

45-60 MINUTES: For **CHOCOLATE CREPES WITH RUM BUTTER**, break the chocolate into squares and divide between the pancakes. Fold them in half and then in half again, tucking the chocolate firmly inside the pancake. Melt the butter and sugar in a spacious frying pan over a low heat. Stir in the rum and turn off the heat. Meanwhile, heat a ridged griddle pan for several minutes until very hot. Cook 3 tuna fillets at a time for 2 minutes each side. Transfer to a plate. When all 6 fillets are cooked, cover the plate with a stretch of clingfilm.

TO SERVE: Stir the diced tomatoes into the lentils and divide between 6 plates. Lift one egg at a time onto kitchen paper to drain then rest over the lentils; finish with a swirl of extra-virgin olive oil. Serve the tuna next to a scoop of guacamole and a lime wedge. To finish the pancakes, reheat the sauce and slip the folded pancakes into the pan. Cook for a couple of minutes, encouraging the sauce over the pancakes, until the chocolate is melted. Serve with crème fraîche.

SHOPPING LIST

GREEN GROCERIES

1 kg floury potatoes

4 Belgian chicory

3 under-ripe bananas

2 lemons

50g bunch flat-leaf parsley

Approx. 25 fresh sage leaves

GROCERIES

1 tbsp vegetable oil

4 tbsp olive oil

½ tbsp red-wine vinegar

1 tbsp smooth Dijon mustard

6 cornichons or 1 pickled cucumber

60g anchovy fillets in olive oil

50g pitted black olives

450g jar Dulce de Leche, preferably Merchant Gourmet

50g walnut pieces

1 tsp instant coffee

Flour for dusting

20cm pre-cooked shortcrust pastry case

CREAMY STUFF

125g butter

150ml milk

300ml whipping cream

MEAT

800g pork fillet/tenderloin

7 slices Parma ham

BREAD

6 thick slices sourdough-style bread

BOOZE

1 glass white wine, approx. 150ml

Generous splash of Marsala

You will also need 12 sheets greaseproof paper approx. 30 x 20cm and tinfoil

Slicing chicory into skinny, long wedges and mixing it with flat-leaf parsley leaves, walnut kernels and scraps of pickled cucumber, makes a lovely salad to serve with salty anchovy crostini. It is a bit of a palaver but very satisfying to turn a fillet of pork into tiny escalopes to sandwich Parma ham and sage leaves. These delicious morsels are very good with lemony mashed potato. Pudding is a terrifically easy cheat's version of banoffi pie – banana, caramelized milk with sugar (Dulce de Leche) and cream – and a guaranteed smash hit.

0-15 MINUTES: Begin with **BANOFFI PIE**. Remove the pastry case from its tin and place on a large plate. Spoon the Dulce de Leche into the pastry case – you may not need it all. Peel the bananas, slice thickly lengthways and nudge up closely over the caramel to cover it entirely. Whip the cream with most of the coffee until firm but floppy. Spoon it over the bananas, using a fork to encourage swirls. Dust with the remaining coffee. Leave to chill.

15-30 MINUTES: To make the **PORK SALTIMBOCCA WITH LEMON MASH**, trim any fat or sinew from the pork and cut 36 slices, each no thicker than a 50p coin. Lay out 6 sheets of greaseproof paper and on each one arrange 6 slices with plenty of space around them. Cover each with a second sheet of paper and, using a rolling-pin, gently but firmly beat into very thin escalopes, almost double the original size.

30-45 MINUTES: Season 3 escalopes on each sheet with black pepper, lay a sage leaf on top and cover with a bit of ham that fits as neatly as possible. Cover with the 3 remaining escalopes, return the greaseproof paper and lightly beat again to sandwich together. Carefully remove to a plate. Repeat with the remaining escalopes until you have 18 saltimbocca 'sandwiches'. Chill until required. Heat the oven to 150°C/300°F/gas mark 2.

45-60 MINUTES: Peel the potatoes, cut into even-sized chunks, rinse and cook in boiling salted water for about 15 minutes until tender. Begin **CHICORY AND PARSLEY SALAD WITH ANCHOVY CROSTINI**. Reserving the oil from the anchovy can, chop the anchovies. Slice the olives and mix the two together, set aside. Chop the cornichons into small pieces. Trim the chicory, halve lengthways and slice down the halves into ½ cm-strips. Pick the leaves off the parsley stalks. Add the mustard to a salad bowl. Mix with the vinegar, then whisk in the olive oil gradually to make a thick vinaigrette, thinning it with 1 tbsp water. Toss the chicory, parsley leaves, walnuts and cornichons in the dressing. Drain the potatoes. Heat 50g butter with the milk in the potato pan and when the butter melts, remove from the heat, return the potatoes and mash. Beat the juice of 1 lemon into the mash. Taste and add more lemon juice if you think necessary. Cover and keep warm.

TO SERVE: To make the crostini toast the bread, dribble one side with anchovy oil from the can, and then top with the anchovy mixture. Serve with the salad. Dust the saltimbocca with flour. Heat 75g butter with the vegetable oil between two frying pans. When it is very hot, cook 4 saltimbocca at a time, frying for 1 minute each side until golden. Keep warm, covered with foil, in the oven. Quickly sizzle the remaining sage leaves in the hot fat and drain. Tip away most of the fat from one pan, add the wine and Marsala and allow to bubble and reduce into a syrupy gravy. Pour over the saltimbocca. Garnish with the crisp sage leaves. Serve the lemon mash separately. Remove the banoffi pie from the fridge just prior to serving.

STARTER P121 **MAIN** P135 **PUDDING** P141

THE
RECI

PES

SOUPS

SICILIAN FENNEL AND BROAD BEAN SOUP 01

2 shallots
1 large garlic clove
50g butter
1 tbsp vegetable oil
2 medium fennel bulbs
1 medium-sized potato
2 chicken stock cubes
500g podded broad beans
3 tbsp fresh lemon juice

Peel and finely chop the shallots and garlic. Soften both in the butter and vegetable oil in a spacious, heavy-bottomed pan over a medium heat. Halve, core and chop the fennel. Stir into the shallots and garlic. Add ½ tsp salt, stir again, cover and leave to cook for 5 minutes. Peel, chop and rinse the potato. Dissolve the stock cubes in 1.5 litres boiling water. Add the chopped potato and stock to the pan. Bring to the boil then reduce the heat slightly. Partially cover and boil for 5 minutes. Add the broad beans. Increase the heat and return to the boil. Boil for a further 5 minutes. Add 1 tbsp lemon juice then liquidize in batches, pressing the soup through a sieve into a clean pan. Taste and adjust the seasoning with salt and more lemon juice.

GREEN MINESTRONE WITH PESTO 05

1 onion
3 tbsp vegetable oil
200g podded broad beans
1 celery heart
1 trimmed leek, approx. 150g
200g extra-fine beans
2 courgettes, approx. 200g
1 vegetable or chicken stock cube
2 new potatoes, approx. 150g
200g frozen petits pois
Tabasco
1 garlic clove
130g carton basil pesto
6 tbsp freshly grated Parmesan

Boil the kettle. Peel and finely chop the onion. Heat 2 tbsp vegetable oil in a large pan that can accommodate the finished soup. Stir in the onion and cook gently for

10 minutes. Half fill a medium-sized pan with boiling water, add 1 tsp salt and the broad beans. Boil for 1 minute. Drain, refill the pan with cold water and add the beans to cool and arrest cooking. Trim and finely chop the celery. Slice the leek into thin rounds. Boil the kettle again. Stir the celery and leeks into the onions. Add 1 tsp salt, stir again, reduce the heat, cover and cook for 5 minutes. Chop the beans into 5cm-lengths. Dice the courgettes. Dissolve the stock cube in 1 litre boiling water. Peel, dice and rinse the potatoes. Stir into the onions. Add the stock and bring the soup to the boil. Reduce the heat and simmer for 15 minutes. Drain the broad beans and, in between other jobs, remove their rubbery skin by nicking the edge with your nail, then squeezing out the bean. Add the beans, courgettes and petits pois and boil for 5 minutes. Taste and adjust the seasoning with salt, pepper and Tabasco. Peel and chop the garlic and liquidize it with the pesto. Tip into a serving bowl. Stir the broad beans into the minestrone and serve with the pesto and Parmesan.

THAI-STYLE SWEETCORN CHOWDER 06

1 onion
2 tbsp olive oil
1 small lemon
2 red Bird Eye chillies
2 garlic cloves
1 red pepper
4 large corn-on-the-cob
3 chicken stock cubes
25g bunch coriander

Peel, halve and finely chop the onion. Cook it for 5 minutes in 2 tbsp olive oil in a large pan, stirring occasionally. Remove the zest from the lemon in paper-thin scraps. Trim and finely chop the chillies. Chop the garlic. Quarter the pepper, discard the stalk, seeds etc. and cut into small chunks. Stir everything into the onion. Slice down the cobs to remove the kernels. Dissolve the stock cubes in 1.5 litres boiling water. Add the stock and kernels to the pan, return to the boil, reduce the heat, partially cover the pan and cook for 15 minutes until everything is tender. Taste and adjust the seasoning with salt and lemon juice. Chop the coriander and stir in just before serving.

ROAST TOMATO SOUP WITH SAFFRON AND HONEY 07

2kg medium-sized tomatoes
2 tbsp olive oil
2 red peppers
Generous pinch saffron stamens
1 chicken stock cube
2 tsp runny honey
6 drips Tabasco
You will also need tinfoil

Boil the kettle. Heat the oven to 180°C/ 350°F/ gas mark 4. Halve the tomatoes and lay, cut-side up, on a foil-lined baking sheet. Smear with olive oil. Halve the peppers lengthways and discard the stalk, core and seeds. Arrange, skin-side up, next to the tomatoes. Roast for 45 minutes. Soften the saffron in 2 tbsp boiling water from the kettle. Dissolve the stock cube in 800ml boiling water. Lift the burnished skin off the peppers then tip the tomatoes and peppers into the bowl of a food processor. Blitz to make a thick, smooth purée. Pass through a sieve into a suitable pan, pressing and scraping – don't forget under the sieve – to ensure that nothing is wasted. Add the honey, Tabasco, saffron and stock. Reheat and adjust the seasoning with salt, pepper and lemon juice.

INSTANT BORSCHT 11

4 uncooked beetroot, approx. 750g
2 chicken stock cubes
1 large garlic clove
Juice from 1 lemon
150g crème fraîche or soured cream, to serve
Flat-leaf parsley, to garnish

Trim, peel and grate the beetroot using a food processor or the large hole of a cheese-grater. Dissolve the stock cubes in 1.2 litres boiling water in a medium-sized saucepan. Stir the beetroot into the boiling stock, return to the boil and boil for 7 minutes. Meanwhile, peel and chop the garlic. Sprinkle with ½ tsp salt and crush to make a juicy paste. When the 7 minutes is up, stir the garlic and half the lemon juice into the soup. Taste and adjust the seasoning with more lemon juice and salt if needed. Serve with a dollop of crème fraîche and a parsley garnish.

SPINACH SOUP WITH CORIANDER DUMPLINGS 16

2 medium potatoes
25g butter
2 tbsp olive oil
500g young leaf spinach
2 chicken stock cubes
¼ tsp freshly grated nutmeg
150ml double cream
25g bunch coriander
75g mascarpone
75g soft goats' cheese

Peel, halve and thinly slice the potatoes, rinse and drain. Melt the butter with the olive oil in a spacious pan. Add the potatoes to the buttery oil and cook for about 5 minutes until tender. Fold in the spinach until wilted. Add 1.2 litres cold water, crumble over the stock cubes, with ½ tsp salt and the grated nutmeg. Bring to the boil then simmer for 5 minutes. Liquidise and return to a clean pan. Stir in the cream, reheat and adjust the seasoning. While the soup reheats, chop the coriander and mix it with the mascarpone and the goats' cheese. Pour the soup into 6 bowls and drop 2–3 spoonfuls of the mixture into each bowl of soup.

WHITE GAZPACHO 19

4 large garlic cloves, preferably new-season
100g blanched almonds
3 tbsp white-wine vinegar or sherry
7-8 tbsp extra-virgin olive oil
225g day-old white bread, without crusts
225g seedless white grapes
You will also need clingfilm

Peel the garlic and place in the bowl of a food processor with the almonds, vinegar, 6 tbsp extra-virgin olive oil and 1 tsp salt. Blitz furiously. Have ready 900ml cold water. Tear the bread into pieces. Add some bread to the food processor, then some water, and continue, thus, until the bread and water is used up and you have created a thick, white purée. Taste and adjust the seasoning with more vinegar, salt and olive oil. Pour into a bowl. Peel and halve the grapes lengthways, if time permits. Stir them into the soup. Cover with clingfilm and chill. Just before serving give the soup a final stir and splash with a little extra-virgin olive oil.

GAZPACHO 28

3 large garlic cloves
150g white bread, without crusts
1 cucumber
1 red chilli
2 red peppers
1 red onion
1 kg very ripe tomatoes
2 tbsp sherry or wine vinegar
100ml extra-virgin olive oil, plus 2 tbsp
3 plum or vine tomatoes
Juice of 1 lemon
20 mint leaves
You will also need 300ml iced water

Peel the garlic. Tear the bread into pieces. Place both in the bowl of a food processor and blitz to make fine breadcrumbs. Meanwhile, peel the cucumber. Halve it horizontally and use a teaspoon to scrape out the seeds. Chop half of it roughly. Trim and split the chilli. Scrape out the seeds. Set aside half of one red pepper and chop the rest, discarding seeds and white filament. Peel and halve the onion. Coarsely chop one half and add to the breadcrumbs with the chopped cucumber, chilli and chopped red pepper. Remove the cores from the 1 kg tomatoes and chop roughly. Add to the food processor with the vinegar, iced water, most of the mint, 100ml olive oil, ½ tsp salt and a generous seasoning of black pepper. Blitz for several minutes until liquidized. Keeping separate piles, finely dice the remaining cucumber and red pepper. Finely chop the remaining onion. Quarter the plum or vine tomatoes, discard the seeds and finely chop. Taste the gazpacho and adjust the seasoning with salt, pepper and lemon juice. Whisk in the 2 tbsp extra-virgin olive oil. Transfer to a serving bowl. Chill until required. Serve the gazpacho with the garnishes in small bowls, adding the mint to the chopped tomato.

MINTED PEA AND LEMON SOUP 29

125g spring/salad onions
1 lemon
50g butter
2 chicken stock cubes
1kg frozen petits pois
1 tbsp concentrated English mint sauce
Tabasco (optional)
Crusty bread and butter, to serve

Boil the kettle. Trim, peel and finely slice the onions. Pare fine strips of zest from half the lemon. Melt the butter in a medium-sized pan, stir in the onions and lemon zest. Season with salt and pepper. Cover and cook over a medium-low heat for about 5 minutes, until soft. Measure 2 litres boiling water into a jug. Add the stock cubes, stirring to dissolve. Add the stock then peas to the pan, increase the heat and boil for 5 minutes, until the peas are tender. Add the mint sauce. Liquidize in batches and pour into a clean pan. Reheat and adjust the seasoning with salt, lemon juice and a smidgen of Tabasco. Serve with the crusty bread and butter.

ROASTED RED PEPPER SOUP WITH SAFFRON 30

6 red sweet pointed peppers, preferably Ramiro
3 medium-small red onions
1 red Bird Eye chilli
1 chicken stock cube
Generous pinch saffron stamens
2 lemons
1 tsp runny honey
Crusty bread and butter, to serve
You will also need clingfilm

Heat the oven to 200°C/400°F/gas mark 6. Boil the kettle. Arrange the peppers on a baking sheet. Halve the onions and position them near the edges. Place the chilli in the middle of the peppers. Roast for 30 minutes, leaving the onions for a further few minutes if not entirely soft. Meanwhile, dissolve the stock cube in 750ml boiling water. Add the saffron. Lift the peppers onto a plate and cover with clingfilm. Leave for 5 minutes and then peel off the blistered, blackened skin. Remove the core and seeds. Scrape the soft onion flesh out of the skin. Place the peppers, onions, what remains of the chilli (without the stalk and seeds) in the bowl of a food processor. Add the saffron stock and blitz. Pass through a sieve into a suitable pan, scraping underneath so nothing is wasted. Reheat and adjust the seasoning with salt, pepper, lemon juice and the honey. Serve with the crusty bread and butter.

BROCCOLI AND LEMON SOUP WITH GARLIC BREAD 38

1 medium onion
1 garlic clove
25g butter
1 tsp vegetable oil
1 lemon
2 chicken stock cubes
1 kg frozen broccoli florets
3 garlic baguettes
60g grated Parmesan
Crème fraîche, to serve

Boil the kettle. Peel, halve and finely chop the onion and garlic clove. Melt the butter with the vegetable oil in a spacious frying pan and stir in the onion and garlic. Cook briskly, stirring often, for 5 minutes. Meanwhile, use a zester to remove the zest from half the lemon and add to the pan together with 1 tsp salt. Stir, reduce the heat, cover and cook for 10 minutes. Dissolve the stock cubes in 1.3 litres boiling water. Add the stock to the onions followed by the broccoli. Return to the boil – this will take several minutes – and boil for 5 minutes. Heat the oven to 200°C/400°F/gas mark 6. Liquidize the soup in batches and return to a clean pan. Add the juice from the lemon and adjust the seasoning with salt. Lay the garlic loaves on an oven tray, prise apart the slices and dredge generously with grated Parmesan. Bake for 10 minutes. Serve the soup in bowls with a scoop of crème fraîche and hot garlic bread.

HUMMUS SOUP WITH MINT AND GARLIC 39

3 garlic cloves
3 x 400g cans chickpeas
9 tbsp olive oil
3 tbsp fresh lemon juice
25g bunch mint
25g bunch flat-leaf parsley
4 tbsp extra-virgin olive oil
Crusty bread, to serve

Peel and roughly chop the garlic cloves. Drain the liquid from the chickpea cans into a measuring jug and make up the amount to 1.3 litres with water. Heat, then purée in batches in a blender with the chickpeas, chopped garlic, olive oil and lemon juice. Simmer for 5 minutes. Season to taste with salt, pepper and lemon juice. Finely chop the mint and parsley leaves. Stir the herbs into the (very) hot soup and serve with a swirl of extra-virgin olive oil and some crusty bread.

CAULIFLOWER AND LEMON SOUP WITH THYME 46

1 large cauliflower
150g spring/salad onions
1 large garlic clove
1 lemon
25g butter
1 tsp chopped fresh thyme
2 chicken or vegetable stock cubes
150g double cream

Cut the cauliflower into small florets, each with a bit of stalk. Trim the spring onions and finely chop, including all the tender green. Peel the garlic and chop coarsely. Remove the zest from the lemon in wafer-thin scraps. Melt the butter in a 2-litre capacity pan and stir in the onion, garlic, lemon zest and thyme. Add ½ tsp salt and stir thoroughly. Cover and cook gently, stirring occasionally for 5 minutes until the onion has begun to soften. Dissolve the stock cubes in 1.2 litres boiling water. Stir the cauliflower into the onion mixture. Add the stock to the cauliflower and bring to the boil. Immediately reduce the heat, partially cover the pan and cook for 10–15 minutes, until the cauliflower is tender. Blitz the soup in batches and return to the pan. Stir in 100g double cream. Reheat, taste and adjust the seasoning with salt, pepper and lemon juice. Serve with a swirl of cream.

STARTERS

CARPACCIO OF TUNA WITH THAI AVOCADO SALAD 02

2 x 200g tuna steaks
2 limes
2 tbsp Thai fish sauce (nam pla)
½ tbsp toasted sesame oil
1 tbsp sweet chilli dipping-sauce, preferably Blue Dragon
10cm cucumber
3 small ripe but firm avocados
25g bunch coriander

Put the tuna in the freezer for 15 minutes to firm it up and make slicing easier. Squeeze the juice of 1 lime into a bowl. Add the fish sauce, sesame oil and sweet chilli dipping-sauce. Mix together. Finely slice the tuna, cutting across the grain (as if slicing smoked salmon). Arrange in a single layer on 6 plates. Peel and split the cucumber lengthways. Use a teaspoon to remove the seeds. Thinly slice into half-moons. Run a knife round the avocados, twist apart and remove the stone and skin. Slice across the avocados and season with the juice of 1 lime. Mix the avocado with the cucumber and pile next to the tuna. Prettily dribble over the dressing. Garnish with a freshly chopped coriander.

COCKLES WITH TOMATO AND LINGUINE 03

200g jar cooked and pickled cockles (drained weight 100g)
1 medium onion
2 large garlic cloves
1 red Bird Eye chilli
50g butter
1 tbsp olive oil
Glass of white wine, approx. 150ml
4 medium vine tomatoes
400g linguine
20g bunch flat-leaf parsley

Tip the cockles into a sieve and rinse well. Shake dry. Peel, halve and finely chop the onion and garlic. Split the chilli lengthways, scrape away the seeds, slice into batons and then into tiny scraps. Melt half the butter with 1 tbsp olive oil in a small, heavy pan. Stir in the onion, garlic and chilli. Cook gently, stirring occasionally, for 10–12 minutes until the onion is soft but not coloured. Stir the drained cockles into the onions, add the wine and bring to the boil. Reduce the heat and simmer for 8–10 minutes until the liquid has reduced by half. Turn off the heat. Finely chop the flat-leaf parsley leaves. Meanwhile, place the tomatoes in a bowl and cover with boiling water. Count to 20, then drain, splash with cold water, skin and core. Quarter, deseed and slice each piece into strips, then dice. Cook the linguine in plenty of boiling water for 6 minutes, or until *al dente*. Drain and return to the pan with the remaining butter. Quickly reheat the cockles and stir into the linguine. Add the tomatoes and parsley. Transfer to a warmed serving bowl.

PISSALADIERE WITH ROCKET 04

1 tbsp olive oil
Flour for dusting
350g puff pastry
3 tbsp tomato purée
400g can Eazy fried onions
2 x 50g anchovy fillets in olive oil
75g pitted black olives
150g wild rocket
Bottles of extra-virgin olive oil and wine vinegar (for the table)

Heat the oven to 200°C/400°F/gas mark 6. Generously smear a 24 x 34cm baking tin with the olive oil. Dust a work surface with flour and roll the pastry to fit the tin. Use the tines of a fork to pierce the dough in several places to stop it rising. Smear the tomato purée then onion, right up to the edges. Split the anchovies lengthways. Make a wide lattice with the anchovies over the onions. Place an olive in each lattice. Dribble the tart with the oil from the anchovies and bake in the oven for about 20 minutes until the pastry is cooked. If it billows, pierce it with a knife to encourage it to flatten. Remove from the oven and leave until required. Cut slabs of the warm pissaladière and serve with a handful of rocket, offering extra-virgin olive oil and wine vinegar for guests to do their own anointing.

PORTABELLO BRUSCHETTA 08

250g large flat mushrooms, preferably portabello
25g butter
2 tbsp olive oil

3 large garlic cloves
3 unwaxed lemons
25g bunch flat-leaf parsley
6 thick slices sourdough
3 tbsp extra-virgin olive oil

Wipe the mushrooms clean and slice thickly. Melt the butter with the olive oil in a frying pan. Place the sliced mushrooms in the pan – you may need to do this in two batches – and cook for a few minutes before turning. Cook for 10–15 minutes until shrunken, juicy and just cooked through. Meanwhile, peel and finely chop 2 garlic cloves. Remove the zest from half a lemon in wafer-thin sheets. Finely chop. Chop the parsley leaves. Make a pile of garlic, lemon zest and parsley and chop everything together. If necessary, return the first batch of mushrooms to the pan. Add half the parsley mixture. Toss and turn off the heat. Toast the bread and rub one side with the remaining peeled garlic clove. Place on plates and dribble with extra-virgin olive oil. Add the remaining parsley to the mushrooms, squeeze over the juice from half a lemon and cook briskly to reheat and absorb the juices. Pile onto the toast and serve with a lemon wedge each.

ASPARAGUS, BROAD BEAN AND PRAWN SALAD 09

1 unwaxed lemon
1 tsp runny honey
3 tbsp olive oil
200g cooked, peeled prawns, preferably North Atlantic
200g podded broad beans
155g asparagus tips
150g sugar snap peas
25g bunch mint
200g feta cheese

Boil the kettle. Remove the zest from half the lemon and chop finely. Measure 2 tbsp lemon juice into a wide-based serving bowl and stir in the honey. Add the olive oil and whisk to amalgamate. Stir in the lemon zest. Add the prawns. Pour a 5cm-depth of boiling water into a wide-based pan. Add 1 tsp salt and return to the boil. Add the broad beans and boil for 2 minutes. Have ready a bowl of cold water. Scoop the beans out of the pan into the cold water. Add the asparagus tips to the boiling water and boil for 2 minutes.

Meanwhile, drain the broad beans, nick the edge of each bean with your thumb and squeeze the bright green beans into the salad, continuing as you cook the asparagus and then the sugar snap peas, separately for 2 minutes each. Lift the asparagus out of the boiling water. Rest on kitchen paper to drain. Add the drained sugar snap peas and asparagus to the salad. To finish, finely chop the mint leaves and add to the salad. Gently toss everything together. Crumble the feta over the top. Loosely toss before serving.

MIDDLE EASTERN MEZZE 10

6 medium-sized tomatoes
1 tsp sugar
3 tbsp olive oil
2 garlic cloves
200g natural yoghurt
2 large lemons
400g small boiled beetroot
20g bunch coriander
150g pot organic hummus
Generous pinch ground cumin
70g pitted black olives
175g couscous
1 generous pinch saffron stamens
200g cherry tomatoes
2 shallots
50g bunch flat-leaf parsley
200g ready-made falafel
2 Greek sesame seed loaves (daktyla)

Heat the oven to 200°C/400°F/gas mark 6. Preheat the grill. Halve the medium-sized tomatoes and season with salt, pepper, the sugar and a splash of olive oil. Grill, adjusting the heat so they cook evenly, for 10 minutes until soft and weeping. Leave to cool. Peel, chop and crush the garlic with a little salt to make a juicy paste. Place the paste in a bowl, add the yoghurt and stir in 1 tbsp olive oil and a squeeze of lemon. Halve the beetroot and place on one end of a platter. Season with salt and a squeeze of lemon. Spoon the yoghurt over the beetroot. Chop the coriander and sprinkle over the top. Arrange the grilled tomatoes next to the beetroot. Spoon the hummus next to the tomatoes and season both with cumin. Scatter with the olives and splash the tomatoes with olive oil. Place the couscous in a bowl and add 250ml boiling water, the saffron, 1 tbsp lemon juice and

1 tbsp olive oil. Stir, cover, and leave for 5 minutes to hydrate. Quarter the cherry tomatoes. Peel and finely chop the shallots. Finely chop the flat-leaf parsley leaves. Mix everything into the couscous. Pile onto one end of a second platter. Cook the falafel in the oven for 10 minutes. Turn off the oven but put the loaves in to get crusty. Arrange the falafel next to the couscous with 1 lemon cut into wedges. Serve together.

PEAR, SPINACH, GORGONZOLA AND WALNUT SALAD 12

350g young leaf spinach
5 ripe pears
3 tbsp lemon juice
170g creamy gorgonzola
50g walnut pieces
1 tbsp runny honey
4 tbsp olive oil

Arrange a bed of spinach leaves on 6 starter plates. Peel, core and quarter the pears lengthways. Thickly slice lengthways into a bowl. Toss with 1 tbsp lemon juice to avoid discolouration. Arrange the slices over the spinach. Add slices of cheese and scatter with walnut pieces. Make the salad dressing by whisking together 2 tbsp lemon juice, the honey and olive oil. Spoon it over the salad just before serving.

ROASTED PEPPERS WITH FETA AND BLACK OLIVES 13

6 red peppers, preferably pointed variety
2 tbsp aged balsamic vinegar, preferably Belazu
4 tbsp extra-virgin olive oil
200g Greek feta cheese, preferably Pittas
12 pitted black olives
Crusty bread and butter, to serve
You will also need clingfilm

Heat the oven to 200°C/400°F/gas mark 6. Arrange the peppers on a roasting tin and roast for 30 minutes, turning halfway through cooking. Transfer to a plate, cover with clingfilm and leave for 5 minutes. Remove the skin, stalk and seeds from the peppers and arrange, shiny-side uppermost, on a serving platter. Zig-zag with balsamic vinegar and extra-virgin olive oil. Crumble the feta over the peppers and scatter with torn black olives. Serve with crusty bread and butter.

INSALATA TRICOLORE WITH BALSAMICO 14

9 medium-sized ripe vine tomatoes
4 buffalo mozzarella
3 large, firm but ripe avocados
Juice of 1 lemon
1 tsp aged balsamic vinegar
6 tbsp extra-virgin olive oil
About 20 basil leaves

Making separate piles, core and thickly slice the tomatoes. Thickly slice the mozzarella. Halve the avocados, twist apart, remove the stone and peel. Slice thickly across the halves. Make individual salads by alternating the slices of tomato, mozzarella and avocado or present on a large platter for sharing. Whisk together the juice of 1 lemon, the honey, a generous seasoning of black pepper, the olive oil and balsamic vinegar and spoon over the salad. Tear the basil leaves over the top.

ASPARAGUS RISOTTO WITH PARMESAN 15

750g asparagus
75g butter
Squeeze of lemon juice
½ chicken stock cube
1 shallot or small onion
250g arborio rice
Glass of Noilly Prat vermouth or white wine, approx. 150ml
4 heaped tbsp freshly grated Parmesan, plus extra for serving

Trim the asparagus, discarding the woody ends. Snap off the tips and cut the stalks into 5cm-lengths. Boil the tips for 2 minutes in 1.2 litres water. Remove from the water. Boil the stalks for 4–6 minutes until tender. Scoop into the bowl of a food processor with a cupful of cooking water and a large knob of butter. Blitz into a smooth purée. Pass the purée through a sieve into a small pan, scraping underneath so nothing is wasted. Season with salt, pepper and lemon juice. Dissolve the stock cube in the rest of the asparagus water and leave on a low heat. Peel and finely chop the shallot. Melt 25g butter in a heavy-based, wide saucepan. Gently cook the shallot for 3 minutes until soft but uncoloured. Add the rice and cook, stirring constantly, for a couple of minutes

until it is glistening and semi-translucent. Add the vermouth, stirring as it seethes and bubbles. Add a ladleful of the hot stock. Stir as it sizzles, cooking for a couple of minutes until the rice has absorbed most of the liquid. Add a second ladleful of stock and stir until all the liquid has been absorbed, adjusting the heat to maintain a gentle simmer. Continue in this way, stirring constantly, until the rice is almost tender but firm to the bite; 17–20 minutes in total. Quickly reheat the asparagus purée and stir into the risotto. Cook for a few minutes until the risotto is creamy and porridge-like. Stir in the asparagus tips, remaining butter and 4 tbsp Parmesan. Cover and leave for 5–10 minutes. Give the risotto a final stir and serve dusted with Parmesan.

AVOCADO WITH TOMATO MAYONNAISE 17

1 shallot or small red onion
2 tbsp red-wine vinegar
2 medium vine tomatoes
6 firm but ripe small avocados
1 lemon
1 tbsp mayonnaise, preferably Hellmann's
3 tbsp olive oil
15g chives
Thinly sliced brown bread and butter, to serve

Boil the kettle. Peel, halve and finely chop the shallot. Place in a bowl and just cover with vinegar. Place the tomatoes in a bowl and cover with boiling water. Count to 30, drain, halve, remove the skin and scrape away the seeds. Dice the flesh finely. Run a sharp knife round the avocados. Twist apart, remove the stone and skin, and then slice across the halves to make 1cm-wide half-moons. Pile the avocado onto 6 plates and season with lemon juice to avoid discolouration. Place the mayonnaise in a bowl. Drain the shallots, reserving ½ tbsp vinegar. Add the shallot and reserved vinegar to the mayonnaise then beat in the olive oil to make a thick and creamy dressing. Scatter the diced vine tomatoes over the avocado and spoon over the dressing. Finely slice the chives and scatter over the top. Serve the avocado and tomato mayonnaise with brown bread and butter.

ROAST AUBERGINE WITH ASIAN DRESSING 18

4 aubergines, long rather than fat

2 tbsp lemon juice

3 tbsp peanut oil

1 red Bird Eye chilli

2 large garlic cloves

2 tsp caster sugar

1 tbsp Thai fish sauce (nam pla)

4 tbsp chopped coriander

About 20 small mint leaves

Heat the oven to 200°C/400°F/gas mark 6. Trim then quarter the aubergines lengthways. Arrange, cut-side up, on a roasting tin and roast for 20 minutes until the flesh is scorched and soft. Leave to cool. Whisk together the lemon juice and peanut oil. Trim and finely chop the chilli, discarding the seeds. Peel and finely chop the garlic, sprinkle with a generous pinch of salt and crush into a paste. Add the chilli, garlic, sugar and half the fish sauce to the lemon juice and oil, and stir. Add the remaining fish sauce if insufficiently salty. Stir in the coriander. Strip the skins off the aubergine and cut into 2cm cubes. Pile onto a platter and spoon over the dressing. Scatter the mint over the top.

ASIAN CHANTENAY CARROTS 20

500g Chantenay or regular carrots

50g fresh ginger

3 tbsp vegetable oil

1 tbsp mustard seeds

½ tsp cayenne pepper

1 lime

4 garlic and coriander mini naan breads

2 tbsp coarsely chopped fresh coriander

500g natural yoghurt

Boil the kettle. Rinse the Chantenay carrots. If you are using regular carrots scrape and cut them into 6cm-long chunky pieces. Boil in salted water for 5 minutes until *al dente*. Drain. Meanwhile, peel the ginger and slice into thin pieces no larger than a shirt button. Heat the oil in a wok or large frying pan. Add the mustard seeds and ginger and stir-fry for about 60 seconds before adding the carrots, cayenne and the juice from the lime. Stir-fry for 2 minutes. Sprinkle the naan with water and grill for 1 minute on each side. Cut into quarters. Give the carrots a final stir-fry so that they are piping hot. Pile

onto a serving dish and scatter with the chopped coriander. Serve the carrots with the naan and yoghurt.

CORN ON THE COB WITH CHILLI AND LEMON BUTTER 21

2 red Bird Eye chillies

150g butter

A generous squeeze of lemon juice

6 corn-on-the-cob

You will also need clingfilm

Trim and finely chop the chillies. Dice the butter and cream together with a squeeze of lemon and the chopped chilli. Form into a log, cover with clingfilm and pop into the freezer. Boil the kettle. Halve the sweetcorn. Boil the sweetcorn for 5–8 minutes until tender. Drain. Remove the butter log from the freezer. Serve the sweetcorn with pats of chilled chilli butter.

CHICKEN LIVER PATE WITH PICKLES 22

1 shallot

1 large garlic clove

75g butter

400–500g chicken livers

1 tsp finely chopped thyme leaves, plus 2 sprigs

2 tbsp brandy, whisky, sherry, port or white wine

100g double cream

1 bay leaf

18 silverskin pickled onions

4 sweet-sour pickled cucumbers

6 slices sourdough or crusty bread for toast

Peel and chop the shallot very, very finely. Peel and chop the garlic. Sprinkle with a little salt and use the flat of a knife to work into a paste. Gently soften the shallot in 25g butter in a frying pan. Meanwhile, sort through the livers discarding any sinew and fatty bits. Coarsely chop the livers and season with salt, pepper and the chopped thyme. Tip into the pan with the shallot, increase the heat and quickly brown all over. Add the garlic. Toss again and then add the booze. Cook for a few more minutes, stirring and tossing, as the juices turn syrupy. Tip into the bowl of a food processor. Add the cream and blitz briefly until smooth. Pour into a 600ml/1pt-capacity

gratin dish and smooth the top. Decorate with the bay leaf and the sprigs of thyme. Melt 50g butter and pour over the top to cover thinly. Pop in the freezer for 20 minutes (set the timer!) to set the butter, and then chill in the fridge until required. Drain the silverskin onions into a bowl. Slice 4 pickled cucumbers on the slant and mix with the silverskin onions. Serve the pâté with hot toast and pickles.

ORANGE AND AVOCADO SALAD 23

5 medium-large oranges, preferably navel

1 large egg yolk or 1 tbsp mayonnaise, preferably Hellmann's

2 tbsp smooth Dijon mustard

8 tbsp extra-virgin olive oil

6 little gem lettuce hearts

4 firm but ripe large avocados

Squeeze the juice from 1 orange into a mixing bowl. Beat in the egg yolk and mustard, then add the extra-virgin olive oil, beating until thick and glossy. Trim, separate, rinse and shake dry the lettuce hearts. Arrange the best leaves into a 'nest' on 6 plates. Peel and cut segments from the oranges (leaving segment skin behind). Peel the avocados and cut into big chunks. Arrange the orange and avocado in and around the lettuce. Spoon over the dressing. Season with freshly ground black pepper.

LIME-PICKLED PRAWNS WITH FENNEL 24

400g cooked, frozen extra-large shelled prawns, preferably North Atlantic

3 tbsp lime juice

1 tbsp red-wine vinegar

1 tsp fennel seeds

1 tsp dried chilli flakes

3 tbsp olive oil

2 medium-sized red onions

60g bunch coriander

Crusty bread and butter, to serve

Cover the prawns with warm water for a few minutes to defrost. Drain, sprinkle with ¼ tsp salt and leave. Put the lime juice, vinegar, fennel seeds, chilli flakes, ½ tsp salt and several grinds of pepper in a mixing bowl. Whisk in the olive oil. Peel, halve and slice the onions very finely. Mix the onions into the dressing and leave, stirring occasionally, for about 30 minutes until limp, soft and pale. Finely chop the coriander leaves. Give the prawns a quick squeeze to remove any excess water. Stir the prawns and coriander into the onions and transfer to a serving dish or platter. Serve with crusty bread and butter.

VIETNAMESE DUCK SALAD 25

2 duck breasts
3 tbsp lime juice
2 tbsp Thai fish sauce (nam pla)
2 tbsp rice-wine vinegar
1 tsp sugar
1 red onion
½ cucumber
2 medium carrots
2 little gem lettuce hearts
A few mint leaves
A few sprigs of coriander

Heat the oven to 200°C/400°F/gas mark 6. Place the duck breasts skin-side down in an oven-proof pan over a high heat. Cook for 2–3 minutes until the skin is crisp. Turn to seal the other side, cooking for 1–2 minutes. Cook in the oven for 10–15 minutes (for pink meat), until the meat feels springy when pressed. Transfer the breasts to a plate. Leave for 10 minutes then slice thickly on the diagonal. Meanwhile, in a salad bowl, mix together the lime juice, fish sauce, rice-wine vinegar and sugar. Peel, halve and finely slice the onion and stir into the dressing. Peel the cucumber and split it lengthways. Scrape out the seeds and slice finely. Scrape the carrots and slice finely on the diagonal. Stir both into the dressing. Separate the lettuce leaves. Make a nest with the lettuce in the middle of 6 plates. Spoon the dressed salad into the nest, top with mint leaves and the duck. Garnish with coriander and any remaining dressing.

SMOKED SALMON AND FENNEL SALAD 26

½ cucumber
2 plump fennel bulbs
2 tbsp fresh lemon juice
2 tsp smooth Dijon mustard
100ml vegetable oil
6 slices smoked salmon or trout
1 tbsp finely snipped chives
Crusty bread, to serve

Split the cucumber lengthways. Use a teaspoon to scrape out the seeds then slice into 5cm-batons. Trim and halve the fennel, cut out the core and slice thinly across the middle. Chop any fronds. Make a dressing with the lemon juice, salt, pepper, mustard and vegetable oil. Place a slice of salmon in the middle of 6 plates. In separate bowls toss the fennel and cucumber in the dressing. Pile the fennel topped by the cucumber over the salmon. Garnish with chopped fennel fronds and the chives. Serve with some crusty bread.

GREEK SALAD WITH LIME HALLOUMI 27

150g wild rocket
1 small cucumber
1 medium red onion
6 ripe tomatoes
20 pitted black olives
1 tbsp chopped coriander
2 red Bird Eye chillies
2 tbsp olive oil
3 tbsp lemon juice
8 tbsp extra-virgin olive oil
250g halloumi cheese, preferably Pittas
1 lime
Crusty bread, to serve
You will also need clingfilm

Rinse the rocket and shake dry. Peel then split the cucumber lengthways, and, using a teaspoon, scrape out the seeds. Slice into chunky half-moons. Peel and halve the onion and slice wafer-thin. Quarter the tomatoes. Place everything in a salad bowl with the black olives and coriander. Cover with clingfilm and chill. Trim and finely chop the chillies and place in an eggcup covered with 2 tbsp olive oil. Whisk together 3 tbsp lemon juice and 7 tbsp extra-virgin olive oil and pour over the salad. Cut the halloumi into 18 chunky slices, about 1cm thick. Heat a non-stick frying pan over a high heat and brown the halloumi in two batches, cooking for about 30 seconds on each side, until crusty and golden. Slip onto a platter and glaze with the chilli and its oil, a generous squeeze of lime and a splash of extra-virgin olive oil. Toss at the table. Serve the salad with the halloumi and some crusty bread.

PIEDMONTESE PEPPERS 31

3 decent-sized red peppers
3 large garlic cloves, preferably new-season
6 plum or other firm ripe tomatoes
2 tbsp olive oil
6 anchovy fillets
Crusty bread and butter, to serve

Boil the kettle. Heat the oven to 200°C/400°F/gas mark 6. Halve the peppers, slicing evenly through the stalk. Remove any white membrane and seeds. Rinse and arrange, cut-side uppermost, on a heavy, shallow baking tray. Peel the garlic and slice very thinly. Lay the slices in the peppers and season with salt and pepper. Pour boiling water over the tomatoes, count to 20, drain, remove the cores and peel. Halve the tomatoes lengthways and place two pieces, cut-side down, in the peppers, covering the slices of garlic and nudged up closely together. Splash with olive oil. Bake the peppers for 30–40 minutes until tender and charred at the edges. Split the anchovies lengthways. Decorate the peppers with an anchovy cross and leave to cool in the baking tray. Use a fish slice to scoop the peppers onto a serving platter and spoon over the juices. Serve with crusty bread and butter.

ASPARAGUS WITH LEMON BUTTER 32

800g asparagus, preferably British
200g butter
2 tbsp lemon juice

Snap the woody ends off the asparagus spears – they will magically snap exactly where tender meets woody. Melt the butter in a small pan and remove from the heat. Boil the kettle. Cook the asparagus in 2 batches in plenty of salted boiling water for 4 minutes until just *al dente*. Lift onto kitchen paper to drain. Arrange the asparagus on two serving platters. Quickly remelt the butter, whisk in the lemon juice and divide between 2 small jugs. Pour some of the butter over the tips and serve the rest for people to help themselves.

LEMON AND TOMATO PRAWNS WITH WILD RED RICE 33

300g Camargue wild red rice
125g spring/salad onions
2 garlic cloves
1 unwaxed lemon
25g bunch flat-leaf parsley
4 tbsp olive oil
400g cooked, peeled prawns, preferably North Atlantic
3 tbsp whisky
2 x 400g cans chopped tomatoes
100g feta cheese

Boil the rice in plenty of salted water for 40 minutes. Trim and finely slice the spring onions, including the green. Peel and finely chop the garlic. Remove the zest from half the lemon and chop very finely. Finely chop the parsley leaves. Heat 1 tbsp olive oil in a medium-sized, heavy-bottomed pan and stir in the prawns. Add the whisky and squeeze over the lemon. Bubble up for 30 seconds then tip into a bowl. Warm 3 tbsp olive oil in the pan. Add the spring onion and garlic and cook for about 5 minutes, stirring a couple of times before adding the lemon zest and 1 tbsp of the chopped parsley leaves. Add the tomatoes, stir well and leave to simmer for 10 minutes. Return the prawns and their juices to the pan and cook for 5 minutes more. Turn off the heat. Add the remaining chopped parsley and crumble the feta over the top. Divide the hot rice between 6 warm serving plates. Give the prawns a quick blast of heat, whilst you fold in the parsley and feta, and serve over the rice.

TENDERSTEM WITH PARMA HAM 34

600g tenderstem or purple sprouting broccoli
1 tbsp aged balsamic vinegar
4 tbsp extra-virgin olive oil
12 slices Parma ham

Half fill a large, wide-based pan with boiling water. Add 1 tsp salt and the tenderstem. Boil for 3–4 minutes until just tender. Drain thoroughly. Arrange bundles of tenderstem in the middle of 6 plates. Whisk the balsamic vinegar with the olive oil and spoon most of it over the top. Drape a couple of slices of ham over the tenderstem. Dribble the rest of the dressing over and round the food.

BANG BANG CHICKEN 35

150g smooth peanut butter
1 tbsp sweet chilli dipping-sauce, preferably Blue Dragon
3 tbsp toasted sesame oil
2 tbsp vegetable oil
2 tbsp sesame seeds
4–6 cooked chicken thighs, approx. 400g
1–2 carrots
½ cucumber
4 spring onions
1 lime

Boil the kettle. Begin with the peanut sauce. Place the peanut butter in a metal bowl placed over a small pan half-filled with boiling water from the kettle. Stir in the sweet chilli dipping-sauce then gradually beat in the toasted sesame oil and vegetable oil to make a thick pouring sauce. Set aside but do not refrigerate. Briefly stir-fry the sesame seeds in a frying pan until light golden. Discard the chicken skin and shred the flesh into 5cm-lengths. Peel and cut the carrots into 5cm-batons. Split the cucumber lengthways, remove the seeds with a teaspoon and cut into 5cm-batons. Trim and finely slice the spring onions into 5cm-lengths. Mix the carrot, cucumber and onion together with the juice of the lime and arrange in the middle of 6 plates. Place the chicken on top. Spoon the peanut sauce over the chicken and garnish with sesame seeds.

POACHED CELERY WITH CAPERS AND ANCHOVY SAUCE 36

4 celery hearts
2 garlic cloves
75g butter
75g anchovy fillets in olive oil
1 scant dsp smooth Dijon mustard
6 tbsp olive oil
3 tbsp capers in vinegar
2 x ciabatta, or other crusty bread and butter, to serve

Boil the kettle. Cut the celery into 8cm-lengths and boil in plenty of salted water for 10 minutes. Drain and spread out on a platter. Meanwhile, peel and chop the garlic. Sprinkle with a little salt and crush into a juicy paste. To make the sauce, melt the butter in a small pan, stir in the garlic paste and cook gently while you chop the

anchovy. Add the anchovy and continue stirring for a few minutes until smooth. Add the mustard and then beat in the olive oil. Just before serving, gently reheat the anchovy sauce and spoon it over the celery. Scatter the capers over the top. Serve with crusty bread and butter.

HUMMUS WITH DUKKAH AND TOMATO TOAST 37

50g bunch coriander
600g organic hummus
About 10 tbsp extra-virgin olive oil
1 large lemon
35g Egyptian Dukkah, preferably Seasoned Pioneers
6 slices sourdough or similarly rustic bread
6 very ripe tomatoes
1 large garlic clove

Finely chop the coriander leaves. Spoon the hummus into two shallow dishes. Douse with extra-virgin olive oil and lemon juice, scatter with the Dukkah and cover with the chopped coriander. Toast the bread. Cut the tomatoes in half. Vigorously rub one side of the toast with the garlic clove and then with the cut tomato, rubbing until only the skin remains. Season the tomato bread with salt and extra-virgin olive oil. Serve with the hummus.

LEEKS VINAIGRETTE WITH EGG AND CHIVES 40

1 kg trimmed long, thin leeks
1½ tbsp smooth Dijon mustard
2 tbsp red-wine vinegar
150ml peanut oil or other flavourless oil
2 eggs
1 tbsp snipped chives
Crusty bread, to serve

Boil the kettle. Fill the sink with cold water. Trim and cut the leeks into 10cm-lengths and agitate them in the cold water. Half fill a large saucepan with boiling water and add 1 tsp salt. Boil the leeks for about 6 minutes until they are tender. Stand in a colander to drain. Make the vinaigrette by briefly blitzing the mustard, 3 tbsp warm water and the red-wine vinegar in a blender. With the motor still running, add the peanut oil in a thin stream until thick and creamy. Boil the eggs for 10 minutes. Crack them under running water and peel. Halve the leeks lengthways – discarding the outer layer if, as sometimes happens, it's stiff. Arrange cut-side up on a platter. Drizzle with the vinaigrette. Grate the eggs over and sprinkle with the chives. Serve with crusty bread.

CRUDITES WITH BOCCONCINI AND ANCHOVY SAUCE 41

3 large garlic cloves
75g butter
75g anchovy fillets in olive oil
1 dsp smooth Dijon mustard
6 tbsp olive oil
2 large, ripe but firm avocados
3 Little Gem lettuce hearts
1 small cucumber
200g small green tomatoes, preferably Tiger tomatoes
250g bocconcini
Juice of 1 lemon
A few sprigs of flat-leaf parsley

Peel, chop and crush the garlic with a large pinch of salt. Melt the butter in a small pan. Stir in the garlic paste and cook gently while you chop the anchovy. Add the anchovies to the pan. Continue stirring for a few minutes until smooth. Stir in the mustard and then beat in the olive oil. Quarter the avocados lengthways, remove the skin and stone and halve each quarter. Trim and quarter the lettuce hearts. Peel the cucumber, halve lengthways, scrape away the seeds and slice thickly on the diagonal. Halve the tomatoes. Divide the vegetables and bocconcini between 6 plates or arrange on a platter. Season with lemon juice and black pepper. Chop the parsley and scatter over the top. If necessary, reheat the anchovy sauce and serve in a separate bowl.

BRUSCHETTA OF RED PEPPER AND GOATS' CHEESE 42

8 thick slices sourdough bread
1 large garlic clove
1 tbsp extra-virgin olive oil
150g soft fresh goats' cheese
340g jar roasted red peppers/pimientos in olive oil

Toast the bread and rub one side with the garlic clove. Splash with olive oil to moisten, then spread lavishly with the goats' cheese. Cover with slices of pimientos and cut into big pieces. Arrange on a platter.

MELON SALAD WITH LIME, MINT AND PROSCIUTTO 43

1 cantaloupe melon
1 yellow melon
Juice from 2 limes
12 slices prosciutto crudo
20 mint leaves

Quarter the melons, scrape away the seeds and remove the peel. Use a melon-baller or cut the melon into small chunks. Place in a bowl and toss with the lime juice. Tear the prosciutto into 5cm-strips. Shred the mint leaves. Make piles of melon in the middle of 6 plates. Spoon over the juices and scatter with mint. Fold the prosciutto on the side.

AVOCADO SALAD WITH LIME AND HALLOUMI 44

3 ripe ready-to-eat Hass avocados
2 limes
250g halloumi cheese, preferably Pittas
3 tbsp capers in vinegar
Approx. 1 tbsp extra-virgin olive oil
25g bunch flat-leaf parsley

Run a sharp knife round the avocados. Twist apart, remove the stone and peel. Place on a board, flat-side down, and thinly slice along the length of the avocado. Arrange in the middle of 6 plates and squeeze lime juice over the top to season and prevent discolouration. Cut the halloumi into 30 wafer-thin slices. Tear the slices in half and strew over the avocado. Squeeze the capers to remove most of the vinegar and scatter over the top. Zig-zag with the olive oil. Chop the flat-leaf parsley. Give the salad a final squeeze of lime and scatter with parsley before serving.

MUSHROOMS A LA GRECQUE 45

750g small white cap mushrooms
1 red Bird Eye chilli
1 large lemon
2 tsp coriander seeds
2 bay leaves
3 sprigs of fresh thyme
3 tbsp olive oil
2 glasses dry white wine, approx. 300ml
4 vine tomatoes
2 tbsp chopped flat-leaf parsley
6 slices sourdough, to serve
1 garlic clove

Boil the kettle. Wipe the mushrooms. Chop the chilli finely. In small scraps, remove the zest from 1 lemon. Lightly crush the coriander seeds. Add the mushrooms, chilli, lemon zest, coriander seeds, bay leaves, thyme, olive oil and wine to a pan. Bring slowly to the boil – allow at least 10 minutes. Reduce the heat, stir, cover and simmer for 30 minutes. Tip into a wide serving bowl and leave to cool. Place the tomatoes in a bowl. Cover with boiling water and leave for 30 seconds. Drain, cut in half and remove the skin, core and seeds. Finely chop the flesh. Toast the sourdough. Rub garlic on one side. Stir the chopped tomatoes and parsley into the mushrooms. Serve in shallow bowls, with spoons and forks, and the toast.

AVOCADO LAYER CAKE 47

3 large ripe avocados
2 large garlic cloves
2 limes
300g jar hot salsa dip, preferably Doritos
300g soured cream
150g mature Cheddar cheese
A few sprigs of coriander

Run a sharp knife round the avocados, twist apart, remove the stone and scrape the flesh into a bowl. Peel and finely chop the garlic. Dust with ¼ tsp salt and crush into a paste. Mash the garlic paste and the juice of 1 lime into the avocados. Taste and add more lime juice if you think it needs it. Smooth the avocado onto a platter or in the middle of 6 side plates. Spoon tomato salsa over the top. Stir the soured cream and gently spread it over the salsa. Grate the cheese over the top and decorate with coriander sprigs. Chill until required. Serve the avocado dip with tortilla chips, advising your guests to scoop through the layers.

SMOKED MACKEREL PATE WITH BEETROOT RELISH 48

250g–300g smoked mackerel fillets
200g crème fraîche
1 lemon
4 tbsp creamed horseradish
100g cherry tomatoes
500g cooked baby beetroot
3 tbsp capers in vinegar
1 tbsp red-wine vinegar
1 tsp aged balsamic vinegar

Peel the mackerel off its skin into a food processor. Add 100g crème fraîche, plenty of black pepper, juice from the lemon and the horseradish. Blitz briefly until smooth. Transfer to a serving bowl and stir in the remaining crème fraîche to make a thick, fluffy pâté. Adjust the seasoning with extra lemon juice and black pepper. Chill until required. To make the relish, cut the cherry tomatoes and beetroot into quarters. Transfer to a serving bowl and mix with the drained capers, red-wine vinegar and balsamic vinegar. Season with salt and pepper and toss thoroughly.

LENTILS WITH SPINACH AND POACHED EGG 49

1 medium red onion
2 tbsp olive oil
½ tsp chopped thyme
2 x 400g cans green lentils in water
1 chicken stock cube
1 tbsp aged balsamic vinegar
150g young leaf spinach
5 medium tomatoes
Splash of wine vinegar
6 large fresh organic eggs
2 tbsp extra-virgin olive oil

Boil the kettle. Peel, halve and finely slice the red onion. Heat the olive oil in a medium-sized pan and stir in the onion. Add the thyme and cook gently, stirring occasionally, for about 8 minutes until the onion is soft. Meanwhile, tip the lentils into a sieve, rinse and shake dry. Dissolve the stock cube in 400ml boiling water. Stir the balsamic vinegar into the onion and add the lentils and stock. Simmer, uncovered, for 10 minutes. Stir the spinach into the pan. When wilted, turn off the heat. Cover the tomatoes with boiling water, count to 20, drain and splash with cold water. Remove their skins, cut out the cores and dice the flesh. Pour a 10cm-depth of boiling water into a wide saucepan. Add the wine vinegar. One at a time, crack 4 eggs into a teacup and slip them into the simmering water. Have a bowl of cold water ready. Cook the eggs for 1½ minutes until the white is set but the yolk is still soft; press one egg gently to test. Use a perforated spoon to transfer the eggs to the cold water. Cook the remaining 2 eggs and place in the cold water with the others. Stir the diced tomatoes into the lentils and divide between 6 plates. Lift one egg at a time onto kitchen paper to drain. Place on top of the lentils and finish with a lavish swirl of extra-virgin olive oil.

CHICORY AND PARSLEY SALAD WITH ANCHOVY CROSTINI 50

60g anchovy fillets in olive oil
50g pitted black olives
6 cornichons or 1 pickled cucumber
4 Belgian chicory
50g bunch flat-leaf parsley
1 tbsp smooth Dijon mustard
½ tbsp red-wine vinegar
4 tbsp olive oil
1 tbsp water
50g walnut pieces
6 thick slices sourdough-style bread

Reserve the oil from the anchovy can and chop the anchovies. Slice the olives and mix the two together. Chop the cornichons into small pieces. Trim the chicory, halve lengthways and slice down the halves into ½ cm-strips. Pick the leaves off the parsley stalks. Add the mustard to a salad bowl. Mix with the vinegar then whisk in the olive oil gradually to make a thick vinaigrette, thinning it with 1 tbsp water if necessary. Toss the chicory, parsley leaves, walnuts and cornichons in the dressing. To make the crostini, toast the bread, dribble one side with anchovy oil from the can, and then top with the anchovy mixture.

SEAFOOD

ROAST SMOKED HADDOCK WITH A POTATO CRUST 01

4 tbsp olive oil
6 thick fillets undyed smoked haddock
5 medium-sized potatoes
1 tbsp smooth Dijon mustard
2 tbsp crème fraîche
750g trimmed green beans
2 lemons

Heat the oven to 230°C/450°F/gas mark 8. Smear a heavy-duty baking tray with 1 tbsp olive oil. Place the fish fillets, skin-side down, about 5cm apart, on the tray. Slice the unpeeled potatoes as thinly as if making crisps – a mandolin is ideal for this. Rinse the slices, shake dry and pile over the fish to entirely cover in a smooth layer. Season with salt and pepper and dribble with 3 tbsp olive oil. Boil the kettle. Cook the fish in the oven for 35 minutes – checking after 20 minutes – until most of the potatoes are crusty and all are cooked through. Mix the Dijon and crème fraîche in a warmed serving bowl. Ten minutes before the fish is ready, boil the beans for 2 minutes in plenty of salted, boiling water. Drain but retain 1 tbsp of the water and stir it into the Dijon mixture together with any juices from the fish. Fold in the beans. Using a fish slice, lift a portion of fish and potato onto 6 warmed plates. Add a lemon wedge. Serve the beans separately.

MISO COD WITH MANGETOUT 03

1 tbsp olive oil
6 fillets cod, haddock or whiting
90g Japanese miso soup paste sachet, preferably Yutaka
4 tbsp grated Parmesan
400g mangetout or sugar snap peas
You will also need tinfoil

Boil the kettle. Line a grill-pan with tinfoil and lightly smear with olive oil. Lay out the fish fillets on the foil then spread each one with the miso soup paste, making an even but not overly thick covering. Carefully dust the paste with Parmesan to cover entirely. Turn the grill to its highest setting and cook the fish for 4–8 minutes depending on the thickness of the fillets until just cooked through with a crusty topping. Meanwhile, rinse, then boil the mangetout in plenty of salted water. Drain thoroughly and arrange in the middle of 6 warmed plates, then drape the fish over the top.

ALMOST SALMON PIE WITH LEMON CRUSHED POTATOES 05

1kg organic new potatoes, preferably Nicola
1 tbsp vegetable oil
350g young leaf spinach
6 salmon tail fillets
2 tbsp olive oil
2 lemons
350g Neopolitan-style tomato sauce
1 tbsp runny honey
200g cooked, peeled prawns, preferably North Atlantic
25g butter
25g flour
250ml milk
2 tbsp chopped flat-leaf parsley
2 tbsp extra-virgin olive oil

Heat the oven to 200°C/400°F/gas mark 6. Boil the potatoes in salted water for 10–15 minutes until tender. Heat the vegetable oil in a wok. Add the spinach and stir-fry for a couple of minutes until it has wilted. Tip into a colander and squeeze with the back of a wooden spoon to remove any excess liquid. Divide into 6 salmon-sized mounds close together in a small baking tin. Place the salmon on a plate, smear with olive oil and squeeze the juice of 1 lemon over the top. Arrange the salmon over the spinach. Tip the tomato sauce into a bowl and stir in the honey and prawns. Spoon the sauce over the fish. Drain the potatoes. Melt the butter in a small pan. Stir in the flour until smooth, then gradually add the milk, whisking as it comes to a boil. Season with salt and pepper and simmer gently for 5 minutes. Cool for 5 minutes then spoon the thick sauce over the fish. Skin the potatoes and return to the pan. Add the juice of 1 lemon and crush lightly with a potato-masher or fork. Pile the potatoes over the fish to evenly cover and dribble with olive oil. Cook in the oven for 25–35 minutes until the potatoes are crusty and the salmon is cooked. Use a fish slice to plate the salmon. Serve with a scattering of parsley and a splash of extra-virgin olive oil.

PAN-FRIED SALMON TABBOULEH 07

225g bulgar cracked wheat
4 firm medium-sized vine tomatoes, approx. 500g
Juice of 1 lemon
125ml olive oil, plus 2 tbsp
125g bunch of spring onions
25g bunch coriander
80g bunch flat-leaf parsley
250g fine beans
6 salmon fillets
2 tbsp extra-virgin olive oil

Boil the kettle. Measure 400ml boiling water into a bowl and stir in the bulgar wheat. Cover and leave for 20 minutes. Place a sieve over a bowl. Quarter the tomatoes lengthways and scrape the seeds and juices into the sieve. Press the debris through the sieve using the back of a spoon to extract maximum juice. Whisk the lemon juice and 125ml olive oil into the tomato juice. Chop the tomatoes. Finely chop the spring onions. Chop the coriander and parsley leaves. Cut the beans in half. Using water from the kettle, boil the beans in salted water for 2 minutes. Drain and set aside. Heat 2 tbsp olive oil in a frying pan over a medium-high heat and fry 3 salmon fillets for 2 minutes each side, pressing down to encourage crusty edges, until just-cooked but still moist. Lift onto a plate and cover with clingfilm. Repeat with the remaining fillets. Give the tomato dressing a final whisk and stir it into the bulgar wheat. Add the tomatoes, spring onions, beans and herbs. Stir thoroughly. Serve a pile of bulgar in the middle of 6 plates and drape a salmon fillet over the top. Decorate with a swirl of extra-virgin olive oil.

SALMON WITH TOMATO AND CORIANDER VINAIGRETTE 09

6 salmon tails
6 tbsp olive oil
½ lemon
1 large garlic clove
1 tbsp red-wine vinegar
400g cherry tomatoes
50g bunch coriander
500g stringless runner beans, traditionally sliced (long, thin and on the diagonal)

Heat the oven to 200°C/400°F/gas mark 6. Boil the kettle. Smear the fish on both sides with olive oil and place on an oven tray. Squeeze over the juice from the lemon. Peel and chop the garlic. Sprinkle with salt and crush into a paste. Add to a bowl that can accommodate the tomatoes. Stir in the vinegar and add 4 tbsp olive oil. Whisk to amalgamate. Quarter the tomatoes and stir into the dressing. Roast the fish for about 15 minutes until it is just cooked through. Finely chop the coriander and stir into the tomatoes. Boil the runner beans in a big pan of salted water for 2 minutes. Drain. Make a pile of beans in the middle of 6 warmed dinner plates. Lay a piece of salmon over the top and spoon the dressing over the fish.

HADDOCK WITH A CHIVE AND MUSTARD SAUCE 13

75g butter
25g flour
1 tbsp smooth Dijon mustard
600ml milk
6 fillets of haddock, cod or smoked haddock
2 tbsp olive oil
1 lemon
1 kg baking potatoes, preferably King Edward
20g chives

Heat the oven to 200°C/400°F/gas mark 6. Melt 25g butter in a medium-sized pan and stir in the flour, stirring until smooth. Now stir in the mustard. Remove from the heat and add 500ml milk. Return to the heat and stir constantly as the sauce comes to the boil. Beating the sauce with a globe whisk can quickly disperse any lumps. Reduce the heat and simmer for 5 minutes. Taste and adjust the seasoning with salt and plenty of pepper. Arrange the fish on an oiled baking tray. Season with salt, a squeeze of lemon and splash of olive oil. Roast for 15 minutes. Keep warm. Peel the potatoes, cut into even-sized chunks, rinse and boil in salted water for about 15 minutes until tender. Drain and set aside. Add 50g butter and 100ml milk to the potato pan. Heat the milk and when the butter has melted, remove from the heat. Return the potatoes to the pan and mash. Beat with a wooden spoon to make a fluffy mash, adding a little extra milk or butter as you think fit. Spoon the potato into the middle of 6 warmed plates and top with a piece of fish. Quickly reheat the sauce and spoon over the top. Garnish generously with snipped chives.

BABY SQUID WITH GARLIC AND LEMON 15

80g bunch flat-leaf parsley
6 large garlic cloves, preferably new-season
1 kg baby squid, cleaned, tentacles tucked inside the sac
750g fine green beans
50g butter
2 tbsp olive oil
3 large lemons
Crusty bread and butter, to serve

Boil the kettle. Pick all the leaves off the parsley and chop finely. Chop the garlic, sprinkle with ½ tsp salt and crush into a paste. Trim the green beans. Remove the tentacles from inside the squid sacs. Split the tentacles and slice the sac into 1cm-wide rings. Boil the beans with 1 tsp salt for 2 minutes. Drain and keep warm. Melt the butter in a large frying pan with the olive oil and stir in the garlic paste, letting it sizzle briefly before stirring in the squid. Stir-fry over a high heat for about 5 minutes until just cooked and very tender. Toss with half the parsley. Serve immediately, sprinkled with the rest of the parsley, giving each person half a lemon to squeeze over the top, and the beans in a separate bowl. Serve with crusty bread and butter.

LE GRAND AIOLI 19

2 large garlic cloves, preferably new-season
6 large eggs, plus 2 large egg yolks at room temperature
350ml olive oil
5 lemons
750g small new potatoes
18 young carrots
400g fine green beans, trimmed
400g podded broad beans
18 bulbous spring onions
6 cod fillets, 175–200g each
20g curly parsley
2-3 tbsp extra-virgin olive oil
A bowl of sea salt flakes, to serve

Boil the kettle. Begin with the aïoli. Peel and finely chop the garlic cloves. Sprinkle with ¼ tsp salt and work into a paste. Place in a bowl with the 2 egg yolks. Beat together with a wooden spoon until thick and creamy. Add 300ml olive oil gradually, alternating with the juice of 1 lemon, until thick and wobbly. Cover and keep at room temperature. Heat the oven to 200°C/400°F/gas mark 6. Boil the potatoes and eggs until the potatoes are tender. Drain. Using water from the kettle, boil the carrots, beans, broad beans and onions separately for 2 minutes. Keeping them apart, drain and keep warm. Arrange the fish on a baking tray, squeeze over the juice of 1 lemon and splash with a little olive oil. Season with salt and pepper. Roast for 15 minutes. Turn off the oven and leave the door open. Remove the rubbery skin covering the broad beans by nicking the edge with your nail, then squeezing out the bean. Peel and halve the eggs. Halve the lemons. Arrange the fish on a serving platter and intersperse with individual piles of all the vegetables, the eggs, lemon wedges and the parsley. Splash the vegetables with extra-virgin olive oil. Serve the aïoli and a small bowl of sea salt flakes separately.

FISH IN A PACKET WITH GOAN GREEN SAUCE 20

198g block creamed coconut
4 large garlic cloves
50g fresh ginger
3 green chillies
80g bunch coriander, stalks trimmed
25g bunch mint
2 tsp ground cumin
2–3 tbsp vegetable oil
6 whiting, plaice or sole fillets
400g basmati rice
3 limes
You will also need tinfoil

Heat the oven to 200°C/400°F/gas mark 6. Grate or crumble the creamed coconut into a mixing bowl. Moisten with 100–150ml hot water, stirring to make a thick cream. Peel the garlic. Peel and coarsely chop the ginger. Trim and split the chillies and scrape away the seeds. Place the coriander, mint leaves, garlic, ginger, chilli, cumin and coconut cream into the bowl of a food

processor. Blitz for several minutes to make a stiff green paste. Cut 12 pieces of tinfoil, each approx. 24cm-square. Lightly oil the centre of 6 pieces of foil. Generously pile the green paste onto the fish then fold the ends together, pressing to make a sandwich. Divide between the 6 oiled sheets of foil. Cover with a second sheet, folding the sides to make a secure but not overly tight parcel. Place on a baking sheet and cook in the oven for 15 minutes. Meanwhile, wash the rice and place in a lidded pan with 600ml cold water. Bring to the boil then turn the heat very low. Cover and cook for 10 minutes. Turn off the heat and, without removing the lid, leave for 10 minutes. Fork up the rice and divide between 6 plates. Serve the foil packets individually, with a wedge of lime, for guests to open themselves.

ROAST HADDOCK WITH BORLOTTI BEANS 22

3 x 400g cans of borlotti beans
½ chicken stock cube
2 tbsp coarsely chopped oregano or marjoram
3 tbsp olive oil
6 haddock fillets, approx. 200g each
6 sprays of cherry tomatoes on the vine
2 tbsp aged balsamic vinegar
½ lemon

Boil the kettle. Heat the oven to 220°C/425°F/gas mark 7. Tip the beans into a sieve or colander, rinse with cold water and shake dry. Place the drained beans in a medium-sized saucepan. Dissolve the stock cube in 300ml boiling water. Add the stock, half the oregano or marjoram and 1 tbsp olive oil to the pan. Season lightly with salt and generously with pepper, stir well and leave to simmer gently. Meanwhile, smear the base of a large oven tray with olive oil and lay out the fish fillets. Arrange the sprays of tomatoes around them and splash everything with the remaining olive oil. Sprinkle the fish with the balsamic vinegar and squeeze the lemon over the top. Season with salt and pepper. Roast the fish for 10–15 minutes, depending on the thickness of the fillets, until just cooked through and the tomatoes are beginning to split and weep. Carefully drain all the juices into the beans and stir well. Divide the beans between 6 large, shallow bowls. Arrange a piece of fish on top and decorate with a spray of tomatoes.

COD WITH PUY LENTILS AND SALSA VERDE 24

350g Puy lentils
1 chicken stock cube
1 small onion
1 clove
1 bay leaf
2 large garlic cloves
80g bunch flat-leaf parsley
1 tbsp smooth Dijon mustard
6 anchovy fillets
1 tbsp capers in vinegar
150ml olive oil
3 lemons
6 cod fillets
Extra-virgin olive oil, to serve

Boil the kettle. Rinse and drain the lentils and place in a pan with 700ml boiling water. Crumble the stock cube over the top. Peel the onion. Use the clove to spear the bay leaf into the onion then bury it in the lentils. Bring to the boil then reduce the heat. Partially cover the pan and simmer for 30 minutes. To make the salsa verde, peel the garlic, coarsely chop and dust with a large pinch of salt. Use the flat of a knife to work into a paste. Remove the leaves from the parsley. Transfer the garlic to the bowl of a food processor and add the mustard, anchovies, squeezed capers and parsley leaves. Blitz briefly, scraping down the inside of the bowl then, with the motor running, add the olive oil in a thin stream to make a thick sauce. Season with salt and pepper and transfer to a serving bowl. Pour a depth of 7.5cm boiling water into a large frying pan and return to the boil. Add 1 tsp salt and the juice of ½ lemon. Immerse the fish into the simmering water, bring back to the boil and switch off. Leave for 5 minutes, then lift the fish onto a warmed plate. Cover with clingfilm to keep warm until required. Discard the onion from the lentils and quickly reheat. Spoon the lentils into the middle of 6 warmed dinner plates and cover with a fillet of cod. Top with a scoop of salsa verde and decorate with a swirl of extra-virgin olive oil, adding a lemon wedge.

CRAB AND PRAWN JAMBALAYA 25

2 red onions
2 garlic cloves
2 tbsp vegetable oil
2 red peppers
1 bay leaf
1 tsp chilli flakes
500g ripe tomatoes
300g basmati rice
1 chicken stock cube
3 dressed crabs, producing about 250g brown crabmeat and 200g white crabmeat
200g cooked, extra-large prawns, preferably North Atlantic
1 lemon
Tabasco
400g fine green beans
25g bunch flat-leaf parsley

Boil the kettle. Peel and finely chop the onions and garlic. Heat the oil in a large frying pan or similarly wide-based pan and stir in the onions and garlic. Cook gently for about 5 minutes while you chop the peppers, discarding the stalk, seeds and white membrane. Stir the pepper into the onions, together with the bay leaf and chilli flakes. Cook for about 15 minutes until the onion is soft and slippery and the pepper softened. Meanwhile, place the tomatoes in a bowl and cover with boiling water. Count to 20, drain, peel and chop the flesh. Rinse the rice in several changes of water. Dissolve the stock cube in 600ml boiling water from the kettle. Stir the rice into the vegetables then add the brown crabmeat. Cook for a couple of minutes then add the tomatoes, ½ tsp salt and plenty of pepper. Now add the stock and bring the liquid to the boil. Stir, reduce the heat, cover the pan and cook for 15 minutes. Turn off the heat and leave the pan with its lid on for 10 minutes. Boil the kettle again. Stir the white crabmeat and prawns into the rice. Heat through and taste the juices. Adjust the seasoning with salt and lemon juice, adding a shake or two of Tabasco if it isn't hot enough. Using water from the kettle, boil the beans for 2 minutes. Drain. Chop the parsley and stir it into the jambalaya. Serve risotto-style with the beans served separately.

CUMIN MACKEREL WITH GOOSEBERRY COUSCOUS 28

1 chicken stock cube
Generous pinch of saffron stamens
3 tbsp olive oil
2 lemons, plus 2 tbsp juice
350g couscous
2 tbsp blanched almonds
25g butter
12 small fresh mackerel fillets
2 tbsp ground cumin
2 x 200g cans gooseberries, drained
A few sprigs of coriander
You will also need tinfoil

For the couscous dissolve the stock cube in 550ml boiling water in a mixing bowl. Stir in the saffron, 2 tbsp each of olive oil and lemon juice and the couscous. Cover the bowl and leave to hydrate. Quickly stir-fry the almonds in the remaining tbsp of oil until golden. Tip onto a fold of kitchen paper to drain. Cover the grill-pan with foil and smear with the butter. Lay the fish, skin-side down, and dust liberally with cumin. Preheat the grill and cook the mackerel for 2–4 minutes – depending on the thickness of the fillets – until just cooked through. Fork up the couscous, stir in the almonds and loosely fold in the gooseberries. Pile into the middle of a warmed platter and arrange the fish around the couscous. Decorate with a few sprigs of coriander and lemon wedges.

ROAST SALMON WITH PESTO POTATOES 29

1 kg scrubbed small salad potatoes
350g trimmed extra-fine green beans
6 salmon tail fillets
2–3 tbsp olive oil
6 sprays cherry tomatoes on the vine
130g basil pesto
2 lemons
Your best olive oil, to serve

Boil the potatoes in salted water for about 15 minutes until tender. Turn off the heat and leave in the hot water. Rinse then halve the beans. Heat the oven to 200°C/400°F/ gas mark 6. Smear the salmon with olive oil and arrange on a heavy-duty baking tray. Arrange the 6 sprays of tomatoes next to the fish. Pierce each tomato to avoid bursting. Tip the pesto into a mixing bowl. Boil the kettle. Roast the salmon and the tomatoes for 15 minutes. Use some of the water from the kettle to boil the beans for 2 minutes. Drain the beans and the potatoes and stir them into the pesto. Divide between 6 warmed dinner plates. Arrange a piece of salmon over the top and drape with a spray of tomatoes. Dribble any fish juices over and finish with a swirl of your best olive oil and a lemon wedge.

CRAB LINGUINE WITH WILTED CUCUMBER 32

2 red Bird Eye chillies
8 tbsp extra-virgin olive oil
375–400g dressed crab, brown and white meat
50g bunch flat-leaf parsley
2 large lemons
1 small or ½ large cucumber
500g linguine

Trim and split the chillies. Scrape away the seeds. Slice into long, thin batons and then into tiny scraps. Place in a small bowl and cover with 2 tbsp extra-virgin olive oil. Place the white and brown crabmeat in a mixing bowl. Coarsely chop the flat-leaf parsley leaves. Boil the kettle. Tip the chilli and its oil and the chopped parsley into the crab. Season lightly with salt, and generously with freshly ground black pepper. Add the juice from 1½ lemons and mix thoroughly. Slowly stir in 4 tbsp extra-virgin olive oil to make a thick but slack mixture. Use a potato peeler to remove the skin from the cucumber. Split it in half lengthways and use a teaspoon to scrape out the seeds. Slice thinly into half-moons. Cook the pasta in plenty of salted boiling water until *al dente*. Two minutes before the end of cooking add the cucumber. Drain, return to the saucepan and stir in 2 tbsp extra-virgin olive oil. Add the crab mixture and stir well, adding more lemon juice or oil or black pepper to taste.

TERIYAKI SALMON WITH SESAME NOODLES 34

4 x 125g bunches salad/spring onions
2 tbsp sesame seeds
200ml teriyaki sauce
2 tbsp soy sauce
6 salmon fillets
375g medium egg noodles
1 tbsp toasted sesame oil/

oriental sesame oil
You will also need tinfoil

Trim the spring onions, retaining the pale green and white. Heat a frying pan over a medium heat and stir-fry the sesame seeds for a couple of minutes until pale golden. Tip onto a saucer. Pour the teriyaki sauce into the pan. Add the spring onions and simmer for 3–4 minutes until tender. Scoop the spring onions onto a plate and cover to keep warm. Boil the teriyaki sauce for a few minutes until it is thick and has reduced to about one-third. Line the grill-pan with foil and lay out the salmon. Boil the noodles in plenty of salted water for 4 minutes; stir a couple of times to loosen the noodle coils. Drain and return to the pan with the toasted sesame oil, the 2 tbsp soy sauce and half the sesame seeds. Stir and keep warm. Baste the salmon liberally with the reduced teriyaki sauce. Turn the grill to its highest setting. Grill the salmon for 2 minutes, baste again then cook for a further 2–3 minutes until just cooked through. Toss the noodles again and place in the middle of 6 warmed plates or shallow bowls. Top with the warm spring onions and lay a fillet of salmon over the top. Sprinkle the remaining sesame seeds over the fish.

CHINESE WHITE FISH WITH COCONUT RICE 35

2 tbsp vegetable oil
2 garlic cloves, preferably new-season
5 tbsp soy sauce
1 tbsp toasted sesame oil
150g spring/salad onions
6 fillets cod, haddock, whiting or huss
50g fresh ginger
50g bunch coriander
400g basmati rice
100g creamed coconut
2 limes
You will also need 12 pieces tinfoil approx. 24cm-square

Boil the kettle. Heat the oven to 200°C/400°F/gas mark 6. Lay out 6 sheets of tinfoil. Smear the middle with a little of the vegetable oil. Peel and finely chop the garlic. Sprinkle with ¼ tsp salt and crush into a paste. Place in a bowl; add 1 tbsp vegetable oil, the soy sauce and the sesame oil. Trim and slice the spring onions on the slant, including the green. Peel and finely

slice the ginger. Arrange the fish over the smear of oil. Scatter with spring onions and ginger and spoon over the dressing. Set aside a few sprigs of coriander and arrange the rest over the top. Place a second sheet of foil on top and fold the edges firmly, but not too tightly, to secure. Place on a baking sheet. Rinse the rice and place in a pan with 600ml cold water. Crumble the creamed coconut over the top. Bring to the boil, stirring to dissolve the coconut. Reduce the heat to very low and cover the pan. Cook for 10 minutes. Turn off the heat, do not remove the lid, and leave for 10 minutes. Meanwhile, bake the fish parcels for 15 minutes. Fork up the rice and transfer to a serving platter. Decorate with lime wedges and sprigs of coriander. Serve the fish parcels for guests to open at the table.

COD NICOISE WITH GREEN BEANS 38

6 cod fillets
2 red onions
2 garlic cloves
4 tbsp olive oil
2 red peppers
1 scant tsp chilli flakes
2 x 400g cans chopped tomatoes
150g jar pitted black olives in brine, preferably Cypressa
25g bunch flat-leaf parsley
1 lemon
500g fine green beans

Boil the kettle. Lightly season the fish fillets with salt and set aside. Peel, halve and chop the onions. Peel and thinly slice the garlic in rounds. Heat 3 tbsp olive oil in a spacious, heavy bottomed pan and stir in the onion and garlic. Cook briskly, stirring often, for 5 minutes. Reduce the heat, add 1 tsp salt, cover and cook for 5 minutes more. Use a potato peeler to remove the bulk of the skin from the peppers, then discard the stalk, seeds and white filament. Coarsely chop the flesh and add that to the pan. Cook, covered, for a further 10 minutes. Stir the chilli flakes into the onions and peppers and then add the chopped tomatoes. Drain the olives and cut in half. Add them to the pan. Cook briskly, stirring occasionally, for 10 minutes. Coarsely chop the parsley. Pat the fish fillets dry with kitchen paper. Arrange on an oiled baking sheet and brush first with olive oil and then with a squeeze of lemon. Roast them for 15 minutes, then remove from the oven and keep warm. Stir the parsley into the sauce. Boil the beans in plenty of salted water for 2 minutes. Serve the fish topped with the sauce and the beans separately.

GREEN SALMON WITH CAULIFLOWER CREAM 41

1 very large cauliflower
100g double cream
100g grated mature Cheddar
1 lemon, plus an extra squeeze
150g white bread, without crusts
25g bunch flat-leaf parsley
4 tbsp flour
2 large eggs
6 salmon fillets or tails
4 tbsp vegetable oil
500g stringless runner beans, traditionally sliced (long, thin and on the diagonal)
You will also need clingfilm

Cut the cauliflower into florets and cook, covered, in boiling salted water for about 5 minutes until soft. Drain, but reserve 2 tbsp of the cooking water. Place the cauliflower, reserved water, double cream and grated Cheddar in the bowl of a food processor and blitz to make a smooth, thick, creamy white purée. Scrape into a pan. Taste and adjust the seasoning with salt and a squeeze of lemon, adding extra cream if the mixture is too stiff. Remove the zest from the lemon. Tear the bread into chunks and place in the food processor with the parsley leaves and lemon zest. Blitz to make green crumbs. Tip the crumbs into a cereal bowl. Sift the flour into a second bowl and whisk the eggs in a third. Pat the salmon fillets dry, then dip each one first in the flour, shaking off any excess, then in the egg and, finally, press into the crumbs. Lay out on a plate as you go. Cover with clingfilm and chill until required. Fry the fish in batches in hot oil for a couple of minutes on each side until nicely crusty and cooked through. Meanwhile, using water from the kettle, boil the beans for 2 minutes. Drain. Quickly reheat the cauliflower cream and serve alongside the salmon, adding a lemon wedge, with beans served separately.

SQUID WITH TOMATOES AND PEAS 43

2 medium onions
4 tbsp olive oil
3 large garlic cloves
12 ripe, firm vine tomatoes, approx. 1 kg
1 kg small squid, cleaned and tentacles inside the sac
500g frozen petits pois
50g bunch flat-leaf parsley
3 lemons, to serve
Crusty bread and butter, to serve

Finely chop the onions. Heat the oil in a spacious, heavy-bottomed pan that can hold all the ingredients and stir in the onion. Cook over a medium heat, stirring occasionally, for 10–15 minutes until they begin to soften and turn golden. Meanwhile, peel and finely chop the garlic. Place the tomatoes in a bowl and cover with boiling water. Count to 25, drain, peel and halve. Scrape out the seeds and chop the flesh. Stir the garlic into the onion; cook for a couple of minutes then add the tomatoes. Cook at a steady simmer for 15 minutes, until the tomatoes begin to thicken with the onions. Don't worry if it seems dry. Meanwhile, remove the tentacles from inside the squid sacs. Cut the tentacle clusters in half. Slice the sacs into 1cm-wide rings. Stir both into the sauce. Season with salt and pepper, stir well, cover and cook gently for about 20 minutes or until the squid is tender. Taste and adjust the seasoning. Stir the peas into the squid and cook, uncovered, for 5–10 minutes. Coarsely chop the parsley leaves and stir into the squid. Serve in shallow bowls with a lemon wedge and crusty bread and butter.

ROAST COD WITH WATERCRESS MASH 44

1.4 kg floury potatoes
6 cod fillets
6 tbsp olive oil
3 lemons
2 large garlic cloves
160g watercress
Approx. 4 tbsp extra-virgin olive oil

Heat the oven to 200°C/400°F/gas mark 6. Peel the potatoes and cut into large, even-sized chunks. Boil in plenty of salted water for about 15 minutes until tender. Season the cod with salt. Leave for 10 minutes then pat dry. Use 1 tbsp olive oil to smear a small, heavy-duty roasting tin that can accommodate the fish. Place the fish fillets in the roasting tin and splash with 2 tbsp olive oil. Squeeze over the juice from 1 lemon and season with salt and pepper. Roast the fish in the hot oven for 10-15 minutes, depending on the thickness of the fillets, until just cooked through. Meanwhile, peel the garlic cloves, chop finely, sprinkle with a little salt and use the flat of a knife to work into a paste. When the potatoes are ready, drain them in a colander. Put the garlic paste and 3 tbsp olive oil in the potato pan and stir-fry over a medium-low heat for about 30 seconds without letting the garlic brown. Remove from the heat and return the hot potatoes and watercress to the pan. Use a fork to mash, mix and amalgamate; you want the potatoes crushed rather than mashed smooth, and the watercress to wilt in the heat. Cover and keep warm. Carefully drain the juices from the cooked fish into the potatoes, season with salt and pepper and give a final mash. Spoon the mash into the middle of 6 warmed plates and lay the fish over the top. Finish with a generous swirl of extra-virgin olive oil over and around the food and serve with a lemon wedge.

SQUID, CHORIZO, CHICKPEA AND BEAN STEW 48

2 medium onions
4 large garlic cloves
4 tbsp olive oil
1 chicken stock cube
2 x 400g cans organic chickpeas
1 kg small prepared squid, tentacles inside the sacs
150g sliced chorizo
Glass red wine, approx. 150ml
2 x 400g cans chopped tomatoes
50g bunch coriander
400g fine green beans
1 lemon

Boil the kettle. Peel, halve and finely slice the onions. Peel and slice the garlic in wafer-thin rounds. Heat the olive oil in a spacious, heavy-bottomed pan, stir in the onion and garlic and cook, stirring occasionally for 10–15 minutes until soft.

Meanwhile, dissolve the stock cube in 600ml boiling water. Rinse the chickpeas thoroughly in a sieve or colander with cold water. Remove the tentacles from the squid sac and cut the sac lengthways into 3 chunky strips. Stir the chorizo into the onions; cook for a couple of minutes then add the squid strips and tentacles. Cook gently, stirring continuously for a few minutes, until the squid begins to curl. Add the wine. Increase the heat and let it boil before adding the chopped tomatoes and stock. Return to the boil, immediately reduce the heat and leave to simmer gently for 30 minutes. Chop the coriander. Top and tail the beans and halve them. Stir the chickpeas into the stew, reheat and adjust the seasoning with lemon juice and salt. Boil the beans for 2 minutes. Drain, then stir into the stew with the coriander.

TUNA WITH CHERRY TOMATO GUACAMOLE 49

4 large firm but ripe avocados
3 limes
200g cherry tomatoes
2 shallots
2 red Bird Eye chillies
1 large garlic clove
25g bunch coriander
6 thick tuna fillets
You will also need clingfilm

Run a sharp knife round the avocados. Twist apart and remove the stone. Dice the avocados in their shells, then use a spoon to scoop the flesh into a bowl. Squeeze over the juice of 1 lime. Quarter the cherry tomatoes then halve the quarters. Peel and finely chop the shallots. Finely dice the chillies. Peel and chop the garlic. Sprinkle with a little salt and crush into a paste. Coarsely chop the coriander. Stir the garlic into the avocado whilst coarsely mashing it; you want lumpy rather than smooth. Mix in the tomatoes, onion, chilli and coriander. Taste and adjust the seasoning with salt, pepper and more lime juice. Cover with clingfilm, letting it sag against the guacamole to avoid discolouration. Heat a ridged griddle pan for several minutes until very hot. Cook 3 tuna fillets at a time for 2 minutes each side. Transfer to a plate. Serve the tuna next to a scoop of guacamole and a lime wedge.

POULTRY

THYME SPRING CHICKEN 02

6 poussins/spring chickens
3 tbsp olive oil
Large bunch of thyme
2 garlic cloves
175g butter
3 lemons
50g bunch flat-leaf parsley
400g asparagus spears
200g trimmed fine beans
You will also need clingfilm

Heat the oven to 230°C/450°F/gas mark 8. Boil the kettle. Snip out and discard the poussins' spines. Open up the birds and flatten slightly with the heel of your hand. Smear generously with the olive oil and season both sides with salt and pepper. Lay the birds over the thyme on roasting trays. Roast for 30–40 minutes. Peel and finely chop the garlic. Sprinkle with ¼ tsp salt and crush to make a paste. Dice 150g butter. Cream the butter with a squeeze of lemon juice and the garlic paste. Chop the parsley leaves and stir into the butter. Form into a small log, cover with clingfilm and pop into the freezer. Check the poussins, remove from the oven when ready and keep warm. Snap off the woody asparagus ends. Cook the beans and asparagus tips separately in plenty of boiling salted water for 2 minutes. Drain and toss together with 25g butter. Arrange the asparagus and beans in the middle of 6 warmed dinner plates and drape a poussin over the top. Make a couple of slashes in the birds and insert a thick slice of garlic butter. Serve with lemon wedges.

THYME-ROAST QUAIL WITH ROSTI 06

3 garlic cloves
1 large lemon
25g bunch of thyme
6 quail
18 rashers pancetta or 12 rashers thin-cut smoked streaky bacon
25g butter
2 tbsp vegetable oil
700g baking potatoes
6 tbsp double cream
½ chicken stock cube
½ glass white wine, approx. 75ml
150g white seedless grapes, approx. 30 grapes
1 tbsp mayonnaise
1 dsp wine vinegar
3 tbsp olive oil
3 little gem lettuce hearts
1 tbsp finely snipped chives

Heat the oven to 220°C/425°F/gas mark 7. Peel then halve the garlic cloves. Halve the lemon and cut each half into 3 pieces. Rinse out the cavity of the birds, shake dry and season with salt and pepper. Pop the garlic, a few sprigs of thyme and piece of lemon into the cavity of each quail. Wrap in 3 rashers of pancetta, making sure that the breast is thoroughly covered. Arrange on a baking tray, breast up and with the bacon joins underneath. Dot with butter. For the rösti, smear a heavy baking tray with the vegetable oil. Coarsely grate the potatoes. Squeeze them in a cloth to remove as much liquid as possible and place in a mixing bowl. Season with salt and pepper and stir in the cream. Spoon 6 mounds onto the tray and flatten to make ½ cm-thick patties. Place on the top shelf of the oven with the quail below. Cook for 15 minutes. Flip the rösti and continue for 15 more minutes until they are very crisp. Roast the quail for 25–30 minutes until the pancetta is crisp and shrunken, the breast feels springy when pressed and the legs feel loose. Remove from the oven and keep warm. Turn off the oven but leave in the rösti. Dissolve ½ a stock cube in 300ml boiling water. Drain most of the fat from the quail pan, leaving about 1 tbsp. Add the wine and simmer briskly for 2 minutes. Add the stock and simmer for 5 minutes more. Halve the grapes lengthways. Add to the pan and cook for 2 minutes. For the salad, place the mayonnaise in a bowl and stir in the vinegar and olive oil. Separate the lettuce, rinse, shake dry and arrange on a platter. Spoon the vinaigrette over the salad and garnish with chives. Place a rösti in the centre of 6 warmed dinner plates, top with a quail and spoon over the gravy, settling the grapes around the edge. Serve the salad after the quail.

MOROCCAN CHICKEN, EGG AND ALMOND TAGINE 10

6 eggs
6 tbsp olive oil
25g butter
400g Eazy fried onions
2 generous pinches saffron stamens
1½ tsp ground cumin
2 tsp ground coriander
12 skinned, boned chicken thighs
2 garlic cloves
4 tbsp roasted Marcona almonds
1 lemon
60g bunch coriander

Boil the eggs for 10 minutes. Heat 2 tbsp olive oil and 25g butter in a spacious, heavy-bottomed pan over a high heat. Add the onions and stir-fry for 5 minutes. Soften the saffron in a little boiling water. Add the cumin, ground coriander and saffron to the onions. Reduce the heat, cover and leave to cook for 10 minutes. Meanwhile, cut each chicken thigh into 4 or 5 strips. Peel and chop the garlic, sprinkle with a little salt and crush to a paste. Stir 3 tbsp olive oil into the garlic paste and smear all over the chicken. Heat 1 tbsp olive oil in a frying pan and quickly stir fry the almonds until golden. Drain on kitchen paper. Stir the chicken into the onions, increase the heat and stir until all the pieces have turned white. Add just enough water to cover. Bring to the boil, reduce the heat, cover and cook for 15 minutes. Taste and adjust the seasoning with salt, pepper and lemon juice. Chop the coriander. To finish the tagine, stir in the almonds and chopped coriander and garnish with halved, hard-boiled egg.

TURKEY TOM YAM 12

80g bunch coriander
2 large garlic cloves
3 green Bird Eye chillies
2 tsp white sugar
7 tbsp Thai fish sauce (nam pla)
5 limes
25g fresh ginger
2 lemongrass stalks
4 red Bird Eye chillies
1 chicken stock cube
250g button mushrooms
8 turkey steaks
400g extra-fine beans

Boil the kettle. Slice the unpeeled ginger, smash the lemon grass with something heavy and place both in a pan with the red chillies. Dissolve the stock cube in 750ml boiling water and add that, too. Bring to the boil, reduce the heat, cover the pan and simmer for 15 minutes. Wipe the mushrooms. Stir 2 tbsp Thai fish sauce and the juice from 2 limes into the stock, and then add the mushrooms. Simmer for 5 minutes. Add the turkey. Simmer very gently for 10 minutes, turn off the heat, cover the pan and leave for 10 minutes. Meanwhile, make the coriander relish. Remove the coriander stalks. Peel and chop the garlic. Deseed and coarsely chop the green chillies. Place the coriander leaves, garlic, chilli, sugar, 5 tbsp Thai fish sauce and the juice of 3 limes in a food processor. Blitz until amalgamated. Pour into a serving bowl. Refill the kettle and boil again. Rest the turkey fillets on a chopping board for 5 minutes then slice on the diagonal into 3 or 4 thick pieces. Return to the pan and cover. Cook the beans in boiling water for 2 minutes. Drain then stir into the tom yam. Spoon into wide soup bowls with a scoop of the coriander relish.

CHEAT'S CHICKEN CONFIT WITH RED ONION MARMALADE 16

6 medium red onions
5 tbsp olive oil
3 heaped tbsp seedless raisins or sultanas
½ tbsp dark brown muscovado sugar
1 tbsp aged balsamic vinegar
18 chicken drumsticks or 12 large thighs
Sea salt flakes, preferably Maldon
1.5 kg floury potatoes
125ml milk
75g butter
Freshly grated nutmeg

Heat the oven to 230°C/450°F/gas mark 8. Trim, quarter and peel the onions and slice very thinly. Heat 3 tbsp oil in a wok over a high flame, add the onions and toss constantly for 5 minutes, stir-frying until they begin to wilt and glisten. Add ½ tsp salt, stir-fry for a further 5 minutes then tip into a 2 litre-capacity heavy-bottomed pan. Add sufficient water to just cover. Bring to the boil, reduce the heat, cover and simmer for 10 minutes. Add the raisins. Boil, uncovered, for 10 minutes until most of the water has evaporated. Stir in the muscovado sugar. When melted add the balsamic vinegar. Boil for 5 minutes until thick. Leave to cool. Smear the drumsticks with olive oil and sprinkle generously with sea salt. Roast on a cake rack placed over an oven tray for 30 minutes until the skin is crisp and golden. Meanwhile, peel the potatoes and cut into even-sized chunks. Rinse, then boil for 15 minutes in salted water until tender. Drain. Heat the milk with the butter. Remove from the heat then mash the potatoes into the pan, beating thoroughly to get a fluffy, creamy consistency. Season with the nutmeg. Serve a mound of mashed potato in the centre of 6 warmed plates, spoon over a dollop of onion marmalade and top with 3 drumsticks.

CHICKEN KEBABS WITH GREEK POTATO SALAD 21

1 kg skinless chicken fillet
4 garlic cloves, preferably new-season
4 sprigs thyme
1 tbsp lemon juice
3 tbsp olive oil
1 kg small new potatoes
1 medium red onion
2 tbsp wine vinegar
4 tbsp Greek or other fruity olive oil
80g bunch coriander
2 red peppers
150g sliced chorizo
3 limes
6 ripe tomatoes
1 tbsp aged balsamic vinegar
3 tbsp extra-virgin olive oil
You will also need 12 metal kebab sticks

Heat the oven to 400°F/200°C/gas mark 6. Slice the chicken into kebab-sized pieces. Peel 3 garlic cloves and chop finely. Dust with ½ tsp salt and use the flat of a knife to work into a juicy paste. Transfer to a suitable container that can hold the chicken. Add the thyme. Stir in the lemon juice and olive oil. Mix the chicken into the marinade, stirring to coat all the pieces thoroughly. Cover and chill for at least 30 minutes and up to 24 hours. Meanwhile, scrub, rinse and cook the potatoes in salted water until tender. Drain. Peel, halve and finely slice the onion and the remaining garlic clove. Pour the wine vinegar into a salad bowl and add a generous pinch of salt and several grinds of pepper. Swirl the vinegar around the bowl until the salt dissolves. Whisk in the Greek olive oil to make a thick and luscious dressing. Stir in the garlic and onion. Trim the coarse stalk from the coriander and, keeping the bunch shape, finely chop the stalks. Let the chopping get progressively coarser as you work up the bunch into the leaves. Stir the hot potatoes into the dressing. Quarter the peppers discarding the stalk, seeds and white membrane. Chunk. Thread the chicken onto skewers, interspersing with a folded slice of chorizo and a piece of pepper, shaking off any excess marinade. Arrange the skewers on a cake-rack resting on a baking tray. Halve the limes and place next to the kebabs. Cook in the oven for about 15 minutes, turning the kebabs halfway through, until crusty; take care not to overcook them. Meanwhile, core and slice the tomatoes thickly and arrange them on a serving platter. Season with salt and pepper then zig-zag with the balsamic vinegar and the extra-virgin olive oil. Add the chopped coriander to the potato salad and give it a final stir just before serving with the tomato salad, kebabs and lime wedges.

HARISSA CHICKEN WITH GREEN COUSCOUS 27

3 tbsp harissa, preferably rose harissa by Belazu

500g Greek strained yoghurt

6 organic chicken legs, jointed and skinned

3 limes

1 chicken stock cube

2 generous pinches saffron stamens

350g couscous

2 tbsp olive oil

2 tbsp lemon juice

200g mangetout

300g frozen petits pois

80g bunch coriander

2 tbsp extra-virgin olive oil

You will also need tinfoil

Heat the oven to 200°C/400°F/gas mark 6.

Boil the kettle. Line a roasting tray with tinfoil. Mix the harissa with 1 tbsp Greek yoghurt and smear over the chicken. Arrange the chicken on the roasting tray. Roast for 15 minutes. Halve the limes and tuck around the chicken. Roast for a further 15 minutes. Remove from the oven and keep warm. For the couscous, dissolve the stock cube and saffron in 550ml boiling water in a spacious serving bowl. Stir in the couscous with the olive oil and lemon juice, then cover. Halve the mangetout lengthways on the diagonal. Use the remaining kettle water to boil the peas and mangetout for a couple of minutes until tender. Drain. Set aside a few sprigs of coriander and chop the rest. Fork up the couscous and stir in the peas, mangetout and coriander. Transfer to a platter. Zig-zag with extra-virgin olive oil. Arrange the chicken and lime wedges around the couscous. Decorate with sprigs of coriander. Dribble with any juices and serve with the yoghurt.

CHICKEN WITH SHALLOT VINAIGRETTE 33

6 free-range chicken legs

2 tbsp olive oil

4 shallots

1 tbsp smooth Dijon mustard

2 tbsp red-wine vinegar

300ml vegetable oil

4 Little Gem lettuces

½ large or 1 small cucumber

15g chives

You will also need tinfoil

Heat the oven to 220°C/425°F/gas mark 7. Smear the chicken legs with olive oil and lay out on a baking tray. Roast in the oven for 35 minutes until the skin is golden. Meanwhile, peel, halve and finely chop the shallots. Place in a bowl. Put the mustard, vinegar, a decent seasoning of salt and pepper in a blender. Add 3 tbsp water and blend together. With the motor still running, pour in 300ml vegetable oil in a thin stream until thick and homogenized. Transfer to a bowl. Separate then rinse and dry the lettuce leaves. Arrange them lengthways on a platter. Peel and thinly slice the cucumber and scatter over the top. Finely snip the chives over the salad. Remove the chicken

from the oven. Scatter the shallots over the chicken pieces and lavishly cover with some of the vinaigrette. Cover loosely with tinfoil and leave for 10 minutes before serving. Spoon the remaining dressing over the salad just before serving with the plated chicken and its shallot vinaigrette.

MALAYSIAN CHICKEN RENDANG WITH BASMATI 37

2 onions

20g fresh ginger

2 lemongrass stalks

8 red Bird Eye chillies

1 tsp ground turmeric

1 tsp ground coriander

2 tbsp vegetable oil

1 kg chicken thigh fillets

400ml can coconut milk

2 limes

4 tbsp desiccated coconut

400g fine green beans

400g basmati rice

A few sprigs of coriander, to garnish

Boil the kettle. Peel and quarter the onions. Peel the ginger. Remove the tough outer layers from the lemongrass and coarsely chop the inner stem. Trim and split the chillies. Scrape away the seeds and coarsely chop. Place everything in the bowl of a food processor and add 150ml cold water. Blitz to a smooth, carrot-coloured purée flecked with red chilli. Add the turmeric, ground coriander and 1 tsp salt and blitz briefly to blend. Heat the oil in a wide-based, spacious pan over a medium heat. Stir in the purée. Cook briskly, stirring occasionally, for 10–15 minutes until the water evaporates, the purée darkens and turns paste-like, and all the ingredients cook thoroughly. Meanwhile, cut the chicken into chunky, bite-sized strips. Stir the chicken into the paste, cooking until sealed. Stir in the coconut milk and bring the sauce to the boil. Adjust the heat so the curry simmers steadily but gently. Cook, stirring often, for about 20 minutes until the chicken is cooked through and the sauce has thickened considerably and darkened in colour. Taste and adjust the seasoning with salt and lime juice. Stir-fry the desiccated coconut in a frying pan, until evenly golden brown. Tip onto a plate to cool and arrest cooking. Boil the kettle. Trim the beans and cut them in half. Wash the rice and place in a pan with 600ml cold water. Bring to the boil, turn down the heat, cover and cook for 10 minutes. Leave, without removing the lid, for 10 minutes. Using water from the kettle, boil the beans for 2 minutes. Drain. Stir the juice of 1 lime into the curry, followed by the desiccated coconut and beans. Taste and adjust the seasoning with a little more lime juice and salt if necessary. Garnish with the reserved coriander. Fork up the rice just before serving.

MOROCCAN SPATCHCOCK WITH TZATZIKI 40

2 tbsp sultanas
½ tsp saffron stamens
7 large garlic cloves
4 lemons
About 10 tbsp olive oil
4 tbsp ras al hanout (Moroccan spice mix)
6 poussins/spring chickens
1 chicken stock cube
350g couscous
400g can chickpeas
500g Greek yoghurt
1 medium-large cucumber
25g bunch coriander

Boil the kettle and heat the oven to 220°C/425°F/gas mark 7. Place the sultanas and saffron in a cup and cover with boiling water. Peel and chop the garlic and pound to a paste with ½ tsp salt. Set aside 1 tsp paste in a serving bowl. Mix the remaining garlic with 2 tbsp lemon juice and 6 tbsp olive oil, then stir in the ras al hanout. Use scissors to remove the poussins' spines. Open out the birds and flatten slightly with the heel of your hand. Smear generously with the spice-mix and lay on a couple of heavy-duty roasting trays. Dribble with olive oil. Roast the poussins on the upper shelves, juggling the shelves if necessary for even cooking, for 30–40 minutes. Meanwhile, dissolve the stock cube in 550ml boiling water in a serving bowl. Add the sultanas and saffron, the couscous and 2 tbsp each olive oil and lemon juice. Stir thoroughly then cover. Rinse the chickpeas in a colander. Make the tzatziki by stirring 1 tbsp each olive oil and lemon juice into the garlic paste in a serving bowl. Beat in the yoghurt.

Peel the cucumber, split lengthways and scrape out the seeds with a teaspoon. Cut into chunky pieces and stir into the yoghurt with 1 tbsp chopped coriander. Remove the poussins from the oven. Fork up the couscous and mix in the chickpeas. Serve the poussins draped over the couscous with lemon wedges and the sprigs of coriander. Serve the yoghurt separately.

POACHED CHICKEN WITH CHERRY TOMATO VINAIGRETTE 42

6 free-range chicken leg portions
2 onions
2 carrots
A few sprigs of thyme or rosemary
4 black peppercorns
1 bay leaf
4 cloves
2 glasses white wine, approx. 300ml
250g cherry tomatoes
2 large garlic cloves
½ tbsp red-wine vinegar
200ml extra-virgin olive oil
Handful of basil, mint, coriander or flat-leaf parsley leaves
200g trimmed fine beans

Skin the chicken. Peel, halve and thickly slice the onion and carrot. Place in a large pot with the chicken, thyme or rosemary, peppercorns, bay leaf, cloves and 2 tsp salt. Add the white wine and sufficient cold water to cover. Put on a high heat and bring to the boil. Skim the surface to remove any grey froth, turn down the heat and leave to simmer gently for 30 minutes. Quarter the tomatoes and place in medium-sized bowl. Peel the garlic and slice in wafer-thin rounds. Add the garlic and vinegar to the tomatoes. Season with salt and pepper. Toss and leave to macerate for 30 minutes. Boil the beans for 2 minutes. Drain and keep warm. Stir 200ml extra-virgin olive oil into the tomatoes and tear the basil leaves over the top. If using mint, flat-leaf parsley or coriander, chop the leaves. Make piles of beans in the centre of 6 warmed plates. Place a drained chicken leg on top. Stir the tomato vinaigrette and spoon over the chicken and beans.

LEMON CHICKEN WITH POTATOES AND SPINACH 45

8 medium-sized potatoes
7 tbsp olive oil
6 free-range chicken legs
80g bunch flat-leaf parsley
1 tbsp dried oregano
2 medium-large onions
1 bay leaf
2 large lemons
½ chicken stock cube
500g young leaf spinach
2 tbsp extra-virgin olive oil
You will also need tinfoil

Heat the oven to 200°C/400°F/gas mark 6. Peel the potatoes, cut into big chunks and boil in salted water for about 10 minutes until tender. Drain. Meanwhile, heat 3 tbsp olive oil in a lidded frying pan and quickly brown the chicken in batches, turning after a couple of minutes. Transfer to a spacious earthenware or ceramic gratin-style dish that can accommodate the chicken in a single layer. Season with salt and pepper. Chop the flat-leaf parsley. Scatter over the oregano and most of the chopped parsley. Peel, halve and finely slice the onions. Heat 2 tbsp olive oil in the frying pan and stir in the onions. Cook briskly, stirring constantly, for a couple of minutes then add the bay leaf and 1 tsp salt. Reduce the heat, cover and cook for 10–15 minutes until soft and slippery. Tip the onions over the chicken and squeeze the juice of a lemon over the top. Boil the kettle. Heat 2 tbsp olive oil in the frying pan and briefly brown the potatoes on one side, then squeeze over the juice of 1 lemon. Cook for 5 minutes. Tip the potatoes over the chicken encouraging them down between the legs. Dissolve the stock cube in 300ml boiling water and add to the dish. Cover with foil and cook in the oven for 30 minutes. Boil the kettle. Remove the foil from the chicken and cook for a further 10 minutes. Cook the spinach in boiling water for 1 minute. Drain in a colander, pressing with the back of a wooden spoon to extract excess water. Transfer to a warmed bowl and splash with 2 tbsp extra-virgin olive oil. Scatter the remaining parsley over the chicken and serve from the dish with the spinach.

DUCK WITH QUICK FRENCH PEAS 47

125g bunch spring/salad onions
100g butter
750g frozen petits pois
3 Little Gem lettuce hearts
4 Gressingham duck breasts with skin, approx. 175g each
20g bunch flat-leaf parsley
You will also need clingfilm

Trim and coarsely chop the spring onions. Melt 75g butter in a wide-bottomed pan and stir in the onions. Cook for a couple of minutes to soften then add 150ml water and the petits pois. Add scant 1 tsp salt and a generous seasoning of black pepper. Quarter the lettuce hearts lengthways, rinse, shake dry then shred finely across the quarters. Stir the lettuce into the peas. Simmer, uncovered, for about 10 minutes, until the peas and onion are tender and the lettuce has melted. Place the duck breasts skin-side down in an ovenproof pan over a high heat and cook for 2–3 until the skin is crisp. Turn the breasts over to seal the other side, cooking for 1–2 minutes. Transfer to the oven for 10–15 minutes (for pink meat) until they feel springy when pressed. Remove the breasts to a plate. Cover with clingfilm and leave until required (at least 5 minutes). Chop the parsley leaves. Slice thickly across the duck fillets on the diagonal. Reheat the peas, stir in the remaining 25g butter and, when melted, adjust the seasoning with salt and pepper. Stir the parsley into the peas and spoon into the middle of 6 warmed dinner plates. Arrange the duck slices over the top, adding any of the cooking juices.

MEAT

LAMB KEBABS, SKORDALIA AND PICKLES 04

6 plum tomatoes
300ml olive oil, plus 8 tbsp
600g baking potatoes
5 large garlic cloves, preferably new-season
1 lime
A few sprigs of rosemary
800g lamb neck fillet
800g small boiled beetroot (without vinegar)
2 tbsp aged balsamic vinegar
120g day-old white bread without crusts
3 tbsp red-wine vinegar
1 large cucumber
A small bunch of dill
1 tsp caster sugar
2 tbsp white-wine vinegar
3 lemons
You will also need 2 big sheets of tin foil and 12 metal kebab sticks and clingfilm

Heat the oven to 200°C/400°F/gas mark 6. Halve the tomatoes lengthways and smear the cut surface with olive oil. Arrange cut-side up on a foil-lined baking tray. Bake at the bottom of the oven for 15 minutes until soft and juicy. Set aside until required. For the skordalia, peel the potatoes and boil until tender. Drain. Meanwhile, for the kebabs, peel and chop 2 garlic cloves. Sprinkle with ¼ tsp salt and crush into a paste. Place the garlic in a dish that can accommodate the lamb and whisk in the juice of 1 lime, 4 tbsp olive oil and the rosemary. Cut the lamb into kebab-sized chunks. Stir into the marinade. Cover and chill for at least 30 minutes and up to 24 hours. Place the beetroot on one large sheet of foil, drizzle with 2 tbsp each olive oil and balsamic vinegar. Season with salt and pepper. Place a second sheet of foil on top and seal the edges securely but not too tightly. Tear the bread into pieces and blitz with the remaining peeled garlic cloves. Pass the potatoes through a vegetable press (Mouli-Legumes) or mash until smooth. Stir the garlicky crumbs into the potato. Beat in 300ml olive oil gradually. Finish by beating in the red-wine vinegar. Cover with clingfilm until required. Peel the cucumber and slice

wafer-thin using a mandolin or the side of a cheese-grater. Dredge with 1 tbsp salt and leave for 10 minutes. Thread the kebabs onto skewers and arrange on a baking tin. Place at the top of the oven and the foil parcel of beetroot at the bottom. Cook both for 15 minutes, turning the kebabs halfway through so they end up crusty. Turn off the oven, open the door and leave both until required. Squeeze as much water as possible out of the cucumber. Wrap in a tea towel and squeeze again. Chop the dill leaves. Dissolve the sugar in the white-wine vinegar. Stir the cucumber and dill into the vinegar. Transfer to a serving bowl. Cover and chill until required. Serve the kebabs on warmed plates with a dollop of skordalia and a lemon wedge, offering the pickled cucumber and roast vegetables separately.

JAPANESE PORK FILLET WITH MISO RICE 08

2 medium onions
4 tbsp olive oil
3 sachets Japanese miso soup paste, preferably Yutaka
75ml soy sauce, preferably Kikkoman
100ml Chinese cooking wine, preferably Wing Yip
2 pork fillets, approx. 500g each
Flour for dusting
100g natural fried breadcrumbs, preferably Goldenfry
4 large eggs
400g basmati rice

Boil the kettle. Peel, halve and finely slice the onion. Place in a medium-sized pan with the miso soup paste, soy sauce, cooking wine and 400ml boiling water. Simmer for 40–50 minutes until the onions are soft and the liquid has reduced by half. Meanwhile, cut the fillets in half across the middle. Trim away any fat or membrane. Sift about 4 tbsp flour into a shallow bowl, put the breadcrumbs in another and crack two eggs into a third bowl. Whisk the eggs lightly until smooth. Roll each piece of fillet first through the flour, shaking away any excess, then the egg and, finally, press into the breadcrumbs. Heat the oven to 200°C/400°F/ gas mark 6. Heat 4 tbsp olive oil in a frying pan over a medium heat and brown two pieces of fillet at a time, cooking each side for 3 minutes, until crusty and golden. Transfer to a roasting tin. Wash the rice and place in a pan with 600ml cold water. Bring to the boil then immediately turn the heat very low. Cover and cook for 10 minutes. Roast the pork for 15 minutes. Remove the rice from the heat and leave covered for 10 minutes. Rest the pork for at least 10 minutes before slicing. Crack the remaining eggs into the egg bowl and whisk with any of the leftover egg. Add the beaten egg to the reduced onion gravy. Leave to set, then stir once; it will be streaky. Thickly slice the pork. Spoon the rice in the middle of 6 warmed plates or bowls, cover with the dark, eggy gravy and arrange slices of pork on top.

PORK WITH CRISPY SAGE AND APPLE MASH 11

2 large garlic cloves
25g bunch flat-leaf parsley
6 pork chops
1½ tsp paprika
2 lemons
8 medium-sized potatoes, approx. 1kg
4 large eating apples
50g butter
150ml milk
3 tbsp olive oil
18 large sage leaves

Peel and finely chop the garlic. Chop the flat-leaf parsley leaves. Set aside 2 tbsp to garnish. Cut through the rind of the chops at 2cm-intervals towards the meat, to avoid buckling as they cook. Season both sides with salt and paprika. Place in a shallow dish and squeeze the lemons over the chops. Scatter chopped garlic and parsley on both sides. Leave to marinate. Peel the potatoes, cut into even-sized chunks and place in a pan with 1 tsp of salt and plenty of water. Bring to the boil while you quarter, peel and core the apples. Cut into chunks and add to the potatoes. Boil for 15 minutes until tender. Drain the potatoes and apples. Heat the butter and milk together. When the butter has melted remove from the heat. Add the potatoes and apples and mash smooth. Keep warm. Heat the oven to 200°C/400°F/gas mark 6. Heat the olive oil in a frying pan and quickly fry the sage leaves on both sides. Remove to kitchen paper to drain and crisp. Lift the chops out of their marinade

and brown 2 at a time for 2 minutes each side. Transfer to a heavy-duty roasting tray allowing plenty of space between the chops. Roast for 10 minutes until the fat is crusty and golden. Tip the marinade juices into the frying pan, sizzle up and dribble over the chops. Lay 3 sage leaves over each chop.

PORK CHOPS WITH MALLORQUIN BROAD BEANS 14

1 medium red onion
1 large garlic clove
3 tbsp olive oil
75g pancetta or smoked streaky bacon
400g podded broad beans
½ glass white wine, approx. 75ml
½ tsp chilli flakes
400g can chopped tomatoes
6 loin pork chops
750g new potatoes
25g butter
25g bunch mint

Boil the kettle. Keeping separate piles, peel, halve and finely chop the onion and garlic. Heat the olive oil in a frying pan and gently soften the onion, adding the garlic after 10 minutes. Slice across the pancetta to make skinny strips and stir into the onion. Cook briskly, stirring often, for 5 minutes. Meanwhile, using water from the kettle, boil the broad beans for 1 minute, then drain. Refill the pan with cold water and return the beans. Add the wine to the onions and let it bubble away. Stir in the chilli flakes and then the tomatoes. Season with salt and pepper and cook for 10 minutes. Drain the broad beans. In between other jobs, remove their rubbery skin by nicking the edge with your nail, then squeeze out the bean into a bowl. At 2cm-intervals cut into the fat running round the chops towards the meat, to prevent them from buckling during cooking. Boil the potatoes in salted water until tender. Drain, toss with the butter and keep warm. Stir the podded broad beans into the tomato sauce. Shred the mint leaves. Grill the chops for 8 minutes each side until the fat border is splayed and golden. Season both sides with salt and pepper. Keep warm until required. Reheat the tomato and bean sauce, stir in the mint and spoon it over the chops. Serve the potatoes separately.

CHILEAN STEAK WITH PIMIENTO 17

1 red onion
7 tbsp groundnut oil
1 bay leaf
3 garlic cloves
2 red chillies
2 red sweet pointed peppers
1 kg rump steak
100g pimiento-stuffed green olives
75g raisins
1 glass white wine, approx. 150ml
½ chicken stock cube
500g plum tomatoes
50g bunch flat-leaf parsley or coriander
400g basmati rice

Boil the kettle. Peel and chop the onion finely. Heat 4 tbsp groundnut oil in a spacious heavy-based saucepan and cook the onion with the bay leaf for 5–6 minutes. Meanwhile, peel and thinly slice the garlic. Trim, deseed and chop the chillies. Dice the peppers, discarding the seeds and stalk. Stir the garlic, chilli and peppers into the onions. Cook, stirring occasionally, for 10 minutes while you trim the steak and slice it into 3cm-long strips, approx. 1½cm wide. Heat 3 tbsp groundnut oil in a wok and quickly stir-fry the beef, in uncrowded batches, until browned all over, transferring to a plate as you go. Dissolve the stock cube in 300ml boiling water. Add the olives and raisins to the stew together with the meat, wine and the stock. Season with salt and pepper. Stir well, bring to the boil, then establish a gentle but steady simmer. Partially cover the pan and cook for 20 minutes. Place the tomatoes in a bowl and cover with boiling water. Count to 30, drain and remove the core and skin. Chop the tomatoes and transfer to a bowl. Chop the flat-leaf parsley leaves and add to the tomatoes. Wash the rice and place in a lidded pan with 600ml cold water. Bring to the boil then reduce the heat immediately to very low. Cover and cook for 10 minutes. Remove from the heat but leave covered for a further 10 minutes to finish cooking. Stir the chopped plum tomatoes and parsley into the beef. Quickly reheat and check the seasoning. Fork up the rice and transfer to a serving dish to serve with the beef.

PORCINI AND PORK STROGANOFF 26

3 medium onions
75g butter
1 tbsp vegetable oil
100g dried porcini (funghi porcini secchi)
1 kg pork fillet/tenderloin
2 heaped tsp paprika
½ chicken stock cube
400ml soured cream
Juice of 1 lemon
500g dried tagliatelle
1 tbsp finely chopped dill

Boil the kettle. Peel, halve and finely slice the onions. Melt 50g butter with the oil in a spacious, wide-based, heavy-bottomed pan. Stir in the onions. Cook, stirring occasionally for 15 minutes until soft. Meanwhile, tip the porcini into a bowl and just cover with boiling water. Cover with a plate and leave until required. Trim the pork and cut into ribbons, roughly 5 x 1 x ½cm thick. Season with salt and pepper. Increase the heat under the onions. Add the pork, stirring until all the pieces are white. Drain the porcini (retain the liquid). Add to the pan with the paprika. Stir to cook the paprika. Add 200ml of the porcini water, 200ml boiling water and the crumbled stock cube. Bring to the boil, reduce the heat and simmer gently for 10 minutes. Stir the soured cream into the pork and reheat. Add the lemon juice, taste and adjust the seasoning with salt and pepper. Boil the pasta in salted water according to packet instructions; about 10 minutes. Drain, return to the pan and toss with 25g butter. Stir the dill into the stroganoff before serving.

LAMB WITH SPINACH POLENTA 30

6 large plum tomatoes
5 tbsp olive oil
500g young leaf spinach
6 lamb chump chops
100g grated Parmesan, plus 2 tbsp
75g butter
300g 1-minute polenta, preferably Merchant Gourmet
2 lemons
You will also need tinfoil and clingfilm

Heat the oven to 200°C/400°F/gas mark 6. Boil the kettle. Halve the tomatoes lengthways, and lay them, cut-side up on a baking sheet covered with foil. Smear the cut surfaces with olive oil. Cook in the oven for about 30 minutes. Pour boiling water into a large pan, return to the boil and add 1 tsp salt and the spinach. Boil for 1 minute. Drain and leave to cool. Trim any excess fat from the chops. Smear both sides lavishly with olive oil and set aside. Boil the kettle. When the tomatoes are soft and weeping, but holding their shape, remove from the oven and leave to cool. Squeeze the spinach between your hands to remove excess water. Heat the griddle and, when very hot, cook 2 chops at a time for 2 minutes each side. Transfer to a warmed plate and season with salt and pepper. Cover with clingfilm. When you are ready to serve, pour 1.2 litres boiling water into a large pan. Add 1 tsp salt and return to the boil. Add the polenta in a steady stream, immediately reduce the heat and stir for 1 minute as it instantly thickens. Stir in the butter, 100g Parmesan and then the spinach. Divide between 6 warmed plates, dust with the extra grated Parmesan and add a chop and 2 tomato halves. Swirl with olive oil and add a lemon wedge.

CUMIN-CRUSTED LAMB WITH BROWN RICE PILAFF 36

10 garlic cloves
2 x ½ legs lamb, fillet end, 800g each
4 tbsp olive oil
4 tbsp ground cumin
2 onions
1 tsp ground cinnamon
400g brown rice
50g butter
3 tbsp flaked almonds
3 tbsp raisins or sultanas
1 chicken stock cube
500g Greek yoghurt
About 20 mint leaves

Heat the oven to 220°C/425°F/gas mark 7. Peel the garlic; quarter 4 cloves lengthways. Stab each joint in 8 places and stuff with the garlic pieces. Crush 4 more garlic cloves and mix with 2 tbsp olive oil. Place the joints in a roasting tin, smear lavishly with the garlicky olive oil and dust liberally with the cumin. Roast for 10 minutes. Once the lamb is in the oven, start the pilaff. Finely slice the onions and last 2 garlic cloves. Heat 2 tbsp olive oil in a frying pan. When very hot stir in the onion and garlic. Cook, stirring, for about 2 minutes, then turn the heat to low. Cook until limp, golden and shrivelled (about 30 minutes); don't rush this. When the lamb has been cooking for 10 minutes, reduce the heat to 200°C/400°F/gas mark 6. Cook for a further 30 minutes (longer if you don't like your lamb pink) turning halfway through cooking. Wash the rice. Melt the butter in a medium-sized, lidded pan. Add the almonds and stir-fry until golden. Stir in the rice, the raisins and 800ml water. Crumble in the stock cube. Bring to the boil, stir to dissolve the cube then reduce the heat immediately. Cover the pan and simmer gently for about 45 minutes until the rice is tender and the liquid absorbed. Shred the mint leaves and stir into the yoghurt. Stir the cinnamon into the onions and cook for a minute more. Serve the rice piled on a platter and fork the onions into it. Carve the lamb thickly, slicing towards the bone sharing the cumin crust equally. Pour the juices over the lamb and serve the yoghurt in a separate bowl.

SESAME PORK WITH CHINESE GREENS 39

12 pork medallions
8 tbsp sesame seeds
800g pak choi
50g fresh ginger
50g garlic cloves
6 tbsp sesame oil
100ml oyster sauce
100ml Kikkoman soy sauce
100ml Chinese cooking wine
You will also need clingfilm

Boil the kettle. Pat the pork medallions dry with kitchen paper. Spread the sesame seeds on a plate and press the medallions into the seeds to cover entirely. Transfer to a plate, cover with clingfilm and chill until required. Separate the pak choi leaves and wash well in several changes of water. Peel and thinly slice the ginger then cut into matchsticks. Peel and finely chop the garlic. Quickly stir-fry the ginger and garlic in 2 tbsp sesame oil in a wok or frying pan until light golden. Add the oyster sauce, soy sauce and Chinese cooking wine. Simmer for a few minutes. Heat the rest of the sesame oil in a frying pan over a medium heat. Cook the pork medallions in batches of 4, allowing a couple of minutes on each side, until golden and just cooked through. Transfer to a plate. Cover tightly with clingfilm to keep warm. In a large pan boil the pak choi for 30 seconds. Drain and keep warm. Reheat the soy sauce, add the greens and cook for a minute or so, turning them through the sauce. Plate the pork. Serve the greens on a warmed platter.

DIJON HONEY PORK CHOPS WITH SPINACH 46

6 plum tomatoes
1 tbsp olive oil
6 pork chops
4–5 tbsp double cream
1 tbsp smooth Dijon mustard
2-3 tbsp lemon juice
½ tbsp runny honey
600g young leaf spinach
5 tbsp extra-virgin olive oil
You will also need tinfoil

Heat the oven to 170°C/325°F/gas mark 3. Halve the tomatoes lengthways and arrange, cut-side up, on a foil-covered baking sheet. Smear the cut surfaces with olive oil. Cook in the oven until required, but, after 50 minutes, check they are soft and weeping but holding their shape. Heat the grill to its highest setting. Cut through the fat at the edge of the chops at 2cm-intervals towards the meat to avoid buckling as they cook. Lay on the grill pan. Lavishly season the side to be cooked first with salt and freshly milled black pepper. Place 5cm from the heat and cook for 5–8 minutes, depending on the thickness of the chops, until the fat is crusty and golden. Turn the chops, season the uncooked side and cook as before. Drain 3 tbsp of the fatty cooking juices into a frying pan. When the chops are done remove and keep warm. Stir 4 tbsp double cream, the mustard, lemon juice, 2 tbsp water and the honey into the pan. Do not finish the sauce yet. With water from the kettle boil the spinach, pushing it under the water, for 1–2 minutes until wilted. Drain. Return to the pan and stir with 2 tbsp extra-virgin olive oil. Arrange 6 mounds of spinach on a serving platter; top each with 2 tomato halves. Add a lavish swirl of extra-virgin olive oil. Heat the sauce, stirring, for about 30 seconds to make a rich, caramel-coloured sauce. Taste and add extra cream or lemon juice if necessary. Plate the chops and spoon over the sauce.

PORK SALTIMBOCCA WITH LEMON MASH 50

800g pork fillet/tenderloin
Approx. 25 fresh sage leaves
7 slices Parma ham
1 kg floury potatoes
125g butter
150ml milk
2 lemons
Flour for dusting
1 tbsp vegetable oil
1 glass white wine, approx. 150ml
Generous splash of Marsala
You will also need 12 sheets greaseproof paper approx. 30 x 20cm and tinfoil

Trim away any fat or sinew from the pork. Cut 36 slices, each no thicker than a 50p coin. Lay out 6 sheets of greaseproof paper and on each arrange 6 slices with plenty of space around them. Cover with a second sheet of paper. Use a rolling-pin to gently but firmly beat into very thin escalopes, almost double their original size. Season 3 escalopes on each sheet with black pepper, lay a sage leaf on top and cover with a bit of ham that fits as neatly as possible. Cover with the 3 remaining escalopes, return the greaseproof paper and lightly beat again to sandwich together. Carefully remove to a plate. Repeat with the remaining escalopes until you have 18 saltimbocca 'sandwiches'. Chill until required. Heat the oven to 150°C/ 300°F/ gas mark 2. Peel the potatoes, cut into even-sized chunks, rinse and cook in boiling salted water for 15 minutes until tender. Drain. Heat 50g butter with the milk in the potato pan. When the butter has melted, remove from the heat. Return the potatoes to the pan and mash. Beat in the juice of 1 lemon. Taste and add more lemon juice if necessary. Cover and keep warm. Dust the saltimbocca with flour. Heat 75g butter with the vegetable oil between two frying pans. When very hot, cook 4 saltimbocca at a time, frying for 1 minute each side until golden. Keep warm, covered with foil, in the oven. Quickly sizzle the remaining sage leaves in the hot fat and drain. Tip away most of the fat from one pan, add the wine and Marsala and let bubble and reduce into a syrupy gravy. Pour over the saltimbocca. Garnish with the crisp sage leaves. Serve the lemon mash separately.

VEGETARIAN

CARAMELIZED RED ONION TARTS 18

6 medium-large red onions
4 tbsp olive oil
½ tbsp dark brown muscovado sugar
1 tbsp aged balsamic vinegar
500g ready-made puff pastry
Flour for dusting
200g Dolcelatte
200g organic wild rocket

Heat the oven to 200°C/400°F/gas mark 6. Trim, quarter and peel the onions. Slice them thinly. Heat 3 tbsp oil in a wok over a high flame, add the onions and toss constantly for 5 minutes, stir-frying until they begin to wilt and glisten. Add ½ tsp salt, stir-fry for a further 5 minutes then tip into a 2-litre heavy-bottomed pan and add sufficient water to just cover. Bring to the boil, reduce the heat, cover and simmer for 10 minutes. Boil uncovered for a further 10 minutes until most of the water has disappeared. Stir in the muscovado sugar and, when melted, add the balsamic vinegar. Boil for 5 minutes until thick and luscious. Leave to cool until required. Cut the pastry into 6 equal pieces, dust a work surface with flour and roll the pieces to approximately 16cm x 12cm. Without cutting all the way through, etch a 2cm-border then prick all over the pastry inside the border with a fork. Oil two baking sheets and lay out the pastry oblongs with space between them. Spread with the onion. Divide the cheese into 6, cut each piece into 4 or 5 chunks and put on top of the onions. Bake the tarts for 15 minutes or until the pastry border is puffed and golden. Serve with a handful of rocket.

PINK PASTA WITH LEMON-GRILLED FETA 23

2 x 250g Greek feta, preferably Pittas
3 large lemons
12 tbsp olive oil
2 tbsp smooth Dijon mustard
2 tsp runny honey
125g bunch spring/salad onions
350g boiled beetroot (without vinegar)
400g quick-cook spaghetti

25g bunch chives

You will also need tinfoil

Slice each block of feta lengthways into 4 slabs. Cover the grill-rack with foil and lay out the 8 slabs. Season with a squeeze of lemon and splash of olive oil. Place the mustard in a mixing bowl. Mix with the honey, the juice of 2 lemons, a generous pinch of salt and several grinds of black pepper. Gradually beat in 10 tbsp olive oil until thick and creamy. Trim and finely slice the spring onions and stir into the dressing. Finely dice the beetroot and add that, too. Boil the spaghetti according to packet instructions – probably 5–10 minutes. Drain well and then return to the pan with 2 tbsp olive oil. Toss thoroughly. Tip the spaghetti into the beetroot. Use tongs to turn and mix until the pasta is evenly pink. Just before serving, grill the feta for 2-3 minutes under a fierce heat until it softens and burnishes. Serve the pasta on 6 warmed plates, ensuring an even share of beetroot. Tip the rest onto a platter. Shower everything with finely chopped chives. Arrange a slab of hot, molten feta over each portion of pasta and lay the remaining slices on the excess – for second helpings!

SPANAKOPITTA 31

500g trimmed leeks
8 tbsp olive oil
125g butter
600g young leaf spinach
80g bunch flat-leaf parsley
25g bunch mint
4 large eggs
200g Greek feta cheese
2 tbsp grated Parmesan
½ tsp grated nutmeg
200g filo pastry
200g trimmed green beans
400g cherry tomatoes
1 tbsp aged balsamic vinegar
75g pitted black olives

Heat the oven to 200°C/400°F/gas mark 6. Trim and finely slice the leeks. Agitate in a sink full of cold water and drain. Heat 2 tbsp olive oil and 25g butter in a large, lidded pan over a medium heat. Stir in the leeks and season with ½ tsp salt. Cover and cook, stirring halfway through, for 8 minutes. Stir

in the spinach, increase the heat and cook for 2–3 minutes until the spinach wilts. Tip into a colander to drain. Finely chop the parsley and mint leaves. Beat the eggs in a bowl. Crumble in the feta and add the herbs, the Parmesan, nutmeg and drained vegetables. Stir. Melt 100g butter in a small pan. Brush an approximately 23 x 30 x 5cm oven dish with olive oil. Keeping the pastry covered with a damp towel to avoid drying out, use half the pastry to make layers in the dish, spreading each layer with the melted butter and leaving an overhang. Tip the filling into the pastry case and smooth over the top. Tuck the overhang in towards the middle and continue making layers of filo as before, finishing with a generous smear of olive oil. Use a sharp knife to cut portion-sized squares or diamonds, going through a couple of layers of filo. Bake in the oven for about 30–45 minutes until the pastry is puffed and golden and the filling set but still moist and juicy. To make the accompanying salad, boil the kettle. Trim and halve the beans and boil them for 2 minutes. Drain. Place the cherry tomatoes in a frying pan with 3 tbsp olive oil and the aged balsamic vinegar. Grill for about 5 minutes until the tomatoes soften and the skins begin to split but before they disintegrate. Remove from the heat, tip into a serving bowl and stir in the black olives and beans. Cut the pie into portions and toss the tomato salad before serving it hot, warm or cold.

HOT PUDDINGS

ARMAGNAC PRUNES WITH VANILLA RICE PUDDING 14

1 vanilla pod
900ml milk
150g pudding rice
1 regular tea bag
250g Agen ready-to-eat pitted prunes
75g caster sugar
3 tbsp Armagnac, brandy, whisky or rum
150g clotted or double cream

Place the vanilla pod in a pan with the milk. Bring to boiling point, reduce the heat and simmer gently for 5 minutes. Give the vanilla pod a good bash with a wooden spoon to release the seeds. Add the rice to the milk. Simmer very gently, stirring occasionally, for about 20 minutes, until the rice is tender and most of the liquid absorbed. Pour 150ml boiling water onto the tea bag. Squish once and remove the bag. Simmer the prunes in the black tea with 25g sugar and the Armagnac for 15 minutes. Tip into a serving bowl and leave to cool. Stir the rest of the sugar into the rice pudding. Add half the cream and cook for a couple of minutes until thick but sloppy. Leave to cool a little (and thicken) in the pan. Remove the vanilla pod from the rice pudding and stir in the rest of the cream. Transfer to a serving bowl. Serve warm topped with a scoop of prunes.

PEACH AND RASPBERRY CRUMBLE WITH CLOTTED CREAM 23

5 ripe peaches or nectarines
400g raspberries
125g redcurrants
2 tbsp caster sugar
100g amaretti macaroons (about 10)
25g butter
300g clotted or double cream

Heat the oven to 200°C/400°F/gas mark 6. Cut the peaches into small chunks. Rinse the raspberries and redcurrants. Strip the redcurrants from the stalks directly into a suitable gratin-style china dish. Add half the raspberries and the peaches. Mix together, sprinkle with 1 tbsp sugar and mix again. Tip the macaroons into a dish and use the end of a rolling pin to crush into coarse lumps.

Melt the butter in a frying pan and stir in the macaroons so that they are coated with butter. Spoon the crumbs over the fruit. Cook in the oven for 15 minutes. Turn off the oven and leave the crumble until required. Meanwhile, place the remaining raspberries in a bowl and sprinkle with 1 tbsp sugar. Stir, then leave for a few minutes until the sugar has dissolved. Tip into a sieve placed over a bowl. Use the back of a spoon to force the raspberries through the sieve. Stir, scraping under the sieve so nothing is wasted, to make a thick coulis. Serve the crumble with a dollop of cream, topped with the coulis.

PEARS POACHED IN WHITE WINE, HONEY AND LAVENDER 29

600ml white wine
3 tbsp runny honey
1 lemon
6 lavender flower heads or 2 sprigs of thyme
6 even-sized, firm but ripe pears
250g rich pouring cream, preferably Channel Island

Pour the wine and honey into a lidded pan that can hold the pears in a single layer. Add 2 paper-thin strips of lemon zest and the lavender. Bring gently to the boil over a medium-low heat, swirling the pan until the honey dissolves. Allow to simmer while you carefully peel the pears, leaving the stalk intact. In a small cone shape cut out the core and smear the fruit with lemon juice to avoid discolouration. Place the pears in the pan and reduce the heat. Cover and cook until tender – about 20 minutes – turning halfway through cooking. Stand the pears in a serving dish. Cook the liquid at a steady simmer until reduced by half and slightly syrupy. Strain it over the pears. Serve with pouring cream.

VANILLA PLUMS IN RED WINE 30

6 dark red plums
2 tbsp sugar
2 glasses red wine, approx. 300ml
1 vanilla pod
300ml crème fraîche
You will also need tinfoil

Heat the oven to 200°C/400°F/gas mark 6. Run a sharp knife round the plums, twist

apart and remove the stones. If they are firmly embedded, leave them; they can be removed later. Place the plums in a ceramic gratin dish, that can hold them in a single layer. Sprinkle with sugar, pour on the wine and tuck the vanilla pod between the plums. Cover loosely with a double fold of foil. Cook for 30 minutes until very soft but holding their shape. Serve warm with crème fraîche.

HONEY-ROAST FIGS WITH GREEK YOGHURT 31

12 ripe figs
Knob of butter
4 tbsp runny honey
1 lemon
500g Greek strained yoghurt

Heat the oven to 200°C/400°F/gas mark 6. Cut a deep cross in the top of the figs and squeeze the sides. Place in an oven dish. Add a knob of butter then spoon over the honey. Squeeze the lemon over the top and roast for 15 minutes. Serve the warm figs with their juices and Greek yoghurt.

GRILLED PINEAPPLE WITH ANGOSTURA 36

2 ripe pineapples
2 tbsp Angostura bitters
6 tbsp muscovado or other dark brown sugar
250g crème fraîche, to serve
You will also need tinfoil

Trim the pineapples and cut into quarters lengthways. Slice off the skin and cut off the woody core. Slice each quarter lengthways into 3 chunky pieces. Cover the grill-pan generously with foil and lay out the pieces. About 10 minutes before you are ready for pudding, season the pineapple lavishly with Angostura and dredge with sugar. Heat the grill to its highest setting and cook for 7–10 minutes until the sugar has melted and the pineapple is juicy. Serve with crème fraîche.

ROAST PEACHES WITH AMARETTI 37

6 ripe peaches
1 vanilla pod
Large wine glass Amaretto approx. 250ml
4 amaretti macaroons
350g crème fraîche

Heat the oven to 200°C/400°F/gas mark 6. Run a sharp knife round the middle of the

peaches, twist apart and discard the stones. Split the vanilla pod, scrape out the seeds and stir into the Amaretto. Arrange the peaches, cut-side up, on a small roasting tin. Fill the cavities with some of the Amaretto. Roast for about 30 minutes or until tender. Transfer to a serving dish. Spoon the rest of the Amaretto and vanilla over the fruit. Leave to cool. Crumble macaroons into the cavities of the peaches. Serve with crème fraîche.

TREACLE TART WITH CREME FRAICHE 39

20cm pre-cooked shortcrust pastry case
100g white bread, without crusts
4–6 tbsp golden syrup
Approx. 1 tbsp lemon juice
250g crème fraîche, to serve

Heat the oven to 200°C/400°F/gas mark 6. Blitz the bread into crumbs in a food processor. Tip the crumbs into the pastry case and smooth the surface. Working from the outside, spoon golden syrup over the crumbs until completely covered. Squeeze 1 tbsp lemon juice over the top. Leave in a warm place for the syrup to soak into the crumbs. Bake for 20 minutes. Turn off the oven and leave until required, with the oven door open. Serve warm with crème fraîche.

CARAMELIZED ROAST APPLES 40

6 small eating apples, such as Cox's
50g butter
3 tbsp golden syrup
3 tbsp soft brown sugar
250g pouring cream, to serve

Heat the oven to 190°C/375°F/gas mark 5. Core and halve the apples. Lay them, cut-side up, on a lightly buttered oven tray. Spoon over the golden syrup and dredge with sugar. Top each apple with a piece of the remaining butter. Bake for about 20 minutes until tender. Spoon the syrup over the top and serve the cream separately.

PISTACHIO CREAMED RICE WITH ORANGE SALAD 42

Handful of shelled pistachio nuts
6 navel oranges
1 tbsp runny honey
2 x 400g cans creamed rice
2 tbsp orange blossom/flower water

4 tbsp thick cream

Generous pinch ground cinnamon

Place the pistachios in a plastic bag, seal and bash with a rolling pin to break into small pieces. Using a sharp knife, slice the ends off the oranges, then the remaining skin in 4 or 5 downward sweeps. Slice the fruit off the 'core' in 3 or 4 large pieces. Cut across each piece into 2 or 3 chunky slices. Pile into a serving dish as you go. Squeeze the juice from the skin and core over the top. Dribble the honey over the oranges. Meanwhile, warm the rice in a pan. Stir in the orange blossom water and then, loosely, the cream. Pour into a wide serving bowl. Scatter the pistachios over the top and dust with cinnamon. Serve with the orange salad.

ROAST PEARS WITH MARSALA AND CINNAMON 45

6 small pears

2 tbsp dark brown sugar

½ glass white wine, approx. 75ml

2 glasses Marsala, approx. 300ml

1 cinnamon stick

300g crème fraîche

You will also need tinfoil

Heat the oven to 200°C/400°F/gas mark 6. Halve the pears through the stalk and lay, cut-side down, in a ceramic dish that can hold them in a single layer. Scatter over the sugar. Add the wine, Marsala and cinnamon stick. Cover loosely with foil. Cook in the bottom of the oven for 30 minutes. Remove the foil and cook for 15 minutes more. Cool a little then serve with the crème fraîche.

CHOCOLATE FONDANT PUDDINGS 47

200g dark chocolate (minimum 70% cocoa solids)

150g butter plus an extra knob

4 large eggs, plus 3 large yolks

100g golden caster sugar

50g plain flour, to dust

300g crème fraîche

Heat the oven to 200°C/400°F/gas mark 6. Boil the kettle. Lavishly butter 6 metal 175ml pudding tins. Dust with flour, shaking out the excess. Place on a baking sheet and pop in the freezer. Break the chocolate into a metal bowl fitted over a half-filled pan of simmering water. Add 150g butter and stir occasionally as it melts. Meanwhile, place the eggs, yolks

and sugar in an electric mixer. Mix at high speed for 3–6 minutes until thick, mousse-like and doubled in volume. Gradually fold the chocolate sauce into the mousse until smooth and slackened. Sift the flour over the top and fold through until smooth. Pour into the prepared tins. Bake for 12 minutes until risen and set. Rest for 2 minutes. Run a knife around the inside of the moulds, turn onto the plates and serve with the crème fraîche.

RHUBARB AND ALMOND CRUMBLE 48

500g fresh or frozen rhubarb

100g caster sugar, plus 1 tbsp

1 large orange

100g plain flour

100g ground almonds

100g butter

300g crème fraîche

Heat the oven to 200C°/400F°/gas mark 6. Trim the rhubarb, cut into 5cm-lengths and pile into a 2-litre capacity gratin-style ceramic dish. Sprinkle with 1 tbsp sugar and squeeze the orange over the top. Mix together the remaining sugar, flour and almonds in a bowl then cut the butter in small pieces over the top. Rub the butter evenly into the mixture. Tip the crumble mixture over the rhubarb, spreading it out evenly. Cook in the oven for 25 minutes until the crumble is a pale golden. If you think the crumble is colouring too quickly, cover it loosely with tinfoil. Leave to cool. Serve with crème fraîche.

CHOCOLATE CREPES WITH RUM BUTTER 49

200g dark chocolate, (70% cocoa solids)

6 ready-made pancakes

150g unsalted butter

150g demerara sugar

8 tbsp rum

250g crème fraîche

Break the chocolate into squares. Fold the pancakes in half and then in half again, tucking the chocolate firmly inside the layers. Melt the butter and sugar in a spacious frying pan over a low heat. Stir in the rum and turn off the heat. When ready, reheat the sauce and slip the folded pancakes into the pan. Cook for a couple of minutes, encouraging the sauce over the pancakes, until the chocolate is melted. Serve with crème fraîche.

COLD PUDDINGS

CARIBBEAN PINEAPPLE 01

2 large ripe pineapples

4 tbsp rum or 1 tbsp Angostura bitters

Trim the pineapples and cut into quarters lengthways. Slice off the skin. Slice thinly lengthways and pile onto a platter, collecting any juices to add, too. Sprinkle with the rum, moving the slices to ensure the alcohol touches everything.

STEM GINGER FOOL 02

350g jar stem-ginger in sugar syrup

500g strained Greek yoghurt, preferably Total

300g jar lemon curd

Dice the ginger into a bowl. Add the yoghurt, 4 tbsp ginger syrup and the lemon curd. Mix together then transfer to pretty glasses. Add a splash of the remaining syrup. Chill until required but remove from the fridge 10 minutes before serving.

FROZEN BERRIES WITH WHITE HOT CHOCOLATE 03

400g organic white chocolate, preferably Green & Blacks

400g double cream

750g frozen summer fruits

Break the chocolate into small pieces and place in a double boiler or in a metal bowl placed over a pan of simmering water; do not let the water touch the bowl. Add the cream and stir occasionally over the next 5–10 minutes until the chocolate has melted and the sauce is smooth and very hot. About 5 minutes before serving the pudding, remove the fruit from the freezer and spread out on 6 plates or 2 platters for sharing. Reheat the sauce until very hot, transfer to a jug and pour lavishly over the semi-frozen fruit in front of your guests.

AFFOGATO 04

Hot espresso coffee

500g good quality vanilla ice cream

100ml Amaretto

Just before you are ready for pudding, make a fresh pot of strong espresso coffee. At the table, place a scoop of ice cream in 6 espresso cups, or similar. Add a splash of Amaretto and follow with the hot coffee.

PEACH MELBA 05

150g fresh or frozen raspberries

3 ripe peaches or nectarines

4 tbsp caster sugar

250ml white wine

500g vanilla ice cream

Boil the kettle. If using frozen raspberries, spread them out on a plate to defrost. Plunge the peaches in boiling water for 30 seconds. Peel away the skin and halve them round their middles. Dissolve the sugar in the wine over a medium heat and cook the peaches in it, covered, for 5 minutes. Place the raspberries in a sieve over a bowl, spoon 4 tbsp of the sugary wine over the top and press through with the back of a spoon. Place an upturned peach over a mound of ice cream and cover with raspberry sauce.

LEMON POSSET WITH RASPBERRIES 06

300g double cream, plus 6 tbsp

75g caster sugar

1 large lemon

300g raspberries

Pour 300g double cream into a small pan. Add the sugar and bring slowly to the boil, stirring constantly as it melts. Boil gently for 3 minutes, stirring. Remove from the heat. Stir the juice of the lemon into the cream. Leave for 5 minutes before dividing between 6 glasses or ramekins, leaving space for the raspberries. Chill for at least 40 minutes and up to 24 hours. Top the possets with the raspberries and finish with a scoop of cream.

RASPBERRY AND ROSE-SCENTED SYLLABUB 07

3 tbsp caster sugar

2 large glasses sweet white wine, approx. 300ml

400g very ripe raspberries

1 tbsp rose water or lemon juice

300g double cream or whipping cream

175g packet sponge fingers

Put 6 sundae glasses in the freezer. Dissolve 2 tbsp caster sugar in the wine in a small saucepan. Cook gently until reduced by about one-third. Leave to cool. Place half the raspberries in a bowl and lightly bruise with the back of a spoon. Sprinkle with 1 tbsp sugar and the rose water or lemon juice. Leave until the sugar has dissolved. Beat the cream until floppy then gradually incorporate the cooled wine, beating gently until all the wine is absorbed to end up with soft, peaks. Do not over-beat. Stir 2 large spoonfuls of whipped cream into the bruised raspberries and their juices, mixing thoroughly. Lightly fold the mixture into the cream until streaked with colour then gently fold in the whole raspberries. Spoon the syllabub into the chilled glasses. Chill in the fridge and serve with the sponge fingers.

MARSALA GRAPES WITH MUSCOVADO YOGHURT 08

500g seedless red grapes

350g seedless white grapes

2 tbsp Marsala

500g Greek yoghurt

2 tbsp dark brown muscovado sugar

Slice the grapes in half lengthways. Place in a pretty bowl and stir in the Marsala. Spoon the yoghurt over the grapes and scatter the sugar over the top. Chill until required. Loosely mix the streaked yoghurt into the grapes just before serving.

STRAWBERRY VACHERINS WITH BALSAMICO 09

400g strawberries

1 tbsp sugar

½ tbsp aged balsamic vinegar

150ml double cream

6 meringue nests

6 small mint sprigs

Hull the strawberries and quarter lengthways. Place in a bowl. Sprinkle the sugar over the top, tossing to dissolve, then add the balsamic vinegar. Toss again and leave until required. Beat the cream until holding soft peaks, taking care not to overdo it. Scoop half the strawberries into a sieve to drain. Tip into a bowl. Into another bowl pass the rest of the fruit and the juices through the sieve, scraping underneath so that nothing is wasted. Stir to make a sauce then transfer to a jug. Fill the meringue nests with whipped cream. Pile with chopped strawberries, add a little of the sauce and garnish with a small sprig of mint. Serve the remaining sauce separately for guests to help themselves.

GINGER AND COFFEE ICE CREAM SANDWICHES 10

250g packet thin ginger biscuits

500g tub coffee ice cream

Take the ice cream out of the freezer to soften slightly. Make 12 sandwiches with the ginger biscuits and a generous scoop of ice cream. Pile onto a plate and return to the freezer. Serve directly from the freezer.

APRICOTS WITH VANILLA, ORANGE AND HONEY 11

500g large, soft, ready-to-eat dried apricots

1 vanilla pod

2 tbsp honey

4 large oranges

500g natural yoghurt

Place the apricots in a pan. Split the vanilla pod and add to the pan with the honey. Squeeze over the oranges. Cover and leave to simmer gently for about 20 minutes until the apricots are swollen and soft. Tip into a bowl and leave to cool. Serve the apricots and their honeyed juices over the yoghurt.

CHOCOLATE TART WITH CREME FRAICHE 12

20cm pre-cooked shortcrust pastry case

2 egg yolks

1 whole egg

50g caster sugar

100g dark chocolate (minimum 70% cocoa solids)

75g butter

250g crème fraîche

Heat the oven to 190°C/375°F/gas mark 5. Boil the kettle. For a homemade look, break off the ridge round the top of the pastry case. Place on a baking sheet. Put the egg yolks, whole egg and caster sugar in the bowl of a mixer and beat vigorously until thick and fluffy. Half fill a pan with boiling water and place a metal bowl over the top. Break up the chocolate, cut the butter into pieces and melt together in the bowl; stir until smooth. Remove the bowl and leave to cool for 10 minutes. Pour the chocolate onto the egg mixture and beat the two together. Pour into the pastry case, right up to the lip. Bake for 10 minutes then leave to cool. Carefully lift the tart out of the tin onto a plate. Serve with the crème fraîche.